D0549183

THE COMPLETE GUIDE TO BUSINESS
SCHOOL PRESENTING

THE COMPLETE GUIDE TO BUSINESS SCHOOL PRESENTING

What your professors don't tell you... What you absolutely must know

STANLEY K. RIDGLEY, PhD

ANTHEM PRESS
LONDON · NEW YORK · DELHI

Anthem Press
An imprint of Wimbledon Publishing Company
www.anthempress.com

This edition first published in UK and USA 2012
by ANTHEM PRESS
75-76 Blackfriars Road, London SE1 8HA, UK
or PO Box 9779, London SW19 7ZG, UK
and
244 Madison Ave. #116, New York, NY 10016, USA

British Library Cataloguing-in-Publication Data
A catalogue record for this book is available from the British Library.

Library of Congress Cataloging-in-Publication Data
Ridgley, Stanley K.
  The complete guide to business school presenting : what your professors don't
tell you– what you absolutely must know / Stanley K. Ridgley.
    p. cm.
  Includes index.
  ISBN 978-0-85728-514-0 (pbk. : alk. paper) – ISBN 0-85728-514-9 (pbk. : alk. paper)
  1. Business presentations. I. Title.
  HF5718.22.R536 2012
  658.4'52–dc23
                        2012028257

ISBN-13: 978 0 85728 514 0 (Pbk)
ISBN-10: 0 85728 514 9 (Pbk)

This title is also available as an eBook.

CONTENTS

Preface   vii

Acknowledgments   xi

Introduction   xiii

Part I   The World of Presenting   1
Chapter 1   I *Hate* Presentations   3
Chapter 2   Public Speaking: The Twenty-first Century Presenter   15
Chapter 3   Basics of Your Talk   29

**Part II   The Seven Secrets of Successful Speakers:
From Stick-Puppet to 3D Presenting**   45
Chapter 4   Stance   50
Chapter 5   Voice: "I Feel Especially *Powerful* Today!"   64
Chapter 6   Gesture   86
Chapter 7   Expression   97
Chapter 8   Movement: No More Stick-Puppet Presenting   108
Chapter 9   Appearance   118
Chapter 10   Passion: Evoking Emotion, Displaying Earnestness   128

Part III   The Story   137
Chapter 11   Storytelling I: The Secret Weapon   140
Chapter 12   Storytelling II: What Kinds of Stories?   149
Chapter 13   Storytelling III: How Do We Tell a Story?   162

Part IV Group Presentations   177
Chapter 14 The Curse and Blessing of Group Presentations   179
Chapter 15 Group Presentations I: Getting Ready   187
Chapter 16 Group Presentations II: What to Do?   198
Chapter 17 Tools of Analysis: Orient, Eliminate,
            Emphasize, Compare   213
Chapter 18 The Case Competition   233

Conclusion   243

Glossary   245

Index   255

PREFACE

There's an old joke that says if you want to hide something from college students, put it in a book preface. Thus it is here that I provide buried treasure – my rationale for this book.

I always tell students that buried inside every obstacle is an opportunity. It is there for the seeing, if only you can recognize it. If only you don't turn away simply because hundreds of others turn from it. I wanted this book to be about hope, desires, dreams, imagination, energy, and dynamism, the distillation of years of your predecessors' experience, about grappling with and overcoming the challenges of business school and beyond.

Surely such notions are relevant to how we present ourselves in public? Yes, *surely* how we conceive of ourselves impacts how we present ourselves. Is this book for *every* business school student? You bet!

I wrote this book because so many students come into my classes with only a vague notion of how to deliver a competent business presentation. From pedestrian presentations to the clueless to the awful – I see them all. Perhaps you're in that number? The odds are good that you could be.

But that's not your fault. It's not that you *can't* do it – it's just that no one has shown you how. Let's change that now.

In these pages, I tell and show you exactly how to give a presentation in business school – by yourself *and* as part of a group. In the process, you gain confidence, competence, personal competitive advantage, and you lift yourself into the highly demanded skill zone of the top one percent of presenters in America, student *or* corporate.

This is not a generic "presentations" book. It's written precisely for you: the business school student. The business school presentation has its own special demands and a context that is specific to business school: how to prepare, how to practice, where to stand, what to do, how to do it, working with your visuals, how to engage your audience, and how to conclude.

Sure, there are some general presentation principles, and they *are* valid regardless of the venue, audience, and purpose. You can hear some of these principles in the typical public speaking course where they teach you "How to give a speech" or "Learn to introduce yourself."

General principles can be useful. But – and it's a *big* but – there is a point at which specific and useful direction trumps general suggestions on "How to give a speech."

You *must* know more. Much more.

Yes, this book is loaded with secrets.

For a very good reason, I subtitled this book "*What your professors don't tell you… What you absolutely must know.*" At risk of alienating a significant number of my colleagues, let me state unequivocally here and now that many business school professors simply do not know what constitutes an outstanding presentation. While this statement appears arbitrary, it's one that I stand by. It's one of those white elephants in the middle of the room that everyone sees, but no one acknowledges.

No, I know of no social scientific study to substantiate this generalization, and I offer it only with hesitation. But I know of no other explanation for the sorry state of business presentations in many of today's business schools.

But you ask, "How can you, Dr Ridgley, speak for schools other than your own?"

The answer is that it's my business to know the state of business school presentations across the spectrum of colleges and universities. I view numerous films of student business case competitions throughout the year, and witness presentations of teams from schools across the country. These are supposedly the best that our schools have to offer.

As a general rule, these presentations are pedestrian offerings, predictable in form and sometimes obscure in content. In international case competitions, teams from Asia seem to dominate, and with good reason. It's not that they are so good – it is that our own teams are so lacking.

There are probably substantial reasons for the general malaise that afflicts business presenting. Surely one major reason is that most faculty and administrators view business presentations as an amalgam of what many euphemistically call "soft skills." Perhaps even *you* refer to business presentations as encompassing "soft skills."

But as long as it retains this moniker, it will continue to be viewed as something that can just be "picked up" along the way. As long as presenting is viewed as a "soft skill" rather than as a subject that requires intense study and practice, much like finance or accounting or marketing, the quality of business presentations will remain abysmal. Finance? Marketing? Of course, my finance, accounting, and marketing brethren might chuckle at the notion that business presenting should be accorded great respect – but then, that might be part of the problem, eh? The high-level, sophisticated business presentation skill-set is anything but "soft."

This report on the current abysmal state of business presenting is surely bad news – but all of this bad news is, in reality, *good* news for *you*. If you learn how to give a clear, organized, competent, enthusiastic presentation – an especially *powerful* presentation – this will equip you to excel in the business world far better than any other single skill can prepare you.

Special Note to You, the Student

Despite my unremitting positivity, I caution you that this is not an esteem-building book. It is not designed to make you feel good about your current level of skill. It is designed to help you improve *dramatically*. Given how low the bar rests in the world of public business presentations, I am confident that you can demonstrate tremendous improvement in a short time simply by eliminating your bad habits.

I have also resisted the temptation to serve up my own notions of what sort of person you ought to be. It is a temptation in any book to include *everything* one thinks of. And so I have resisted the urge to transform a how-to book into a quasi-philosophical tract with all sorts of digressions, interesting to me perhaps, but not entirely useful to you. In fact, I discarded thousands of words lecturing and conjecturing on how a good life should be lived. Yet some of these nuggets do remain, for this subject truly *is* about opening minds to the endless possibilities of a limitless world.

It is clear that women have special challenges in the corporate world, a field traditionally dominated by men. The corporate mentality pressures women, and how you respond to these pressures can make or break your career. Tied to this, in the unforgiving venue of the business presentation, how you perform is critical to your future. Minority students and international students also have challenges particular to them, and throughout this book, we overcome the obstacles that nettle the entire gamut of students – men, women, and international students.

This is a how-to manual, straight to the point. Simple and direct, as the late wordsmith Jacques Barzun urged us.[1]

If you embrace the secrets I offer, if you follow the rules and guidelines, and if you practice and seek out opportunities to speak, you *will* become a superior presenter.

And if you adopt all you find here, you will doubtlessly develop a hunger to move up to the apex, the most rarefied level of all – that realm of business presenting that exists in our imaginations. I call it the Power Zone.

How might you reach this next level?

A personal presentations coach can take you to the highest level of business presenting. The time and money spent in acquiring advanced skills is well spent, an investment in a skill that is universally applicable, that is in high demand, and that will serve you for your lifetime.

Throughout these pages, some of the greatest master speakers in history coax you along, and wheedle you and cajole you to be your best, recognizing that the responsibility ultimately rests with you. For instance, I agree wholeheartedly with experts Paul Brees and G. Vernon Kelley, who engaged students in the process of business presenting more than eight decades ago:

> The process is not a simple one, nor is the process easy. You will never learn by reading a book, this or any other, although we suggest a plan by which you can learn. In the first place, you must learn to speak by speaking; and you must learn to be direct by talking directly to your audience. Force yourself to do it and it will become easier.[2]

In the end, it is you and your efforts that transform you into a powerful speaker, not this book or its secrets. This single fact is both liberating *and* your greatest challenge. Turn the page to meet that challenge.

---

1 Jacques Barzun, *Simple and Direct* (New York: Harper Perennial, 1975).
2 Paul R. Brees and G. Vernon Kelley, *Modern Speaking* (Chicago: Follett Publishing Company, 1931), 125–6.

ACKNOWLEDGMENTS

I imagine that most of us who strive to write a book also dream of writing the *perfect* book. But that dream quickly fades as what we put on paper invariably appears inferior to what we imagined it would be. Our thoughts never quite coalesce on the page the way we want them to, and our inner editor, perfectionist that it is, tells us constantly "That sucks."

Yet somehow the book materializes, and it's the best we can do.

This book has been in the preparatory stages for many years, and I thank the hundreds of students who have had the experience – whether pleasurable or not – of delivering hundreds of presentations to me as I sat stone-faced, scrutinizing every movement, hanging on every syllable, squinting at every unreadable PowerPoint slide. I thank these presenters who paved the way for the following lessons, who communicated to me an insatiable desire *to learn what is not taught in business school.*

Business school presenting is one of the most quixotic exercises that bedevil students. Everyone expects you to do it, but no one shows you how.

Or, if you do receive a class in public speaking, it is conducted by someone outside the business school who has no clue what you need to know. Nice people, sure, but the instruction is useless.

So it is that I thank the generations of students who have come through my classes, lamenting their lack of preparation, persevering anyway, and evincing utter delight at the prospect of becoming fabulous presenters through hard work, self-knowledge, and the lessons of the ages contained herein.

I want to recognize the help of my colleague Dr Arun Kumaraswamy and my dear friend Lory Pyle for their editorial and substantive comments. And for their unwavering support, I thank Andrea, Caitlyn, and Nathan Ridgley. All illustrations are by Andrea Lynn Ridgley. Any errors that appear in the book are, despite my best efforts, my own.

INTRODUCTION

If you're reading this, I assume that you're a business school student. Unless you are an errant liberal arts type or a young executive hoping to discover what you missed in school, then most likely you are a business school undergraduate or MBA candidate.

We have never met, but I know the challenges you face in this particular slice of life, because I deal every day with business students just as frustrated as you are with this beast. You are faced with an unenviable situation.

You hate *business school presentations*, and I know why you hate them.

I know why you are average, or even poor, at delivering them, and I know it is not your fault.

I know exactly why your presentations are not as good as they could be and why a tiny minority of students seem so at ease and appear to know exactly what to say.

And I know you are ready to change all of that, starting now.

The Gap

You are bright and energetic about most things, aren't you? You have dreams. You have goals, usually "big, hairy, audacious goals," as business author Jim Collins calls them.[3] Maybe you keep them to yourself, but you still have them.

You take your classes seriously, more or less. You give your classes a chance to pass muster, to show you something new and fresh. Even something "relevant." But you doubtlessly find that most of your business classes have *The Gap*.

---

1 Jim Collins and Jerry I. Porras, *Built to Last: Successful Habits of Visionary Companies* (New York: HarperBusiness, 1994).

That gap is darned big. It's a huge missing piece of the business puzzle. It's frustrating, and it can kill your enthusiasm. Here it is:

Professors in most of your classes expect you to deliver business presentations. But no one tells you how.

That's *The Gap*.

This guide fills The Gap. Quickly – completely – and in a way that answers all of your questions.

But this is *not* just another "presentation" book like the dozens you see on Amazon.com when you search the word. It's not a textbook like the dense "business communication" texts you buy at more than $150 per copy.

This book is for every young person on the cusp of adult life, who wants – who yearns, who *thirsts* – for knowledge, who wants to crack the success code. This book is for the student who has searched his or her entire life for the secrets of success withheld – the blueprints, the plans, the secret tablets.

You just *know* that somewhere is a manual for success that has been hidden from you. Others seem to have read that book, and they appear confident, vibrant, good-looking, competent, and infuriatingly at ease. They are effortlessly successful people. You've seen them your entire life – luck comes to them, good fortune kisses them, and success is a radiant aura worn like a jeweled crown.

We all wonder at their easy confidence. Obviously, they've had access to the secret manual. We gnash our teeth a bit, and we speculate on where to find a copy. And then you discover the uncomfortable "truth." They are delighted to tell you that there *is* no such manual for success in life and business. It's a myth.

Well, there *is* a manual, and this it. Quite possibly the most useful book you will ever read in your entire business school career.

I know the secrets of great business presenting, and I've distilled them to share with you right here. You hold in your hands the essential manual for any student on the launch pad ready to soar to that first job. Not to wax hyperbolic, but this book can make the difference whether you soar gloriously – or crash ignominiously.

Best of all, this book can fix *all* of your business presentation woes right now.

All of them.

I Talk to You and No One Else...

You may have had "business presentations" in a communications course of some sort. In many of these classes, you will find thick, expensive textbooks on "public speaking" or "business communications."

These books typically feature small print, tortured graphics, and colorful artwork that are designed to stimulate and motivate you. They are heavy on abstract concepts. They discuss communication "theory," complete with flow charts and pyramidal schemes, and they focus mainly on writing.

Only on occasion does a business communication course or book tell you exactly what to do, and what *not* to do. Isn't that truly what you want? Just the facts?

Tell me what to do and what not to do.

In these pages you find answers to the most basic of questions:

- **What *is* this beast – the business presentation?**

- **Isn't it really just making "good slides" and then reading from them?**

- **What do I say? How do I say it?**

- **How do I stand? *Where* do I stand?**

- **How do I reduce 20 pages of analysis into a four-minute spiel that makes sense and that "gets it all in?"**

- **How should we assemble a group presentation? How do we orchestrate it?**

- **Where do I begin, and how?**

- **How do I end my talk?**

- **What should I do with my hands?**

- **How do I conquer nervousness once and for all?**

- **How can I tell "what the professor wants?"**

- **How do I translate complex material, such as a spreadsheet, to a PowerPoint slide so that it communicates instead of confuses or bores?**

The Complete Guide answers each of these questions and many more that you haven't even thought of yet. You already see how useful this book is, don't you?

How to Read this Book

I have arranged this book in four parts – The World of Presenting, The Seven Secrets of Successful Speakers: From Stick-Puppet to 3D Presenting, The Story, and Group Presentations.

Part I: The World of Presenting is an opportunity for me to ramble and tell stories from a professor's point of view, to lament over the sorry state of presenting in academia and in the business world generally. I do this to share how widespread and deep the problem is, because frankly, there is a kind of averted gaze in business school with regard to presenting. Few folks recognize that there *is* a problem. Committing heresy here, I'll just say it: many professors simply aren't good presenters. You know it, they know it, administrators know it – but we all simply move forward pretending the problem doesn't exist. And this studied silence can contribute to an attitude of nonchalance with respect to these so-called "soft skills." In this section, we adjust that perspective a bit and cultivate a healthy respect toward the activity of business presenting. I offer you a connection to the long and storied history of presentations, elocution, and oratory. This is validation for our noble and grand endeavor of business presenting.

Part II: The Seven Secrets of Successful Speakers: From Stick-Puppet to 3D Presenting addresses you as a presenter. It focuses on *you* and how you must change and grow. It offers "Seven Secrets" that can transform you as a presenter in the shortest possible time. These are the eternal verities of speaking that, if you apply them, can turn you into a champion. Master these Seven Secrets, which form the Seven Pillars of your personal speaking platform, and you can soar higher in the business world than you possibly could have imagined, and your career can soar farther and faster than you ever thought possible.

Where do these secrets come from? They reside in the collective wisdom of more than 2,500 years of recorded history. This is the link that you share with every great speaker that history has seen fit to remember – you share their *humanity*. All of the challenges you face in business school presenting were tackled centuries ago. Every single one of them. I've collected them and offer them to you here.

Part III: The Story addresses the single most powerful technique ever devised for presenters, but one that has been consciously purged from the business presentation repertoire by folks who don't know better. You can harness the six most powerful words in the English language to create genius presentations that electrify and motivate an audience.

Part IV: Group Presentations tackles one of the most fearsome bugaboos of business school and demonstrates how to turn it into a masterful *tour de force* of your business school career, useful to you for years to come. Group presenting is the most prevalent type of presenting in business school. It's also the most-hated – but we'll fix that. This section also covers business case competitions, and this is the only book in English that does.

Clear, Concise, Memorable

In these pages, you don't learn "communication theory." You learn to give a business school presentation. You learn to give a "show."

You improve your skill in presenting and public speaking, which are required activities in all of your business classes for the last two years of college. You improve your grades as a result of your increased skill.

You achieve a level of personal, competitive advantage that no other skill can provide you today. That's no idle promise, and you discover why.

You increase your competitive advantage as you graduate from business school. You learn the *single most important skill* to lift you into the High-Demand Skill Zone. You create for yourself a personal competitive advantage that lasts a lifetime, and lays the groundwork for your spectacular business career.

Moreover, this book is for you, the business school student. Others can surely thumb through it and benefit from it in some way, but I have resisted the urge from publisher and kibitzer alike to "broaden the message" so as to "broaden the audience."

I've resisted pressure to water down this book, to move its focus from you, the business student, and to "connect it" to a broader spectrum of people, to *all* college students. Perhaps even to young executives as well. I think not.

The business presentation is a rite of passage for every business school student, and you deserve a book of your own. Here you learn how to give business presentations *in business school*, and how to negotiate that rite of passage in the most successful and fruitful way possible.

I hope that you join me in the next chapter, and the next. As you move through this book, you will begin to acquire the power, verbal dexterity, energy, and charisma to grow into a bold presenter – one who is at home on the stage, at ease with themselves, and comfortable with the material. You *will* become a fabulous business presenter.

Let's take those first steps in the next chapter.

PART I

THE WORLD OF PRESENTING

I *HATE* PRESENTATIONS

Classes are changing now, and I step into the elevator with a gaggle of students. They're going to class, but they look as if they're trudging to the morgue to identify a relative. Business school can be like that at mid-semester. From derivatives to depreciation, from value chain to valuation of the firm, gloom hangs in the hallways and dissipates only with the coming of spring.

And on the elevator, snippets of conversation reach me. Two animated girls chatter in grinding cartoon voices, and I catch a conversation mid-sentence. I *think* it was a conversation.

> "...terrible on the mid-term. He's, like, *so* unfair! He, *like*, wouldn't give me credit for–"

> "So *totally*–"

> "–next week with the group project, so I said *whatever*. I *hate* presentations! But it's, *like*, twenty-five percent of our grade and it's, *like*, due next week, and we *have* to rehearse. I *totally* don't have *time* for this, and besides, I *hate* giving presentations!"

> "Like *whatever! Dude needs to chill out.*"

> "Yeah, *like*... I know what you mean. Group work sucks. *Like*, it really sucks! I never get a good group. And I never get, *like*, a good topic!"

> "I *hate presentations!*"

> "*Totally.*"

The elevator doors open, and the ladies exit, the fog of angst wafting out with them. I calculate to myself – six intensive weeks, and these college students could become superior speakers and presenters, at ease with an audience, articulate and sure of themselves, presenting with clarity and with a powerful style unique to each of them. Admired by their peers. Sought by employers across the industry spectrum. No more "hate" for "public speaking." No more slang barbarisms...

No more "like."

No more "totally."

No more "whatever."

But they had disappeared into the jaws of the business school. They faded into that mass of students bustling to wherever you bustle, perhaps to sorority rush, to the next party.

Those ladies carried away with them the same problem that *most* business school students carry in their psychic backpacks, weighing them down without them knowing it – a distaste for everything that involves business presenting.

I hate presentations!

I hate public speaking!

I hate group work! I never get a good group! I never get a good topic!

I hate my group!

I hate it all!

How many times have you said it yourself? You hate public speaking. You hate giving speeches. You hate presentations.

If you happen to be giving a *group* presentation, it's even *worse*. Your imagined failure is multiplied. In group work, others now depend on *you*. And you depend on *them*. And you "never get a good group." All of that, and more.

Now, breathe deep.

If you're nervous about business school presentations...

If you don't even know the point of presentations...

If you *pretend* to know what a good presentation is, but in your heart you have no clue, and you just mimic your way through with your fingers crossed...

If you hope to God you never have to deliver another presentation after you graduate...

Then this book is for you – *just* for you. I wrote this book for you and no one else. It's just for you, the student, because I understand every one of your fears, your doubts, your jittery nerves, and your ignorance of what is desired from you. I understand you perfectly.

Visualization Time: Picture Yourself

Let's talk about the presentation itself. You know a bad presentation when you see one, don't you? We see them all the time, so often in fact, that who can be faulted for believing that presentations are supposed to be dull contrivances? You also know the superb presentation as well, and you surely know the superior presenter when you see him or her. But it's hard to figure out *why* it's so good. You can't quite put your finger on any single factor that imbues a presentation with power, but the whole of it speaks to you. You feel it across a range of emotions.

The speaker moves well, his voice resonates, he doesn't stumble, he dances expertly with his visuals, you never doze off, you remember what he says, and he stops and leaves you wanting more. You understand that you've been in the presence of a master.

Perhaps you believe that the excellence you perceive is the product of a "natural born" speaker. As a result, perhaps you think you have witnessed something that you can *never* be, something beyond your abilities. Perhaps you believe it's a gift.

Yes, it *is* a gift. It's the gift of unlimited potential, and everyone has it. Now visualize *yourself* actualizing this gift. Visualize yourself stepping confidently to the lectern and smiling at your audience. You feel in command and surely feel none of the butterflies that used to make you tremble. You have no fear. You aren't nervous. You exude an aura, or what we call professional presence.

You step out from behind the lectern and into the command position. It is apparent to everyone that *you* control the agenda. That they're about to hear something special, a business case that will yield something that *only you* can tell them and in a way that motivates and moves them to action.

Visualize yourself moving easily to and fro, gesturing precisely as you lay out the situation statement. Your voice hits the right notes with the right emotion as you serve up your value chain analysis.

You pause in the right places as you dramatize compelling story that incorporates financial analysis and the results of your SWOT analysis. Each of your teammates steps up and follows your lead. They shine and interweave their portions of the show seamlessly. Your presentation comes off as a well-orchestrated ballet, flawlessly performed.

Finally, you step up to conclude with a rousing strategic recommendation that electrifies your audience. The audience applauds loudly. Your team fields questions with aplomb, and you articulate crisp answers that satisfy even the most hardened skeptic.

Such is the stuff of a powerful business presentation. If you can visualize it, then you can achieve it. You are *more* than capable of it.

Fully Within Your Grasp

The above scenario of an especially powerful business presentation is yours for the taking. It's not the exclusive province of so-called "natural born" presenters. If you decide you truly want to excel at business presenting, and you earnestly pursue the skills and techniques of this book – the distilled wisdom of 2,500 years of presenting – then you can reach the pinnacle of business presenting.

But before you receive the keys to the kingdom and begin your stewardship, I offer here several prerequisites. Here is the very first lesson in the book before you even turn another page.

Rid Yourself of Negative Talk

We just conjured a spectacular image of ourselves as an especially powerful business presenter. Contrast that image with the kind of negativity we normally associate with business presentations.

Many students who fear, disdain, *hate* presentations have a tendency toward negative self-talk. If you are one of these folks, stop it now.

Negative self-talk serves no useful purpose on the planet, especially when it concerns something as fundamentally important to your career as *public speaking*. A true champion in any sport never tells himself or herself "I'm no good at this" or "I hate my teammates" or "I want to play the sport, but I hate practice and training."

Whether you like it or not, presentations are a major part of business school, just as much as finance, accounting, or management. They are not an "add-on" or a "soft skill." Good presenting is not something you can "pick up" along the way, nor is it a distasteful task you can avoid or foist onto someone else.

In fact, the average business school undergraduate delivers 20–25 presentations and speeches in a college career, and many of them are elaborate semester-ending projects. Given that many students obsess over their grades, consider that these presentations constitute a significant portion of the grade point average (GPA).

Almost *every* business course incorporates group work and group presentations, so presentations aren't going away anytime soon. Then, once you graduate… Well, I've encountered students who believe that once they graduate and get a "real job," their obligations to present in public end. This is 100 percent wrong.

Not *My* Job...

Presenting is considered a skill, and it is a skill that corporate America covets. It is not as involved or as deep as entire subdisciplines such as accounting or risk management, but it is a skill unto itself that harbors principles, laws, rules and best practices.

Much of this you never hear in business school, because teaching "presenting" is always someone else's job. Your professor assumes you've been trained in this mysterious class that you're supposed to have taken, but you never see listed on the course schedule. If such a course actually exists, for some reason it is taught by someone outside the business school or by an administrator type who was assigned the task to "teach presentations" because, well, it's her turn. I know you're familiar with this.

But it wasn't always this way. Contrast your experience with the importance accorded to presentations prior to the dawn of multimedia.

Entire departments of public speaking used to hold proud places in American universities. An entire university called the National School for Elocution and Oratory in Philadelphia thrived on into the late years of the nineteenth century. Books for business speakers used to crowd the shelves. Yes, presenting *is* a skill, and one that is severely neglected today.

So if you find yourself whining about presentations, stop right now. I know that you occasionally gripe. *Every* student does at some point. Let's reverse the dynamic right now and begin thinking positively of how superb business presenting can bestow on us a lasting personal competitive advantage and propel us up into the High-Demand Skill Zone where employers seek the finest candidates.

Let's lay some groundwork for that right now.

The One Superb Skill

If today you discovered that there was one thing – one skill – you could learn that would immeasurably increase your chances of getting a great job after graduation, wouldn't that be great? What would you think of that? That it's too good to be true?

What if you learned that this skill is something that you can develop to a reasonably high level in just a handful of weeks?

Think of it – a skill you can learn in four to five weeks that can provide you with a lasting competitive advantage throughout the rest of your working life. A skill that few people take seriously. A skill in incredibly high demand by America's corporations.

Capable business presenting *is* a highly demanded skill. Companies haven't nearly enough personnel who can communicate effectively, logically, comfortably, clearly, and cogently. And I include C-suite personnel in that number as well. The vast majority of employers seek the following knowledge, skills, and abilities in new MBA hires: communication skills (86 percent); professionalism (78 percent); initiative and integrity (77 percent); motivation (76 percent) and ability to deal effectively with pressure and unexpected obstacles (75 percent).[1]

And this is why you, as a business student, gain personal competitive advantage *vis-à-vis* your peers when you take presenting seriously rather than as a distasteful task. You gain *incredible* advantage by embracing the notion that you *should* and *can* become a powerful business presenter.

In other words, if you actually devote yourself to the task of becoming a superb speaker, you can become one. The task is not as difficult as you imagine (although it isn't easy, either).

Transformation Time

This is about transformation of the way we think, of the way we view the world, of the lens through which we peer at others, of the lens through which we see ourselves. It is a *liberating window* on the world. And it begins with your uniqueness.

---

1 Graduate Management Admission Council, *Corporate Recruiters Survey: General Data Report* (2011), 2.

You *are* unique.

This is not esteem-building snake oil. I am not in the business of esteem building, nor in the feel-good industry. If you had to affix a name to it, you could say that I *am* in the business of esteem-discovery.

I don't teach you to be unique, and I don't teach you to be someone other than who you are. I help you to *discover* who you are, to inventory your gifts and talents and to take stock of your desires and dreams. I help you to respect and learn what the finest public speakers and presenters in history can teach you – and that handful of eternal verities that *will* transform you, if you accept them.

I encourage you to find within yourself the capacity for excellence that you hope and pray you have, but fear you don't have the guts to tap into. I teach you to stop riding the surface, and to plunge into the business life with gusto.

So your belief in this uniqueness is utterly essential to your development as a powerful business presenter.

But given the tendency of modernity to squelch your imagination, to curtail your enthusiasm, to limit your vision, and to homogenize your appearance and your speech, you may have abandoned the notion of uniqueness as the province of the eccentric. Perhaps you prefer to "fit in."

Some truths can be uncomfortable. Often, truths about ourselves are uncomfortable, because if we acknowledge them, we then obligate ourselves to change in some way. But in this case, the truth is liberating.

Your Shrinking World

Recognize that in four years of college, a crust of mediocrity may well have formed on you. It is, at least partially, this crust of mediocrity that holds you back from becoming a powerful presenter. Your world has shrunk incrementally, and if you don't push it out, it will close in about you and continue to limit you.

Recognize that you dwell in a college cocoon. Self-doubt, conformity, and low expectations can attach themselves to you, slowing you down as barnacles slow an ocean liner.

Your self-confidence gets leeched away by a thousand interactions with people who mean you no harm and, yet, pressure you to conform to a standard, a lowest common denominator. People who shape, cramp and restrict your ability to deliver presentations. They lacquer over your innate abilities and force you into a dull conformity.

Their expectations of you are low. They expect you to be like them. They resent your quest for knowledge and try to squelch it. Beware of people who doubt you, your desires and your success. At some point, you might question whether these people actually belong in your life.

Yes, you *are* unique, and in the subsequent pages you discover the power of your uniqueness. You strip away the layers of modern mummification. You chip away at those crusty barnacles that have formed over the years without your even realizing it.

It is time to express that uniqueness in ways that support whatever it is you want to do. I offer you the clear path to success, a way of interacting and engaging with the world that liberates you and empowers you to utilize your gifts to achieve your goals.

Until now, the path has probably *not* been clear, at least with respect to your presentation skills.

Here's Why...

Let me describe your typical presentation experience in business school as you watch a so-called professional who visits to deliver a lecture.

You see a dull business presentation that some people praise as good. A fellow stands in front of you, crouching at a lectern, and he *reads* slide after slide with dozens of bullet points obviously taken from a written paper.

Unreadable spreadsheets appear on the screen, and the presenter begins reading the slides *verbatim*, his head turned away from you. You realize, finally, that he is reading the slides along with everyone sitting in the audience.

You scratch your chin, and say to yourself "That's not hard at all."

Just cobble something like that together, and you think you have a business presentation. And why *wouldn't* you think that? It seems to have all the elements: a speaker-reader of slides (you), a PowerPoint display on the screen with bullet points on it, some numbers, and a five-minute time slot to fill with talk. Stir well and chill before serving.

But what you actually have is something ugh-awful.

You don't know what you want to accomplish, or why. You really have no idea what you should say, or why. You certainly don't view yourself as benefitting from the process in any way. Instead, you see it as something incredibly painful. Because it *is* painful. It's painful because of the way it's been explained to you. Because the explanations are always incomplete. You never seem to get the whole story.

Who Teaches this Stuff, Anyway?

The folks who actually provide you with some sort of presenting instruction are often disconnected from your business courses. They may even be ensconced in another school altogether, such as "communication" or "education."

They typically don't know much about business, and they may well have been assigned to teach the course because… well, *somebody* has to teach it, and since it's a "soft skill," most anybody can fill in. Right?

So they teach you "How to give a speech" or "How to introduce yourself." You seldom have the opportunity to engage in a complex group presentation, and certainly not a presentation about a business case. Because many of these instructors aren't even in the business school, they cannot show you how to incorporate business content into your presentations.

What About Your Professors?

Let me say here that I have great respect for *all* of my colleagues in *all* of the subdisciplines of business, and the tremendous storehouse of knowledge and expertise amassed in our business faculties. What I find, however, is that the skill of business presenting is truly no one's job in the business school, and so it languishes. No business school professor really wants to teach it when it is outside his or her subject area.

The truth is that for most of your professors, presenting is secondary. This makes sense, as each faculty has a specialty or functional discipline they are charged with teaching. "Presenting" is no one's functional discipline, and so it goes unaddressed, orphaned to expediency and neglect. Moreover, many professors in your business courses are often afflicted with the same malaise that plagues business at large. They themselves cannot present well.

It is the same in the business world at large. *Your* presenting woes are the same woes that scourge the American business landscape, from young executives to the C-suite.

The Malaise in Corporate America

I attended a business conference in San Diego not long ago. At this conference, I witnessed some of the worst speaking I have ever heard in my career, coupled with the use of incredibly bad visuals. These visuals were badly done PowerPoint slides. This conference featured:

- **Monotone voices**

- **Busy slides with tiny letters**

- **Motionless speakers planted behind a lectern**

- **Aimless and endless talking with seemingly no point**

- **No preparation and no practice attended these presentations**

- **Papers shuffling in the audience, because handouts were given prior to the talk**

You've seen your own versions of this awful scenario. It is more common than you might imagine.

Communications consultant Andy Goodman conducted major research on the issue in 2005, evaluating more than 2,500 public interest professionals' recent presentation viewing experiences.

The average grade public interest professionals gave to the presentations they attended was C−. The average grade given to the visuals that respondents observed in presentations they attended was also C−. When asked to recall presentations they had seen over the last few months, survey respondents said they were more than likely to see a poor presentation as an excellent one.[2]

This is the current state of presentations in corporate America and business schools. Is it uniformly bleak? No, of course not. Generalizations are just that – general in nature. I have seen a sufficient number of fine presentations to understand that, somewhere, superb instruction holds sway. Or at the very least, young people whose early development has trained them for stage performance have found their way to the business platform. Good for them.

---

2 Andy Goodman, *Why Bad Presentations Happen to Good Causes* (Los Angeles: Cause Communications, 2006), 10.

But for the most part, the situation is as I have described here. This presents you with magnificent opportunity. Now that you understand the situation and why it exists, it's time for you to join the ranks of superior presenters. It's time for your debut.

On the Cusp of Greatness... Or Something Fairly Close

The method I elaborate here is not the *only* way you can deliver a presentation in business school. In fact, some of my colleagues do disagree with various points. *You* might chafe at what you consider "arbitrary" rules. Go your own way then, and I wish you good luck and Godspeed. Continue what you've been doing and see how it goes.

I do not quibble or judge – I only show you *what works*. These are the techniques and tools that have worked for more than 2,000 years *and* which have earned your fellow college students thousands of dollars by winning business case competitions.

I contend that you become a much better speaker if you employ the techniques and commitment offered here. Your improvement is rapid, and with this improvement you *feel* the difference. By this, I don't mean a general aura of well-being. I mean that you *feel power*. You gain a sense of mastery, of confidence, and of *élan*.

Much more than that, you lift yourself into the High-Demand Skill Zone. This is the narrow elite slice of the executive labor market where you can differentiate yourself from 95 percent of your peers, and thus command a higher salary and greater responsibility. These are great expectations for a little book. But the realization of expectations depends on you.

Step-by-step, we build you into a confident and powerful presenter. Step-by-step, you learn to work with your material, the stuff of business presentations, and to frame the story you tell.

Step-by-step, you learn to build especially powerful presentations that play to your strengths and utilize multi-media to tell your story in the most compelling, provocative and powerful way possible.

Big Ideas

This book will mean something different to you than to any other person reading and learning from it. It changes you in a positive way, but the changes are yours and yours alone.

You discover your strengths, you develop your style, and you play to what makes you unique. These are not platitudes or self-help therapy. They are the building blocks to presentation success. And presentation success is the key to career success.

Too many 600-page texts bore you and enrich the publishing company. Here, you find exactly what you must know and do to excel. You are free to listen and learn. And you are free to ignore what is in these pages, if you choose.

But if you search for a key, a single formula that can solve your school challenges and ease your worries about post-graduation career possibilities, this is as close as you will ever come to finding one.

You have *complete control* over implementation of this Big Idea. It's completely up to you whether it works or not. Here in this book, I require that you *do* stuff, and you may conclude that it's too much sacrifice for too little reward in this lab scenario called college.

On the other hand, you may conclude otherwise. You may decide that you want to enter what I call the Power Zone. The Power Zone of constant and steady improvement in presenting that is yours for taking, all with the right attitude and proper perspective.

When you change yourself and your attitude, you succeed in transforming every presentation that you deliver from this point forward.

In these pages, I tell you many secrets, and I'll reveal one here. It is this:

To become a superior speaker, you transform yourself. Once you have transformed yourself, you can never go back to the way you presented before. Once you have learned how to transform yourself, you can never look at presentations the same way.

By reading this book and applying its explicit instructions, it is within your power to change your entire career. Thus, you are about to take an irrevocable intellectual step.

Are you ready?

PUBLIC SPEAKING: THE TWENTY-FIRST CENTURY PRESENTER

We live in the twenty-first century age of multimedia kaleidoscopic presentations, with video clips, sound effects, dazzling animation, laser pointers, remote control clickers and endless bullet points.

Can 3D presentations be next? *Avatar* for the C-suite? A taste of sci-fi effects modified for corporate tastes and sensibilities?

Somehow, I cannot envision the CEO and his staff donning unfashionable glasses to indulge a desire for hi-tech effects of dubious value, but I've learned never to say never. It *could* happen, and it would be disastrous. In fact, most of the bells and whistles that infest our modern presentation culture have degraded the presentation universe.

Why do we even *bother* talking about presenting when the technology does it for us? We have endless templates, courtesy of Microsoft and thousands of individual shareware enthusiasts dedicated to the free flow of information. The human being now appears expendable. The young executive becomes more and more superfluous in the presentation process. She becomes chief slide-reader.

Every occasion for transmitting information to groups of people large-or-small is now an occasion for cobbling together PowerPoint slides. Cutting and pasting from corporate documents. Slides rife with bullet points, boredom, and blandness…

…and bereft of even a whiff of imagination.

These "presentations" are little more than group reading sessions. Everyone sits, watches a lit screen, and reads along with the "presenter." Sometimes you stand in the dark, glad to be invisible to the audience.

And why not? It's accepted. It constitutes ninety-five percent of what passes for presentations in the business world. And you see the same thing in business school. You've *done* the same thing in business school. And you'll do it again.

So this begs the natural question, "Why bother?"

Why not coast along with everyone else, keep your head down, don't attract attention, and make your corporate mark by being a diligent cubicle employee sitting at your computer and punching numbers into spreadsheets all day?

Why don't we just eliminate presentations altogether? Aren't they inefficient and imprecise? The evidence would seem to suggest just that.

Communication coach Lynda Paulson observes that "Most people can read and comprehend more content in half-an-hour than you could ever get across in the same time through speaking. Add the time consumed in going to and from a meeting, and a speech is not the most efficient way to get you content across."[1]

But – and it's a *big* but – the public presentation is packed with potential to deliver a powerful message that no other communication method can match. We still deliver presentations now because the original intent of the presentation was the same intent that has animated public speaking throughout history.

The Power of Personal Presence

Personal presence

Personal presence distinguishes the business presentation as a distinctly different form of communication, and it is the source of its power. I should say *potential* power. For much of the potential power of presentations has been forfeited.

That potential has been squandered out of corporate fear, ignorance, egoism, conformity, and simple habit. Lynda Paulson describes the unique qualities that a business presentation offers, as opposed to a simple written report.

> What makes speaking so powerful is that at least 85 percent of what we communicate in speaking is non-verbal. It's what people see in our eyes, in our movements and in our actions. It's what they hear through the tone of our voice. It's what they sense on a subliminal level. That's why speaking, to a group or one-on-one, is such a total experience."[2]

---

1 Lynda R. Paulson, *The Executive Persuader* (Napa, CA: SSI Publishing, 1991), 26.
2 Ibid.

Here, Paulson has described the impact of *personal presence*. It's the tangible ability of the messenger to conveying a convincing message. A skilled speaker exudes energy, enthusiasm, *savoir faire* – he becomes part of the message. Here is where *you* become part of the message and bring into play your unique talents and strengths.

But modern technology has swept the speaker into the background in favor of naked information and pyrotechnics that miss the entire point of the show – namely, communicating with and persuading an audience. Lots of people are fine with being swept into the background, into that indistinguishable mass of grays. They'd be happy if you faded into the background, too. Who needs competition making everyone else look bad? Most people don't want to compete in the presentation arena, and they would just as soon compete with you for your firm's spoils on *other* terms.

But the true differentiating power of a presentation springs from the oratorical skills and confidence of the speaker. That, in fact, is the entire point of delivering a presentation – a project or idea has a champion who presents the case in public. Without that champion – without that *powerful presence* – a presentation is even less than ineffective. It becomes an incredibly bad communication exercise and an infuriating waste of a valuable resource – time.

Today, we are left only with the brittle shell of this once-powerful communication tool. Gone is any notion of the skilled public speaker, a presenter enthusiastic and confident, articulate and graceful, powerful and convincing. All that remains is an automaton slide-reader in a business suit.

This is surely a far cry from how we imagine it ought to be – powerful visuals and a confident presenter, who commands the facts and delivers compelling arguments using an array of powerful tools.

Perhaps we *do* see great presentations on occasion. Certainly the occasional bright light emerges, a skilled speaker who dazzles us. But that's rare. Today's average business school presentation, just like its modern corporate counterpart, has been leeched of its power and passion. The notion of *personal presence* has faded into the student's generic self-abnegation and vague desire to blend into a background of drab grays and browns. How have we come to this sorry state?

In part, it is a general misunderstanding of the very nature of the presenter's task. General ignorance abounds of the purpose of the presentation and the role of the presenter in accomplishing that purpose. Moreover, many professors and businesspeople alike are unfamiliar with the techniques of power presenting and the notion that a presenter ought to possess high-order skills.

Who is a Presenter?

Before computers. Before television and radio. Before loudspeakers. Before all of our artificial means of expanding the reach of our unaided voices, there was the public speaker. The "presenter."

Public speaking was considered close to an art form. Some *did* consider it art. In 1886 Alexander Melville Bell wrote that "The great arenas of public oratory" were "the church, the courthouse, the legislative chamber, and the theater."[3] Thus public speaking – or the "presentation" – was the province of four key groups of people: preachers, politicians, lawyers, and actors. The first trying to save your soul, the second to take your money, the third to save your life, the fourth to transport you to another time and place, if only for a short spell.

Other, less high-toned professions utilized the powerful communication skills of presenting – carnival barker, vaudevillian, traveling snake oil salesmen. All of them businessmen of a type. These were not the earliest examples of America's business presenters, but they surely were the last generation before modernity sapped the vitality from public speaking. Today, we're left with those initial key professions – preachers, politicians, lawyers, and actors – all of whom today practice a faded version of presenting.

The skills necessary to these four presenting professions were developed over centuries. The ancient Greeks knew well the influence of oratory and argument, the persuasive powers of words. Socrates, one of the great orators of the fifth century BC, was tried and sentenced to death for the power of his oratory, coupled with the "wrong" ideas.

Cicero, acknowledged by many as the ancient world's second-ranking orator, behind Demosthenes, recognized that style is as important as substance in public speaking: "We now see, that it is by no means sufficient to find out what to say, unless we can handle it skillfully when we have found it."[4]

The greatest experts on the planet – the most superb presenters – were those men and women of the 1880s to the 1920s, who propelled us into the information age. They benefitted from 2,000 years of presentation wisdom. They communicated with force and passion, emotion and drive. To a person, they had *personal presence*.

---

3 Alexander Melville Bell, *Essays and Postscripts on Elocution* (New York: Edgar S. Werner, 1886), 149.
4 *Cicero on Oratory and Orators*, trans. J. S. Watson (Philadelphia: David McKay, 1897), 145.

But in our modern twenty-first century smugness, we are apt to think that long-dead practitioners of public speaking and of quaint "elocution" have nothing to teach us. We've adopted a wealth of technological firepower to improve, embellish, amplify, and exalt our presentation message. Yet the result has been something quite different.

Instead of sharpening our communication skills, multimedia packages have served to supplant them. Each new advance in technology creates another barrier between the speaker and the audience.

Today's presenters have latched onto the notion that PowerPoint *is* the presentation. The idea now appears to be that PowerPoint has removed responsibility from you to be knowledgeable, interesting, concise, and clear. Many young people like this just fine, as it takes away the pressure of actually having to do something. The presentation becomes something *outside* the speaker.

The focus has shifted from the speaker to the fireworks, and this has led to such a decline to the point where in extreme cases the attitude of the presenter is: "The presentation is up there on the slides… let's all read them together." And in many cases, this is exactly what happens. It is almost as if the presenter becomes a member of the audience.

PowerPoint and props are just tools. That's all. You should be able to present *without* them. And when you can, finally, present without them, you can then use them to maximum advantage to amplify the superior communication skills you have developed.

In fact, many college students *do* present without PowerPoint every day outside of the university. Some of them give fabulous presentations. Most give adequate presentations. They deliver these presentations in the context of one of the most ubiquitous part-time jobs college students perform – waiter or waitress.

On-the-Job Presentation Training – And Increased Income

For a waiter, every customer is an audience, every welcoming a show. The smartest students recognize this as an opportunity to sharpen presentation skills useful in multiple venues, to differentiate and hone a personal *persona*, and to earn substantially more tips at the end of each presentation.

Most students in my classes do not recognize the fabulous opportunity they have as a waiter or waitress – they view it simply as a job, performed to a minimum standard. Without even realizing it, they compete with a low-cost strategy rather than a differentiation strategy, and their tips at the end of the evening show it.

Instead of offering premium service and an experience that no other waiter or waitress delivers, these students give the standard functional service like everyone else.

As a waiter, ask yourself: "What special thing can I offer that my customers might be willing to pay more for?"

Your answer is obvious… you can serve up a unique and enjoyable experience for your customers. In fact, you can make each visit to your restaurant memorable for your customers by delivering a show that sets you apart from others, one that puts you in-demand.

I do not mean juggling for your customers, or becoming a comedian, or intruding on your guests' evening. I do mean taking your job seriously, learning your temporary profession's rules, crafting a presentation of your material that resonates with confidence, authenticity and sincerity, and then displaying enthusiasm for your material and an earnestness to communicate it in words and actions designed to make your audience feel comfortable – and heroic.

Yes, *heroic*. Every presentation – every story – has a hero and that hero is in your audience. Evoke a sense of heroism in your customer, and you win every time. Evoke a sense of heroism in your presentation audience, and you win every time.

I have just described a quite specific workplace scenario where effective presenting can have an immediate reward. Every element necessary to successful presenting is present in a wait-staff restaurant situation.

Moreover, the principles and techniques of delivering a powerful presentation in a restaurant and in a boardroom are not just similar – they are *identical*. The venue is different, the audience is different, the relationships of those in the room might be different, but the principles are the same.

So back to the early practitioners of oratory and public speaking. Here is the paradox: a fabulous treasure can be had for anyone with the motivation to pluck these barely concealed gems right off the ground.

Adopt the habits of the masters. *Acquire* the mannerisms and the power and versatility of the maestros who strode the stages, who argued in courtrooms, who declaimed in congress, and who bellowed from pulpits. They are your presenting ancestors. And right now, they look down and glower at you. They are unhappy at what they see in the world of business presenting.

They see three groups of people who perpetuate three views of business presenting. Let's look at these three views. With regard to presentations, I deal with two large groups of people. For sake of descriptive simplicity, let's call these two groups "Natural Born" and "McTips!"

"Natural Born" and "McTips!" represent two extreme views of what it takes to become an especially powerful and superior business presenter. Neither is remotely accurate. And neither group is what might be called enlightened in these matters. Members of both groups are frustrating and irritating in their own ways and completely self-serving. Here is why...

We often look for folks to excuse us from what, deep down, we know we ought to do, or know what we *can* do. If we look hard enough, we find what we search for, and excuses are extremely easy to find. Let's look at these two excuses that hold us back from fulfilling our potential as especially powerful presenters.

The Three Groups

Generally, in the business world there are three views of "presenting" and three groups of folks who hold these views. The first two groups are large. They make up about 95 percent of us business types. Their views on presenting are, to be frank, quite destructive.

But there is another group that constitutes the remaining five percent. This group has an incredible competitive advantage in business presenting. As a result, most folks in this group would be satisfied if it stayed small and exclusive and powerful.

They would likely prefer that you *not* join this elite group, as you might increase the competition for them.

Let's look at the first two groups and see if you fall into either category.

Group one: The impossible dream

First, one very large group of people believes that good presenting is impossible unless you have the "gift." Public speaking is the province of the gifted and the charismatic. It's a God-given talent that you cannot hope to replicate. They'll tell you not to try. They'll scoff at your effort. They'll ask you, "How can you 'learn' talent?"

They ask it with a shrug of the shoulders. It's akin to the magical world of art – artists are people who visualize and create masterpieces that the rest of us can only admire. For this large group of naysayers, there is almost something mystical about the easy manner of a Bill Clinton, Barack Obama, Jerry Seinfeld, or Colin Powell. These are "natural born" speakers, and then there are the rest of us.

This view would have us believe that great speakers are born with some arcane and unfathomable gift, combining talent and natural stage facility. That Bill Clinton sprang from the womb declaiming that he feels our pain. That Ronald Reagan was born orating on lower capital gains taxes. That Oprah Winfrey began her talk show career in kindergarten.

If the first view holds that great speakers are born with a gift, then quite logically this view leaves the rest of us to strive with middling presentation skills. It's an excuse for us not to persevere. Why bother to try? Why not, instead, hire some of these natural-born-speaker types to do the heavy presentation lifting? The rest of us can skate along and pretend that we're not actually lazy, or frightened, or disinterested, or unambitious.

One of my colleagues down the hall claims that business presenting is somehow "different."

"It's not oratory or classical rhetoric or acting," he says. "It is something *different.*" Just "different."

And yet it rarely is taught, except in the breach. It is left to "public speaking" classes to instruct business school students. These public speaking classes typically teach generic public speaking. You know the approach – "How to give a speech." This "How to give a speech" approach has a one-size-fits-all character and doesn't do us much good in the business school.

As far as presenting in general, an erroneous attitude persists: "You either have it or you don't." Surely these must be some of the most defeatist words ever crafted. They betray an attitude as well. The lazy attitude they embody has been around a long time.

> Objections on not infrequently raised against the systematic study of oratory. Eloquence, we are told, is the gift of Nature, and must be left to her direction. But... The great oratorios of both ancient and modern times have diligently studied the rules of the art until they acquired the grace of cultivated nature... The incessant labors of Demosthenes, of Aeschines, of Hortentius, of Isocrates, and Gracchus, show that these men agreed with Cicero in the belief that to be in oratory, something more is needed than *to be born.*[5]

---

5 Albert M. Bacon, *A Manual of Gesture* (New York: Silver, Burdett & Co., 1893), 10–11.

"Natural born speaker" has all the musty certitude of cliché, a handy excuse for those disinclined to work hard. Could any more negative a phrase ever have been coined? Actually, there *is* a bit of insidious truth to the phrase – it *is* true that you either have skill or you don't. Or you have a certain level of skill. Or you do not.

But the implication here is that you cannot *acquire* great public speaking skill. There is comfort in such arbitrariness – the false certitude that you cannot succeed and you are therefore absolved from trying.

You get no absolution from me.

Group two: This is easy stuff!

If there is a large group of people who believe that speakers are "born," an equally large group of people believes that public speaking is *easy*. It's an effortless "knack" you can pick up in your spare time. You can "get the hang of it." You can "wing it," because you think you're good at it.

Has the presentation landscape changed so much that what was once taught as a fine skill is now mass-produced in 30-minute quickie sessions of speaking "tips"? I actually saw a headline on an article that offered *12 Tips to Become a Presentation God!*

"Tips?" Really?

Have the demands of the presentation become so weak, have our expectations become so degraded, that we now believe that presenting can be served up in McDonald's-style kid meals… "You want to super-size your speaking McTips?"

People in this "McTips!" group are quite confident and seemingly knowledgeable about it. They believe that anyone can become a good presenter *with minimal effort*, because it is actually "easy."

A colleague of mine falls into this category. He is a man I greatly respect for his business acumen and all-round good humor. But he dismisses presentation skills as something that can be picked up quickly.

"Thirty minutes is all it takes," he tells me sagely. He rocks back in his chair. And he is serious. "Thirty minutes. I can teach someone to present in just 30 minutes. All that other stuff is just BS."

This attitude toward public speaking has persisted for decades. Just as I have written this guide for you, James Albert Winans authored a presentations book for his students more than seven decades ago. Winans was one of the public speaking masters of the 1920s, a professor of public speaking at Cornell University, and he identified the same wrong-headedness that plagues us today:

> The book is perhaps a sufficient answer to the naïve freshman, who when he came to ask me about my course, exclaimed, "Gee, I don't see how you can make that stuff hard!" But while there is no attempt made to dodge natural difficulties and offer "public speaking made easy," neither is there an attempt to make the subject more difficult than an intelligent treatment makes necessary. That would be a sorry business indeed.[6]

Many people are simply ignorant of the depth and breadth of the public speaking domain. So they wax eloquently and ignorantly about it, believing it to be something that it is not.

The idea that, powerful presenting is actually the judicious application of high-order skills of gesture, voice, movement, style, focus, elocution, and even intuition is alien to the "Easy Presenting" group. Moreover, the very *nature* of these skills is foreign to them. The skill-set of the advanced and effective presenter is much akin to that of the actor, and these skills would seem irrelevant to someone with only a superficial understanding of the art of presenting.

After all, business is serious, right? Wheareas mere "acting" is, well, frivolous. Acting is talent-based, right, with no role for learned techniques? Hardly. Acting coach Anita Jesse zeroes in on the basic skills necessary to powerful acting, and they are as easily applied to the art of powerful presenting:

> Almost any proficient actor will tell you that expertise [in acting] depends upon a short list of basic skills. Those building blocks are concentration, imagination, access to emotions, listening, observation, and relaxation.[7]

Concentration, imagination, access to emotions, listening, observation, and relaxation. These are the qualities necessary to an actor's powerful performances, and these are likewise qualities essential to the power presenter. They are elements of *personal presence.* They are qualities you find in abundance in the great speakers we admire for their rhetorical skill and abilities to communicate – Bill Clinton, Ronald Reagan, Barack Obama, Oprah Winfrey, Martin Luther King. Every great speaker has exhibited all of these qualities in greater or lesser degree.

---

6 James Albert Winans, *Public Speaking* (New York: The Century Co., 1926), 17.
7 Anita Jesse, *Let the Part Play You* (Burbank, CA: Wolf Creek Press, 2001), 3.

So those are the two groups of naysayers – the "Natural Born" and the "McTips!" folks. Most people fall into either of these two camps – "presenting" is either impossibly hard to learn or it's a toss-off activity that you can pick up somewhere along the way in business school.

These attitudes can cripple modern business education. Delivering an effective presentation is a deeply personal activity. To criticize a presentation is to criticize a person's ego. And so, the attitude persists.

Group three: Into the Power Zone!

So we have these two perspectives – that great presentations are incredibly *easy* or presentations are impossibly *hard*.

We have remaining to us a narrow slice of the spectrum between "Natural Born" and "McTips!" This is the third group. It's small, and it's where you want to be. It's where you find the truth.

The Power Zone is the province of those who understand that anyone can become a great presenter with work and desire. A deep philosophical, academic, and professional history undergirds public speaking, and public presentations – *great* presentations require study and practice and preparation and technique. This history informs the very best presenters and their work. You dismiss it only to your great loss.

Folks in the Power Zone are privy to the truth, and once you learn the truth about presenting, you can never go back to viewing presentations the same way. Consider this pop culture analogy from the 1999 film *The Matrix*.

In *The Matrix*, humans live in a world that is not what it seems. In fact, everything they believe about the world is false. Morpheus (Lawrence Fishburne) offers to reveal the truth to Neo (Keanu Reeves) about his existence. Morpheus offers Neo a blue pill and a red pill. The process of presentation discovery is much like the red-pill/blue-pill choice that Morpheus offers to the young computer hacker Neo.

> "You take the blue pill, the story ends, you wake up in your bed and believe whatever you want to believe. You take the red pill, you stay in Wonderland, and I show you how deep the rabbit hole goes."[8]

The blue pill returns Neo to his old state of ignorance. The red pill reveals the secret, and once he learns it, he can never return to his old life.

---

8   *The Matrix*, DVD, directed by Andy Wachowski and Lana Wachowski (1999; Burbank, CA: Warner Home Video, 1999).

Likewise, you can stop reading this book this instant – the blue pill – and return to the righteous and relaxing world of "Natural Born" or "McTips!" Both of these viewpoints permit the average presenter to remain mired in mediocrity with an excuse to stay right there.

That's the paradox, the Curse of Freedom. It's completely within your power to seize the fruits of great presenting. It's your choice.

"Natural Born" means you don't try at all, while "McTips!" means you offer token effort as befits a low-level pedestrian task. So, if you choose the blue pill, close this book and go your own way immediately. *Bon voyage!* I wish you a hearty good luck and Godspeed, and perhaps you will be happier for your choice.

But if you are one of the few who thinks for a moment "Hmm. What if the professor is right? What if–?"

Then... take the red pill

Then, read on to the next brief paragraph – the red pill – and be forever shorn of the excuse for mediocrity, of the excuse for settling for less than an absolutely smashing presentation *every time*. For the truth is in the Power Zone, and once there, you will never be satisfied with your old presentation life again. You cannot go back.

Choose the red pill. Step boldly into the Power Zone.

The Power Zone is the province of the privileged few who understand the truth that *anyone* can become a great presenter, with the right kind of hard work and the *desire* to become a great presenter. To join this third group requires you to adopt a new state of mind.

If you already carry this view, that's superb. If you don't... you can decide now to adopt it or forever be relegated to the other two groups – believing you're not good enough, or believing you *are* good enough when you actually are *not*.

You actually *can* become a capable presenter. You can become a *great* presenter. When you enter the Power Zone, you are both cursed and blessed with knowledge. This knowledge represents two sides of the same coin.

You are cursed with the knowledge that the only limitation you have is *you*. You are blessed with the knowledge that you can become a good – even *great* – speaker. An especially powerful presenter.

Now, you have no other real excuse. It's totally up to you.

The Source of Advantage Today

In today's PowerPoint-driven world, the competitive advantage lies with firms that possess greater and more highly skilled human capital – people who are steeped in the nuances of communicating to groups of people both large and small. But these people are rare nowadays. To use the business vernacular, they are in a state of undersupply.

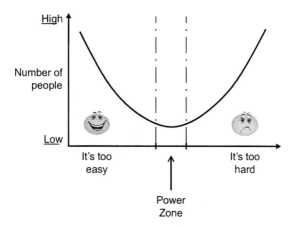

Instead, we see literally thousands of examples of automaton-like executives delivering staid presentations. You can find them on corporate websites, such as Coca-Cola.[9] Presidents, CEOs, and such like are the main culprits in perpetuating bad speeches and worse presentations. It's in the nature of their fiefdoms that these emperors never wear clothes, and surely no one in the firm will tell them of their mediocrity. And this is one reason that mediocrity has become the norm.

In contrast to the business world, the bubbling province of emotional communication is dominated by motivational speakers, preachers, actors, and the occasional maverick lawyer. These communicators touch people's deepest desires and needs and provide a kind of psychic fulfillment. You should strive for this as well in your own slice of the business realm.

Does this mean to adopt a "Price is Right" *persona* in your speaking, with much strutting and exaggeration? Not unless you feel called to it. Extreme speaking is unnecessary to touch people's hearts and feelings.

9 The Coca-Cola Company, "Leadership Viewpoints," http://www.thecocacolacompany. com/presscenter/viewpoints.html (accessed June 18, 2012).

No, it means that you should recognize the opportunity presented by the vast wasteland of corporate public speaking. Perhaps it's time to consciously move to the Power Zone of powerful business presenting.

You need not become a scholar of public speaking. In fact, few people have that deep an interest in the subject and even fewer can claim that kind of knowledge today. But what you *can* and *should* do is this: Open your mind and heart to the possibilities of found treasure.

This book brims with the finest advice and techniques that presenters have perfected over centuries. You don't have to fish for these nuggets in the literature of the past... I've already done that for you. And it's all here, organized logically.

The uncut diamonds have been arranged for you on the ground, and all you need do is pick them up.

BASICS OF YOUR TALK

Structure, Content, Audience

If you look to improve your presentation skills quickly and dramatically, this chapter does that for you. Here I discuss several types of presentations you face in business school, and I offer you a handful of basics that allow you to significantly improve your business presentations *right now*.

It will not take you all the way to the Power Zone, but when you adopt these basics and see and feel your improvement, you should need no more convincing that you can become an especially powerful business presenter.

In all presentations, you apply the three Ps – **principles, preparation**, and **practice**.

This means that you apply the personal *principles* of this book to your own development as a presenter, that you *prepare* diligently using the techniques I give you, and that you *practice* in the prescribed manner.

Your Presentations

You are faced with several types of presentations in business school, but they all share fundamental commonalities, whether in finance, marketing, risk, or strategy. Here, I do not refer to shared subject matter, of course. There are obviously major differences between finance and marketing. I refer to here to the *structural elements* of your presentations.

These elements consist of 1) purpose, 2) length, 3) number of participants, 4) size and type of audience. With regard to subject matter differences – such as those found among, say, marketing, human resources, and international business – these differences do not appreciably affect *how* we present.

Let's look at each of these four elements.

1) Purpose – Your purpose is to *persuade*.

Sure, other reasons for giving a presentation may flit about, offering artificial distinctions that are really of no consequence – to teach, to inform, to demonstrate, and such like. But you are there to *persuade* your audience and call them to action.

Gene Zelazny is the director of visual communications for the consulting firm of McKinsey & Company, and in his book *Say It with Presentations*, he puts it this way. Your purpose is:

...to *persuade* the city council to place the waste dump in their backyard

...to *persuade* the company founder to close down the two plants

...to *persuade* the business unit heads to cut costs by 40 percent.[1]

In business presentations your purpose is almost always to persuade and issue a call to action – this is the case 95 percent of the time. In short, you want your audience to *do* something. Your presentation must persuade the audience to do something and then explicitly call them to act.

Write down your purpose. It should be a clear, one-sentence statement of your objective. This is your mission statement. It is very much like a company's mission statement, which guides a company's strategy.

Likewise, your mission statement guides you to prepare a succinct, direct, convincing presentation. Here are some examples:

• "My objective is to convince the senior leadership of Toughbolt Company to enter the Paraguayan market in the next 12 months by means of a joint venture."

• "My objective is to persuade the rank-and-file members of three unions to compromise on upcoming contracts so that our company can remain financially stable in these difficult economic times."

---

1 Gene Zelazny, *Say it With Presentations* (New York: McGraw-Hill, 2006), 7. I concur with Zelazny and I recommend his book for anyone interested in developing engaging presentations; it is concise and quite useful.

- "My objective is to convince the audience of my presentation that my valuation of the company is correct and, as a consequence, we should accept the acquisition offer that has been made by Toughbolt Company."

2) Length – Quite often you are given a specific length of time for your presentation. It can range, say, from 2 minutes all the way up to 20 minutes for an individual show. Group presentations usually last no more than 20 minutes, and your part of the presentation lasts no more than 4–5 minutes.

Regardless of length, the basic structure I describe here is the same for all of your presentations. For example, let's take an assignment that I give to students in my basic international business course.

In this assignment, students are required to read an article of their choice, synthesize it in one written page, then give a two-minute presentation that summarizes the piece, that relates it to the concepts of the course, and that places it in the context of globalization.

The task that always befuddles them is *what to include in the presentation.*

Almost every student believes he must cover the *entire* article in his presentation. This is a typical approach toward presenting, and it is almost always incorrect. Without explicit instructions to analyze the article and synthesize it, the student produces a long and rambling explication of the article as he remembers it.

Rather than carefully selecting the material for importance and impact, the student attempts to pour *everything* into a two-minute spiel. Inevitably, this leads to the student trying to memorize whole sentences from the article in a kind of rote exercise. The result is a "presentation" that rambles with no real purpose except to "inform" in a kind of vague way.

My remedy to this is the Rule of Three, which structures and limits your presentation. More about this later. Here, the most important point to remember is that *you* actually choose what goes into your presentation so that it is the proper length and makes the point you wish to make – concisely.

Granted, the only persuasion going on here is to convince the student-audience of the relevance of an international business event to their success in the course. Yet it does lay the groundwork for longer, more complex presentations. You will see this example again later when I discuss the structure of your presentation.

3) Number of participants – In business school you are faced with presentation situations that require participation of anywhere from one to six people.

The ideal group presentation is probably 15 minutes long with three speakers. You may, however, be faced with a requirement levied by your professor that "everyone speak." And so larger groups are faced with the conundrum of "passing the baton" from student-to-student in an awkward dance, with each student presenting a narrow slice of the overall presentation pie.

In the chapters on group presentations later in the book, I show you how to handle this task smoothly and how to turn it to your advantage.

4) Size and type of audience – You may find yourself speaking before a handful of people gathered around a conference table. Or you may address a class of 40 or even 100 people. Your audience may consist of fellow students along with your professor, or you may find yourself delivering a show for outside consumption – visiting corporate executives, faculty judges, or even parents and visitors to your school.

You always adjust your presenting techniques and style according to the size and composition of the audience.

Your Framework

Every presentation, every speech, every talk has the same fundamental structure. Like a story, it must have a beginning, middle and end.

Within this three-part framework you find room to maneuver as you progressively increase the complexity of your presentation. You develop subcategories and substantiating points along the way. You refine it with techniques. But you always adhere to the barebones structure of beginning, middle, end.

A simple way of putting this is the three-step adage that provides us rough guidance:

1) Beginning: Tell them what you will tell them.

2) Middle: Tell them.

3) End: Tell them what you just told them.

This is neither double-talk nor backwoods wisdom. This structure provides you focus. It forces you to limit your content to the essentials. Adhere to this framework, and you'll produce presentations that rivet your audience and convey your message with sniper-like accuracy and power.

We Assume Your Paper Is Done...
Now It's Time for the Presentation

In all of this talk about presentation and style, let's not forget that the substance of your message must be superb. You must be in control of your subject matter and have something worthwhile to say. I assume this to be the case. I assume that you have mastered your content and message. Isn't this a reasonable assumption?

Your message, after all, is distilled from what you learn in your classes. Finance. Operations management. Accounting. Marketing. Risk. Human resources. International business. Entrepreneurship. All of these major subjects provide grist for your presentation.

The presentation is your show. The presentation highlights the fruits of your labors. It is *not* a verbatim transcript of a written paper. It is *not* a laundry list of everything you think about. In a sense, it is much like the trailer for a film that provides a mini-movie of highlights that informs and whets the appetite.

The presentation *is* a show. It's a distinct form of communication. It is a communication product distinct from the written work.

So, prepare your paper/analysis/case first, and *then* look to your presentation. If pursued in this way, the task of preparing your presentation will be much easier. With paper in hand, you pick and choose. You cherry-pick the most exciting, the most poignant, the most powerful, the most stimulating points to share in your presentation. In fact, you are obligated to do just that.

This selection process is a major factor in your success – or failure. You do not include everything in your presentation that appears in your paper. The art and craft of power presenting is as much about knowing what to *leave out* as it is about knowing what to *include*.

In the following section, we learn how to select the most powerful points and how to package them to produce a tight, focused, and especially powerful presentation.

Packaging Your Analysis

Your show consists of three basic components – the beginning, middle, end. From your practical standpoint of delivery, we call this **starting**, **staging**, and **stopping**.

You hook your audience with a compelling situation statement and recommendation. From there, you **stage** your talk, weaving a story to substantiate your recommendation and utilizing the many techniques in this book. Then you **stop** with a brief recapitulation of situation statement and, again, your confident recommendation.

Beginning, middle, end.

Starting, staging, stopping

Starting – The Beginning

This may sound counterintuitive, but you begin preparing your talk with your conclusion in mind. Answer the question: What is your ultimate recommendation?

Once you have distilled this conclusion – this *ultimate recommendation* – you place it in the first minute of your presentation. It's part of your introduction. We do this for one primary reason that's dictated by the very nature of our craft – time and attention.

Your audience consists primarily of busy executives who are accustomed to the bottom line. But more than that, your audience consists of reasonable, logical persons who want to understand you. They want to place your recommendation in the proper context. That's why we begin with a recommendation, so that your audience can then understand your reasoning – the facts and analysis that follow make sense when we know the conclusion they lead to. The audience can fasten onto your logic, your listeners can trace your reasoning. It's much easier to bring them along to accept your call to action.

So what do you say first? Just this…

Begin your presentation with a grabber or hook.

Do *not* waste time with "throat clearing." Metaphorical throat clearing is simply a way of edging into a talk sideways – thanking everyone, expressing your delight at being in this city or that school, or by introducing your team, if it's a group show. This kind of warm-up verbiage is a supreme waste of your opportunity. Your throat clearing leeches the energy and anticipation from the room. Your audience has heard it all before, and they truly do not wish to hear it again.

Punch 'em in the gut with a rip-roaring grabber. This "grabber" is directly connected to your thesis and not something that you contrive for dramatic effect. Let's take an example.

In 2009, I coached an all-female team competing in a Target Corporation case competition. Leaving aside the complexity and many particulars of the case, the fundamental issue was how best to design and market women's personal care products. The audience comprised eight judges from Target Corporation, half of them men.

The lead presenter moved into the command position, waited patiently until she had their full attention, and then led off with her grabber. Here was the grabber...

"It's one of the most intimate things a woman can do to herself."

And then she paused.

She paused for only three seconds, but it must have seemed like three minutes to the judges. Do you think this young woman had the judges' attention? She surely did. They could not wait to hear what was to follow, because they could not possibly imagine how she would continue after this line.

"What a woman puts next to her, on her skin, is an intimate act, and we believe it should be natural, safe, and contribute to pure beauty..."

After your grabber has your audience's attention, state your thesis. What's a thesis? It's the point of your talk. It's a *situation statement* that includes your ultimate recommendation. Ask yourself this question: What is the whole point of my talk? The answer to this question is your thesis.

For example, let's say our project case is to recommend the best international entry mode for American company Toughbolt into Brazil. We launch the presentation with our grabber, and then deliver our presentation thesis that contains the question on the table, and our ultimate recommendation:

"This minute, we have no market presence in Brazil. None. But just eight months from today – eight months from today, Toughbolt Corporation can hold 42 percent of the Brazilian widget market. This is not magic. It's not bluster. It's the result of a bold strategy whose first step is the acquisition of Brazilian conglomerate Dorado, Inc.

"Accordingly, we recommend that Toughbolt immediately tender an offer to Dorado for the purchase of 51 percent of stock at a per-share price we show to be prudent for us and equitable for Dorado. Of all the entry modes into Brazil available to us, *this* one promises the greatest return in the shortest time in a way that is consistent with our corporate strategy. This presentation demonstrates that this course of action is fiscally sound, the best use of scarce resources among the considered alternatives, and a basis for rapid growth."

So you see that you begin with your conclusion. You then follow with your staging, which is rock-solid, and airtight reasoning as to how you arrived at it.

Staging – The Middle

Yes, you guessed it – I call this "staging" so as to maintain the alliterative trope of "esses."

Starting.

Staging.

Stopping.

But in point of fact, this section actually *is* a process of staging. You are staging the body of your talk. You create a stage. You build your talk in stages. You make the case for your recommendation. Here I offer controversial advice, and not every presentation guru will agree with it. But with it, *you can never go wrong.*

Apply the **Rule of Three**, and apply it ruthlessly.

For a moment, let's consider this "Rule of Three." This is always successful in structuring this portion of your presentation. The Rule of Three means you select the three main points from the material at hand and use that as the structure for your show.

Although you may never have heard of the Rule of Three, it is one of the most basic frameworks for public speaking, and it derives from something almost existential in the human psyche.

Think about this for a moment. There is something magical about the number three. We tend to grasp information most easily in threes. Consider these examples:

- Stop, look and listen – A well-known public safety announcement

- "Friends, Romans, countrymen, lend me your ears" – William Shakespeare

- Veni, Vidi, Vici (I came, I saw, I conquered) – Julius Caesar

- "Blood, sweat and tears" – Winston Churchill

- "Faith, Hope and Charity" – The Bible

- "Life, liberty, and the pursuit of happiness" – the Declaration of Independence

- *The Good, the Bad and the Ugly* – a Clint Eastwood Western

- "Duty – Honor – Country. Those three hallowed words reverently dictate what you ought to be, what you can be, and what you will be" – General Douglas MacArthur

The Rule of Three is a standard structural model advocated by many presentation coaches, and with good reason. It's a powerful framework, incredibly sturdy. Think of it as a reliable vessel into which to pour your superb beverage. With the Rule Of Three, you can – literally – never err with regard to your presentation structure.

Offer substantiation for your thesis and ultimate recommendation in three main points. Strip down all of your convoluted arguments, all of your evidence, all of your keen analysis to the three major points that you believe make your case.

In the Toughbolt Corporation example above, note that in our thesis statement and ultimate recommendation, we mentioned three positive reasons for our chosen course of action:

> "...this presentation demonstrates that this course of action is fiscally sound, the best use of scarce resources among the alternatives, and a basis for rapid growth."

These three factors serve as your basic Rule of Three structure for the middle of your presentation.

1. Most efficient use of resources over other expansion alternatives

2. Financial analysis of the projected acquisition

3. Projected returns and growth rate

Does this mean that other information is not important? Of course not. It means that you have selected the *most important points* that make your case and that you want to rivet in the minds of the audience. Remember that you select the major facts not to be *comprehensive*, but to be *persuasive* in your presentation.

With respect to other more subsidiary points that appear in your written analysis, you always have the opportunity to address those issues in a question and answer session to follow your show.

Stopping – The Ending

Many presenters often leave the ending of their presentation to chance. They never practice how to stop. As a result, they don't know how to stop. Stopping gracefully and with power is a distinct skill. It must be practiced, because it is the most important part of your persuasive talk. You want your audience to remember the final words you say. It's your last chance to emphasize your most critical message.

> It is the most vital part of a speech, the supreme moment when the speaker is to drive his message home and make his most lasting impression. This calls for the very best that is in a man... it should be short, simple, and earnest. The temptation to make the closing appeal too long should be carefully avoided. Whether the speech be memorized throughout or not, the speaker should know specifically the thought, if not the phraseology, with which he intends to end his address.[2]

There is an old public speaking adage that goes like this: "Check your tie, check your fly, say your piece and say goodbye." Strangely enough, I've found that it's the "goodbye" part that can be extremely difficult for some people – young and old, male and female.

In fact, it's common to see young speakers spiral out of control on the downside of a fine presentation. I have seen *great* student presentations flounder at the last minute, because no one had thought it through *all the way* to the end – no one had thought to prepare or to practice how they would conclude the presentation. And so it ended with a whimper instead of the brief and powerful recapitulation of the main point.

So it remains as one of the most difficult tasks to convey to a young speaker – the importance of knowing *when* and *how* to stop.

Why is this important? Because:

1. The conclusion is the last impression you leave your audience as you call them to action.

2. If not planned, your conclusion can expand into another speech, and few things turn off an audience more.

3. This potentially powerful part of your show becomes, instead, a debilitating albatross that *subtracts* value.

---

2 Grenville Kleiser, *How to Speak in Public* (New York: Funk & Wagnalls Company, 1910), 209.

Despite all of this, the ending remains a neglected aspect of the presentation and one whose chief pathology is the speaker's inability to stop. I let some of the great presentation masters speak to an issue that has plagued speakers for centuries.

> It is well to have an ending in mind. What the speaker says last is remembered first by the audience. When he has hinted that he is about to conclude, he will spoil everything if he continues to plod along looking for a place to stop. The audience is already in the mood to leave and is impatient with this failure to wind up the business promptly. Annoyance is the only response to "one more thing," "as I said before," "I urge you once again," "I forgot to say," and the other pathetic delays of the speaker who is through but does not know it.[3]

From 2,100 years ago, Quintilian tells us this about the conclusion:

> The repetition and summing up is intended both to refresh the memory of the judge, to set the whole cause at once before his view, and to enforce such arguments anybody as had produced an insufficient effect in detail. In this part of our speech, what we repeat ought to be repeated as briefly as possible, and we must, as is intimated by the Greek term, run over only the principal heads; for, if we dwell upon them, the result will be, not a recapitulation, but a sort of second speech.[4]

Don't continue on because you think that you're adding value. You're not. Padding in a speech is no more welcome than is padding in a written paper. "Few speakers discern that length does not indicate depth. Better stop before you are through than go on after you have finished. Only makers of short speeches are invited to speak again."[5]

Do not run off-stage as you deliver your last lines. Do not lose the last sentence in a turn of the head in a rush to leave the stage. Savor the moment, and let your powerful last words sink in.

---

3 William G. Hoffman, *The Public Speaker's Scrapbook* (New York: McGraw-Hill, 1935), 82.
4 William Vincent Byars (ed.), *The Handbook of Oratory* (Chicago: Ferd P. Kaiser, 1901), 104.
5 J. Berg Esenwein, *How to Attract and Hold an Audience* (New York: Hinds & Noble, 1902), 161.

Your Audience

As much as some of us love the limelight and the adulation of the crowd, it is wise to remember that your presentation isn't about you – although our self-indulgence can sometimes make it seem so.

No, you are not in this to please yourself. Your presentation is for your audience members. You *must* address what they want. And you must get them to do what *you* want them to by demonstrating to them that it's what *they* want.

Address the needs of the people in your audience and fulfill their expectations in language they understand, with metaphors and examples that resonate with *them*. Your objective must be expressed in terms of how it best connects with your audience. Speak to their needs and *fulfill* them.

The good news is that your audience generally has low expectations, which means that you can dazzle it with a merely above-average presentation. This is because the level of business presenting is so dismally low that audiences dread listening to them as much as you hate giving them. *No one* seems happy at the prospect of this afternoon's weekly "finance update."

But remember this – regardless of the topic of your talk, every audience wants the same basic thing. You want to tap this desire and satisfy it in your presentation. This desire is to be a hero.

Everyone wants to have a chance to be a hero. No one wants to *hear* from Indiana Jones – everyone wants to *be* Indiana Jones. Or at least believe that, given the chance, we could do great things.

This is a touchstone principle long known to professional speakers. Kenneth Goode and Zenn Kaufman authored a book in 1939 called *Profitable Showmanship*, and their words resonate with stone-cold veracity over the subsequent 70-plus years right up to today and to the next quarter earnings briefing:

> The audience is always on the screen, at the microphone, in the prize-fight, or in the pitcher's box. *You*, the individual member of the audience, are the hero of the day. No selling can ever be completely successful that forgets this principle: that the prospect is the Hero of the Show. And, in fact, the *only hero!*... The minute you slide the spotlight off *him*, off *his* crazy ideas, off *his* pet peeves, particularly off *his* whims, your show is over. You may as well go home, for your audience is gone... The hero of the [presenting] drama is the customer – or prospect. His vanities, his

hopes, his fears, his ambitions – these are the stuff from which your plot is spun and on him – and him alone – must the spotlight shine.[6]

If this message is difficult to digest or threatens to dissolve when you close the book, here is a mnemonic aid to help you stay focused on the audience. Dr John Kline has developed this mnemonic aid, and he calls it TOOTSIFELT. This is a contrived acronym, which stands for: "The object of this talk is for each listener to…"[7]

This keeps the focus on your audience and its needs. This phrase keeps you rooted in your purpose, captures the spirit of your presentation and embodies the audience-centered approach. If you state this question repeatedly throughout the development of your show, you cannot fail to produce a tightly scripted and targeted message.

Bad Advice

I have never been a fan of providing speakers lists of taboos, because it is a negative way of looking at presenting. I want for you to concentrate on the positive words and actions that lift your presentation to its highest possible level. I'd rather you not be thinking of a menu of "Do not do this." It tends to clutter your mind with worries of making "a false move." And then you tighten up.

However, it *is* necessary to review at least once some of the clichéd bad advice dispensed by folks who ought to know better.

I have found that much of becoming a great presenter is bound up in getting students to *stop* what they're doing now as a result of bad habits and bad advice. You have to know the specific behavior that ruins a presentation, so that you can avoid it. If you recognize bad habits and avoid them, you become *de facto* a reasonably competent presenter.

Let's look at some of the most common examples of bad, vague, or incomplete advice you invariably hear during your business school career from the most well meaning of folks. Recognize that in the chapters to come, all of these chestnuts will be corrected in full.

---

6 Kenneth Goode and Zenn Kaufman, *Profitable Showmanship* (New York: Prentice Hall, 1939), 35–6.
7 John Kline, "TOOTSIFELT: How to state your objective," Klinespeak.com (May 2004), http://www.klinespeak.com/columns/years/2004/0405.htm (accessed July 26, 2012).

"Don't put your hand in your pocket... it looks 'unprofessional'"

This is absurd advice and carries the whiff of oral tradition about it. From presidents to preachers, the hand in the pocket – if done properly – conveys assurance and confidence. For many speakers, it also removes one hand from the equation as an unnecessary distracter. Naturally, you don't jingle keys or coins in your pocket.

"Make eye contact"

This advice is insidious in that it actually contains a large kernel of truth. It sounds reasonable. Yet it doesn't tell you *how* to do it. And, yes, there is such a thing as bad eye contact.

"Move around when you talk"

This gem was given to me by a student, passed on from one of his other professors. Again, advice to roam aimlessly about the stage is worse than no advice at all.

"Just the facts"

Really? Which facts are those? Folks who use this phrase believe that it makes them appear no-nonsense and hardcore. But a more pompous and simultaneously meaningless phrase has yet to be devised. What does it mean, "Just the facts?" Which facts? Randomly selected facts? Facts selected according to criteria that I never mention? You mean you don't want context? Or analysis?

"The numbers tell the story"

This is a favorite of finance folks, who seem to believe that the ironclad rules of presentations do not apply to them. "We're special," my finance majors like to say. "We don't deal with all of that soft storytelling... We deal in hard numbers."

There is so much wrong with this, it's difficult to locate a reasonable starting point. Numbers, by themselves, tell no story at all. If they *were* capable of telling a story, it would be a considerably incomplete story, giving a distorted picture of reality.

"You have too many slides"

You can tell *nothing* about a presentation by looking only at the number of slides in it. You will hear this nonsense from folks who believe that the length of a presentation dictates the number of slides you use, as if some kind of mathematical formula is in play.

Absurd on its face, people who use this believe that every slide will be shown a set amount of time. They likely do some sort of calculation in their heads, dividing the time available by the number of slides to yield a number they believe indicates there are "too many" slides."

"Practice your talk in the mirror"

Don't practice in front of a mirror unless you plan to deliver your talk to a mirror. It's creepy to watch yourself in the mirror while talking for an extended period. There is nothing to be gained by rehearsing one way, only to do something entirely different for the actual event.

Of course, you initially observe yourself in the mirror as you adjust your stance and appearance to ensure that what you *feel* is what people *see* while you present. But you do *not* practice your finished talk in front of a mirror. That's just bizarre.

Conclusion

Thus concludes this primer on the basics of business presenting. If you do nothing more than apply the structural precepts in this chapter, you can take your business presentations to a level significantly above the average. To vault your own presenting skill level to stratospheric heights, plunge into Part II: The Seven Secrets.

For further reading on structure and organization, check out:

John A. Kline, *Speaking Effectively: Achieving Excellence in Presentations* (2003)

PART II

THE SEVEN SECRETS OF SUCCESSFUL SPEAKERS: FROM STICK-PUPPET TO 3D PRESENTING

Introduction

This entire section is about you and your *style*. Here, we think hard about your style – what it is, what it means, and how to craft it to your preferences.

Style is a many-faceted concept. We use the term all the time, and yet – what *is* it? Style has so many components that we simply cannot think of it as something *by itself*.

We want to deepen and broaden you as a presenter, to transform you. The effects of this transformation become apparent with you and your performance on the stage. You change from offering a flat, monotonous, two-dimensional presentation to offering a compelling, full-bodied, richly textured message in multiple dimensions.

You become a 3D presenter.

Accordingly, this section offers the Seven Secrets to a superior style, all of which impact you as a speaker in some way – great or small. Here we talk about emotion and passion, drama and earnestness, stage fright and self-consciousness. In the chapters to follow, you find the larger themes and techniques of voice and gesture, movement and expression.

Here, we talk of *style*. It's an indefinable quality, isn't it? And yet we know it when we see it.

To even imagine a style, we must first think of someone who embodies a particular style, whether we hate it or want to emulate it. Bill Clinton.

Jerry Seinfeld. Arnold Schwarzenegger. Michael Jordan. Malcolm X, Sarah Palin. Oprah Winfrey. Simon Cowell. Al Sharpton. Brad Pitt. Barack Obama. You can create your own list.

Think of someone you admire, someone who has *style*. Now ask yourself what that style is *exactly*. What comprises the style? Can you break it into component parts?

Is it hair? Clothing? Voice? Vocabulary? A unique walk? Demeanor? Carriage? Presence?

You see that *style* is abstract. We can't really grasp it in the abstract. It's hard to define, and if we concentrate on it too intently, it begins to dissipate. So how on earth can we even begin to talk about *your* style?

Can you describe your style in a single word?

"Brusque?"

"Cool?"

"Laid-back?"

"Committed?"

Time to Sharpen Your Style

Or maybe your style is too amorphous. It's just too vague to grasp. We can't define our own style in one word or in a dozen, can we? Not so that it means anything relevant. Why is that? Because, just as with the well-known people in our lives whose styles we admire or abhor, our own styles are constructed from many different factors.

An effective style is not contrived. It grows organically from our life experiences, from our expertise, from our desire to achieve.

What do we mean by "organically?" It *grows*. It grows from within us over time. It springs from our unique essence, from everything that has gone into creating our personalities, quirks, habits, humor, tastes, and preferences. It springs from what we choose to wear, what we think about, how we treat other people, what we read, how we choose to spend our time and who we spend it with.

Our vocabulary and our accent leaven our style, becoming an indistinguishable part of it. Our style is inseparable from who we are. It is very much our **brand**.

Ironically, as soon as we become conscious of our "style" – our *brand* – we often become stilted. It's akin to thinking carefully about how we walk, placing one foot in front of another. Suddenly, we become self-conscious about an action which, until that point, was automatic. And if we are unhappy with our style, and we decide we ought to change it, well, that's a tall order. To *consciously* *change* our style, we change who we are.

Embracing Change

Yes, we *can* change our style, and that is a good thing. We can consciously change who we are and what we stand for, *if we so choose*. You can also consciously choose *not* to change.

Complicating this picture is the fact that our style changes a bit every day. It changes with every new habit we pick up, with every new change of clothing, with every adoption of the latest slang and fad, with every new hairstyle.

We change according to the people we meet, the books we read, the entertainment we choose, the dreams we dream. We can either seize control of that process of change, or we can let it drag us along. Or drag us down.

You choose every day. Over time, your choices accumulate, and you *become* your choices.

Style is one product of your choices. Sure, it may not be the most important result of your choices, but your personal style can enhance your professional opportunities, or it can degrade them. Again, your choice of direction is up to you.

You can *choose* to be confident. You can *choose* to be articulate. You can *choose* to be thoughtful. You can *choose* to be calm, polished, and suave. You can *choose* to be confident and interesting. You can *choose* to be composed or professional.

Or you can choose otherwise.

The Secret Elements of Style

All of this bears on your presentation skills and your ability to present in a competent, listener-friendly manner and to convey a compelling case to any audience. I want you to think now of putting together the various components of style – **stance**, **voice**, **gesture**, **expression**, **movement**, **appearance**, and **passion**. They spring from within you, rather than adorn you like a suit of clothes.

Think of them as Seven Secrets – the lost secrets of presenting. I call them "lost secrets" because they have been shunted aside, neglected in favor of modern "communication theory" and the dazzle of PowerPoint.

Now you'll notice that there's overlap among the various style components.

For instance, **expression** seems part of **gesture**, and **appearance** would seem to encompass **expression** and **stance**, and **passion** might incorporate elements from several other principles.

Of *course* there's overlap. This is always a result when you attempt to disaggregate a complex phenomenon into component parts. I have disassembled the various components of presentation style so that we can learn about each one separately.

This is artificial, because you can't separate sincerity from your appearance. You can't eliminate movement from your talk, from your volume, from your nuance. If we consider our style akin to a chain, the reality is that the links of the chain that comprise our distinct style remain connected to each other even as we examine each link separately.

To introduce a second metaphor for the components of our style, think for a moment about an internal combustion engine. An engine doesn't function when it's disassembled, but mechanics take apart an engine to study it, to understand its parts, and to determine the cause of its malfunction so that it might perform at maximum potential and effectiveness.

Likewise, engineers analyze the engine's components so to build better engines and to ensure that they perform with full power. Similar to this process, here we analyze the components of our style so to build a better presenter – *you*.

The components of our style operate interactively to yield a superior product. Each element of our style works in tandem with the other elements to yield a powerful product that is greater than the sum of its parts. This is called synergy.

Style Synergy

Synergy may be one of the most overused words in business. Yet when we have a chance to achieve real synergy, we should seize it. This is one such opportunity.

Together the Seven Secrets achieve what we call *style* synergy. According to the *American Heritage Dictionary*, synergy has its roots in the Greek word *sunergos*, which means, "working together." The results of synergy can be positive or negative, and can be illustrated by the equation $2 + 2 = 5$ or $2 + 2 = 3$.

In the first case, by combining the components of our style and working together effectively, we can produce a greater result than if we relied upon any number of elements separately.

In the second case, the neglect of any of our elements can detract from the overall effect of our presentation, with correspondingly poor results.

The coming chapters reveal the Seven Secrets, which are the internal determinants of your style. Combined, they generate powerful synergy beyond what you could have ever imagined for yourself.

STANCE

The Challenge: A weak and ineffective stance. A stance that is uncertain and constantly shifting, one that saps your confidence and transmits disorganization.

The Solution: A powerful, confident stance that transmits strength and competence, one that invests your message with surety and persuasiveness.

The Benefit: Your presentation rests upon a solid foundation stance of strength that suffuses you with confidence. Your confidence increases from the flow of positive energy – a reversal of the negative energy generated by a weak stance.

How do you stand before a crowd when you speak? Have you ever consciously thought about it? Have you developed, on your own, a ready stance that you always use?

Or do you allow your mood of the moment to dictate your body's posture? Does it vary according to the whim of the moment?

Your stance is an essential part of your presentation that can either enhance or degrade your show. How you stand, how you carry yourself, communicates to others.

Whether you are actually speaking or not, your body language is always transmitting. It transmits a great deal about us with respect to our inner thoughts, self-image, and self-awareness. Whether we like this or not is not the point. The point is that we are constantly signaling to others nonverbally.

Your body is sending nonverbal messages – you are sending a message to those around you, and those around us will take their cues based on universal perception of the messages received. Your stance transmits your inner self, whether confident or timid.

Have you thought about the constant silent messages your posture radiates? What are these messages that you unconsciously send people? And why do we care? Why are we even talking about this?

Nonverbal Signaling – It Can be Intentional or Otherwise

Perhaps you have heard that nonverbal communication is just as important, if not more important, than verbal communication. There is dispute on this point among some fine minds. But there *is* a consensus that powerful nonverbal signals can either enhance your presentation or undermine it.

In fact, five of the Seven Secrets in this part of the book are nonverbal. So doesn't it make sense to master the techniques of nonverbal communication that can add so much to your presentation?

Every aspect of your presentation ought to project strength, competence, and confidence. This goes for your nonverbal communication as well as your verbal delivery of the presentation. You achieve this goal with a number of nonverbal techniques, all working simultaneously and in harmony, including stance, gesture, movement, expression, and appearance.

Your first technique is fundamental to projecting an image of strength, competence, and confidence. This first technique is assumption of the proper *stance*. Think of it as the foundation upon which your presentation rests.

It is impossible to build a lasting structure on a shaky foundation. In fact, quite practical reasons *demand* that you develop a solid foundational stance while delivering your presentation.

Stand Tall – Here's Why

The first reason is confidence, both yours and the audience's. A solid, powerful stance communicates strength, competence, and confidence – the authority that an audience needs to witness in the speaker. Likewise, a solid powerful stance invests the speaker – *you* – with a feeling of strength, competence, and confidence.

The second reason is that a solid stance removes from your thought processes any concern over how or where you must stand at any particular time. Your ready position is a good friend. It's comfortable, like an old pair of shoes.

Nervousness over something as basic as your stance is something that has plagued speakers for centuries. This nervousness and apprehension and uncertainty over stance is one of the verities of public speaking, and the problem was solved centuries ago.

> Young speakers are often embarrassed by not knowing just how they should stand up on the platform. They feel afraid that they may look awkward. Further, when they do mount the platform, they become extremely self-conscious. Their hands seem to be larger than usual, and they "do not know where to put them." Their feet seem to be painfully evident no matter what position they assume. This self-consciousness, and general feeling of awkwardness, can largely be done away with by a few simple directions as to what not to do, and a few suggestions as to what is generally found to be the best practice.[1]

So when nervousness strikes, your ready stance is there for you as a source of stability and familiarity.

The third reason is that your ready position serves as a departure point for various movements throughout your talk. It acts as counterpoint to your repertoire of movements and gestures. It serves as your comfortable base to which you return again and again.

A powerful initial stance is a formidable addition to your personal *persona* and enhances your professional presence. Many of my students have found that a strong ready position combined with confident gestures elevates their presentations so noticeably that their professors compliment them as having "great speaking skills."

Let's start with your present stance and then move to your new, powerful stance.

Your Current Stance – Does It Help You or Hurt You?

How *do* you stand when you converse in a group at a party or a reception or when giving a presentation? What's your normal "bearing?"

---

1 Dwight E. Watkins, *Effective Speaking* (Chicago: Markus-Campbell Company, 1939), volume 2, manual 3, 59.

The importance of a speaker's bearing cannot be overestimated... How an arrogant, conceited bearing repels, and a sympathetic, modest, differential bearing attracts! How an uncertain bearing disturbs, and how a confident bearing imparts ease to the audience![2]

The typical business school student stance for a presentation is not much different from what you see in the business world writ large.

Unsatisfactory stances infest the business landscape, and you've seen them dozens of times. You see it in the typical corporate meeting, after-dinner talk, finance brief, or networking breakfast address – slouching, shifting, odd, arrogant, timid, uncertain stances. Let's look at this pathology of the modern business presentation – the speaker's ineffective stance – and let's correct it.

Bad Business Stance

The speaker stands behind a lectern. The speaker grips the lectern on either side. The speaker either reads from notes or reads verbatim from crowded busy slides projected behind him.

The lectern serves as a crutch, almost like a bunker. And the average speaker, even the corporate VP, appears to be afraid that someone will snatch the lectern away. Many business examples illustrate this. Take, for instance, Mr Muhtar Kent, the chairman of the board and CEO of Coca-Cola.

Mr Kent appears to be a genuinely engaging person on occasions where he is not speaking to a group. But when he addresses a crowd of any size, something seizes Mr Kent and he reverts to delivering drone-like talks that commit virtually every public speaking sin.[3] He grips the lectern. He hunches uncomfortably. He squints and reads his speech from a text in front of him and, when he does diverge from his speech, he rambles aimlessly.

Successful C-suite businessmen and businesswomen, such as Mr Kent, are caught in a dilemma – many of them are terrible speakers, but no one tells

---

2 Edwin Dubois Shurter, *Public Speaking: A Treatise in Delivery* (New York: Allyn & Bacon, 1903), 115.

3 See Mr Kent deliver an October 2010 address at Yale University in which he begins with a rambling apology, grips the lectern as if it might run away, hunches uncomfortably the entire time, and does not even mention the topic of his talk until the 4-minute mark: http://www.youtube.com/watch?v=XLgptCjGP_k&feature=player_embedded#at=21 (accessed July 26, 2012).

them so. No one tells them so, because there's no upside in doing it. Moreover, many business leaders believe their own press clippings. They tend to think that their success in managing a conglomerate, in steering the corporate elephant of multinational business to profitability, means that their skills and judgment are infallible across a range of unrelated issues and tasks.

Mr Kent is by all accounts a shrewd corporate leader and for his expertise received in 2010 almost $25 million in total compensation as Coca-Cola CEO and board chairman. But he is poor speaker. He is a poor speaker with great potential. Many business leaders like Mr Kent could become outstanding speakers and even more powerful advocates of their businesses.

Bad Influence

But as it stands now, executives such as Mr Kent exert an incredibly insidious influence in our schools and in the corporate world generally. Let's call it the "hem-of-garment" effect, where those of us who aspire to scale the corporate heights imitate what we believe to be winning behaviors.

Because our heroes are so successful in having scaled the corporate heights, their "style" of speaking is emulated by thousands of young people who believe that, well, this must be how it's done: "He is successful, therefore I should deliver my own presentations this way."

You see examples of this at your own business school, as in when a VP from a local insurance company shows up unprepared, reads from crowded busy slides, then takes your questions in chaotic and perhaps haughty form. Who could blame you for believing that this is how it should be done? This is, after all, the unfortunate standard.

This relates to you and your presentation trials in this way.

In your business presentations, I'm guessing that your stance is not much different than what I have described here. You stand behind a lectern. You stand there and grip the sides of the lectern and look at a computer screen, either from your laptop or on the screen mounted on one of the ubiquitous smart lecterns. You read your talk and look at the audience infrequently. Your body language exudes discomfort, and every action you make diverts attention from you to somewhere else.

In short, you behave as if your posture and stance have nothing to do with your message. You act as if your words carry the message alone. A part of you actually believes that it is the force of your argument, your compilation of facts, your detailed spreadsheet that will carry the day. Because that's the way it *should* be, right? As a result, you push the presentation outside of yourself.

"*There* it is!" you think, and you gesture behind you. "*There* is the presentation up there on the screen!"

Leave Behind the Herd of Mediocrity

I have described here a kind of worst-case scenario, the results of ignoring your stance and the importance of harnessing body language to your service. Yet this worst-case delivery of presentations goes on thousands of times each day nationwide and doubtlessly throughout the world. I have seen of enough of this pathology in other countries to know that it is practically universal.

You devalue yourself. You become complicit in your own commoditization. You *become* a commodity, and you destroy any possibility of gaining personal competitive advantage from superior presentation skills. You render yourself easily replaceable.

This ugly scenario just described is far too often the norm in our business schools. You can vouch for this yourself. I know that you've seen presentations given in your school that rival that of the hapless Muhtar Kent, and it is more than likely that your own presentation style resembles that of Mr Kent in some ways.

The Power of Body Language – Bend It to Your Will

Body language can be a powerful tool if you understand how it works and bend it consciously to your will. Don't simply avoid negative body language – engage in *positive* body language to enhance your talk. Let it become part of your repertoire of useful speaking techniques.

Unless you want to transmit an uninviting message, seize control of your communication this instant. There is no reason not to. And there are many quite good reasons why you should.

Recognize that much of the audience impression of you is forming even as you approach the lectern. They form this impression immediately, before you shuffle your papers or clear your throat or squint into the bright lights. They form their impression from your walk, from your posture, from your clothing, from your grooming, from the slightest inflections of your face, and from your eye movement. The audience takes silent cues from you, and your posture is one of those subtle cues that affect an audience's mood and receptivity.

All before you utter a single word. "The body, the hand, the face, the eye, the mouth, all should respond to the speaker's inner thought and feeling."[4]

The basis for all of the other nonverbal signals you send is posture. Your posture affects those who watch you and it affects you as well. Those effects can be positive or negative.

So how do *you* stand?

Do you stand with shoulders rounded in a defeatist posture? Do you transmit defeat, boredom, and *ennui*? Do you shift from side-to-side? Do you unconsciously sway back-and-forth? Do you cross your legs without knowing it, balancing precariously upon one foot, your free leg wrapped in front of the other, projecting an odd and wobbly about-to-tumble-down image? Do you dance with choppy steps? "Unless you change your position with an object in view, avoid unnecessary shifting of weight, as it indicates nervousness."[5]

Three Effects

Body language has three powerful effects, two on your *audience* and the other on *you*. We have talked thus far about how your body language affects your overt message to your audience.

There is also a second subtle and covert message, and this is the degree of credibility that you have with your audience. Your *body language* transmits your depression, guilt, fear, lack of confidence to the audience, or it transmits your strength, confidence, and capability.

Are those in your audience confident in what you say, or are they skeptical? Do you inspire confidence, so that when you issue your call to action, the audience will be ready to march?

> Often an audience discounts what a speaker is going to say even before he utters a word. We say: "his appearance is against him." If the speaker stands any physically lazy way, we, often rashly, conclude that he is mentally lazy. If he stands in the attitude of a braggart, we jump to the conclusion

---

4 Grenville Kleiser, *How to Develop Power and Personality in Speaking* (New York and London: Funk & Wagnalls Company, 1912), 105.

5 Frances Putnam Hoyle, *The Ideal Book of Elocution, Oratory, and Entertainment* (W. E. Scull, 1902), 39.

that he is an egotist. If he fidgets on the platform and indulges in many explosive and nervous movements, we conclude he is ill at ease or unused to speaking. Whereas, if the speaker stands erect, chest high, hands hanging in repose, the audience at once decides that here is a man accustomed to speaking, having something worthwhile to say.[6]

The third effect of body language is on *you* and your emotions.

Body language acts as an amplifier of emotion. When you feel depression, guilt, fear, lack of confidence, your body language can take on the physical manifestations of those emotions and amplify them. They can leech away your strength. Much of this initial negative energy comes from the well-known fear of public speaking.

If we fear the act of public speaking, the internal flow of energy from our emotional state to our physical state is negative. Negative energy courses freely into our limbs and infuses us with stiffness, dread, immobility and a destructive self-consciousness. We shift involuntarily into damage-limitation mode. It cripples us.

Your emotions affect your body language. They influence the way you stand, the way you appear to your audience. They influence what you say and how you say it. But you can reverse the process.

Let me say this again, so there is no mistaking the message here. *You can reverse the process.*

Create Positive Energy

You can use your gestures, movement, posture, and expression to influence your emotions. You can turn them around quite handily and seize control of the dynamic.

Instead of your body language and posture reflecting your emotions, reverse the flow. Let your emotions reflect your body language and your posture. Consciously strike a bearing that reflects the confident and powerful speaker you want to be.

Skeptical? A venerable psychological theory contends this very thing – that our emotions evolve from our physiology. It is called the James–Lange Theory,

6 Dwight E. Watkins, *Effective Speaking* (Chicago: Markus-Campbell Company, 1939), volume 2, manual 4, 54.

developed by American psychologist William James and the Danish physiologist Carl G. Lange.

> Count ten before venting your anger, and its occasion seems ridiculous. Whistling to keep up courage is no mere figure of speech. On the other hand, sit all day in a moping posture, sigh, and reply to everything with a dismal voice, and your melancholy lingers... [I]f we wish to conquer undesirable emotional tendencies in ourselves, we must assiduously, and in the first instance cold-bloodedly, go through the outward movements of those contrary dispositions which we prefer to cultivate.[7]

Much more recently, a Harvard study substantiated the James–Lange Theory and found that power posing substantially increases confidence in people who assume them while interacting with others. In short, the way you stand or sit either increases or decreases your confidence. The study's conclusion speaks directly to us.

> High-power posers experienced elevations in testosterone, decreases in cortisol, and increased feelings of power and tolerance for risk; low-power posers exhibited the opposite pattern. In short, posing in displays of power caused advantaged and adaptive psychological, physiological, and behavioral changes, and these findings suggest that embodiment extends beyond mere thinking and feeling, to physiology and subsequent behavioral choices. That a person can, by assuming two simple 1-minute poses, embody power and instantly become more powerful has real-world, actionable implications.[8]

This holds tremendous significance for you if you want to imbue your presentations with power. Your foundation grows out of the notion of what we can call "power posing." This means you should stand the way you *want* to feel.

Affect the posture of confidence. Consciously affect a positive, confident bearing. Square your shoulders. Affix a determined look on your face. Speak loudly and distinctly. In short, let your actions influence your emotions. *Seize control* of the emotional energy flow and make it work for you.

So what is a confident posture? Let's begin with a firm foundation.

---

7 James Albert Winans, *Public Speaking: Principles and Practice* (Ithaca, NY: The Sewell Publishing Company, 1915), 112–13.

8 Dana R. Carney, Amy J. C. Cuddy and Andy J. Yap, "Power Posing: Brief Nonverbal Displays Affect Neuroendocrine Levels and Risk Tolerance," *Psychological Science* 21 (October 2010): 1363.

Building Your Ready Position

For any structure to endure, we must build on solidity and strength. And I mean this both in the metaphorical and literal sense with regard to business presentations. "The posture should give the appearance of self-assurance and ease, without egotism or antagonism."[9] You must not only project strength and stability, but you must also *feel* strength and stability. The two are inseparable, and let me reveal to you why.

Think first of the confident *man*.

To appear unstable and fearful before an audience, a confident man must make a conscious effort to strike such a pose. Likewise, it would take a conscious effort for a man, who has planted himself firmly in the prescribed confident posture, to feel nervous, uncertain, or unsure of himself. That is, if he affected the confident pose and maintained it relentlessly against all of the body's involuntary urges to crumple and shift, to equivocate and sway.

Think as well of the confident *woman*.

How does the confident woman's demeanor different from that of the confident man? Virtually not at all. Affect the pose you want. Consciously control your appearance. The point and the goal is to establish a foundation that exudes strength, competence, and confidence. Strength, competence, and confidence that flow from the stance itself.

This strong personal foundation is your *ready position*, your standard posture for your presentation. Your ready position is the default stance you assume when giving your talk, when not emphasizing with movement and gesture.

I give you two options for your ready position. They are equally powerful and radiate confidence. They are, in fact, based on body language that is associated with confidence and power. They are the *basic stance* and the *classic stance*.

To learn both of these stances, you need a full-length mirror. Practicing your stance in front of a mirror will ensure that your feeling of how you appear to others matches your actual appearance.

This is one of the *few* times I advocate use of a mirror. It is essential that your impression of how you look matches your actual appearance. You would be surprised at how many students are unaware of the image they project. It is necessary for you to verify visually that you appear how you wish to appear.

---

9 Paul R. Brees and G. Vernon Kelley, *Modern Speaking* (Chicago: Follett Publishing Company, 1931), 175.

Here is the technique, which has served speakers for more than a century, and as described by public speaking master Dwight Watkins in 1939:

> He should look at himself in a large mirror to see if he is plumb; to see if his body is symmetrical with respect to a vertical plane drawn through the center of his chest and the center of his image in the glass. He should examine himself to see if his head wilts forward or is cocked on one side or the other, if one shoulder is lower than the other, if one side of the body is turned toward the image in the glass more than the other. As he stands before the mirror he should adjust himself until he looks symmetrical and direct; until he looks as strong, as self-possessed, as worthy of respect and confidence as is possible. In this way he should study himself as an audience would see him.[10]

The Basic Stance

Take a position in front of the mirror, and stand with your feet shoulder-width apart. Plant yourself as you would a paving stone in a garden.

Look down at your feet. Distribute your weight evenly over each foot. Your heels should be no closer than 6 inches to each other. Your heels should be no farther apart than 12 inches. Find comfort somewhere between these parameters.

Do not slouch or put more weight on one foot than on the other. Point your toes slightly outward. Do not let your body slump, nor stiffen.

Keep your shoulders back, head up, expectant.

Do not allow your head to settle down betwixt your collar bones. If you do, it will compress your neck like a concertina. It cramps your voice box, cuts the flow of air you need to speak.

Basic stance   Your hands? To begin with, let your hands hang loosely at your sides. You have plenty to do with your hands later.

Now, look at yourself again in the mirror. *This* is your ready position – the basic stance.

This is the foundation upon which we will now build your new repertoire of presentation skills. It offers the natural advantages of a powerful base that invests you with confidence and stability.

---

10 Dwight E. Watkins, *Effective Speaking* (Chicago: Markus-Campbell Company, 1939), volume 2, manual 4, 50.

You can also utilize the classic stance, which is equally desirable and has the additional benefit of eliminating the tendency to sway while speaking.

The Classic Stance

The classic stance is called this for obvious reasons – it takes its origins from the oratorical tradition of ancient Greece, which produced the finest presenters in history. We find excellent reasons for this stance to have evolved over time. It takes advantage of everything we know about positive body language and its association with conveying a message with confidence and credibility.

Classic stance

Again, stand in front of a full-length mirror. This time, stand with one foot in front of the other, offset by about 4 inches. Your toes are again pointed slightly outward. See the diagram.

Your weight is shifted primarily to the back left foot, and you should be able to lift and easily tap the toe of your right foot. In this position, it's almost impossible for you to sway or rock side-to-side.

Again, let your hands hang loosely at your sides for now. Shoulders straight, held erect, your back straight, head up, expectant.

This position will infuse you with confidence. You should actually feel positive energy flowing through you.

Burn Your Stance into Your Consciousness

Back to the mirror. You have selected your stance. You have adjusted your position in the mirror until you are satisfied with it. Now, it is time to adopt this stance as your own so that you can strike this pose when you need it. Here's the technique:

When he has adjusted his image in the glass until it looks the best to him, he should shut his eyes and tried to get the general physical and moral sensation that belongs with that image. He should practice until the feeling that goes with the image is fixed upon him and he is able to reproduce the image and self without the aid of the mirror. He should walk about the room sustaining this feeling of strength and ease, occasionally returning to the mirror to see if the image is right.[11]

Adjust your stance in the mirror, ridding yourself of tics and awkwardness. If it feels "unnatural," that's only because it may be new to you. You have old stance habits. *Break* them and develop new habits – positive stance habits.

By adopting the basic stance or the classic stance, you eliminate odd tics. This is a positive process, developing good habits, and it is much better than trying to memorize a list of "don't do this."

Now that you have your new stance, it is worth taking a moment to examine some of the more common pathologies that affect presenters.

Do *not* engage in the following tics and habits:

Do not!

Do not cross your leg in front of you while you balance on the other leg. This "standing cross" is more prevalent, for some reason, among female presenters than among males. Some males have this habit as well. This is a debilitating movement from both the standpoint of the audience and for you. It projects instability. It makes you *feel* unstable, because you *are* unstable. This movement removes your sure foundation. For some reason, you balance yourself on one leg. You teeter back and forth. You rock precariously. No one benefits from this posture.

Do not cock your hip to one side – this is called a "hip-shot." Again, this action undermines your foundation. This hip-shot posture degrades your presentation in multiple ways. It shouts nonchalance. It denotes disinterest and impatience. It cries out to the audience a breezy bar demeanor that is completely at odds with the spoken message you want to convey.

The hip-shot says: "I'm really laid-back about this topic. I am so laid-back, in fact, that I truly don't want to be here telling you about it and I'm counting the seconds until I can sit down and be done with it."

Do not engage in little choppy steps. This side-to-side dance is common. It telegraphs nervousness.

---

11 Watkins, *Effective Speaking*, 50–51.

Do not slump your shoulders. Few things project lack of confidence like rounded shoulders. Slumping shoulders can be a reflexive response to nervousness that leads to a "closed body position."

You Have Your Foundation – Time to Build

Your goal at this point is to maintain a solid physical foundation. You want to project an image of confidence to the audience and to imbue yourself with confidence in point of fact. You have begun to do this with your stance – solid and confident.

To summarize, square your shoulders and distribute your weight evenly over your feet in your basic stance or 80-20 back-front in your classic stance. Your toes should be pointed slightly outward. Arms are loosely at your sides. This is your ready position. Your foundation.

Now here is the first addition to your ready position.

The First Step – Your Hands

Stand as described, and place your left hand in your pants pocket, out of the way. This position, which is illustrated in Chapter 6, should be your default position. This position carries a multitude of positives and no negatives. It can carry you through any presentation occasion.

It imbues you with confidence. To your audience, it projects competence, confidence, reassurance, and sobriety: "Here is someone who knows their stuff."

In the chapter on gesture, we build on your foundation to create a powerful platform *persona*. In the meantime, absorb the words of Arthur Stevens Phelps, whose belief in a grandiose stance is captured here:

> Gracefulness of carriage, if not innate, may be cultivated, as every observer of the military recruit, the dancing school, and the transformation between college freshman and senior years, knows. To acquire the habit of carrying yourself erect, it is necessary only to hold the head high, and your body will follow… Get athletic grace by athletic exercises. Eliminate all awkward positions when in private, or in social converse, such as arms akimbo, or awesomely folded, or clasped across the chest like the corpse of Tutankhamen, or grasping the abdomen like the Indian God of pain.[12]

---

12 Arthur Stevens Phelps, *Speaking in Public* (Cleveland: F. M. Barton Company, 1930), 202.

VOICE: "I FEEL ESPECIALLY *POWERFUL* TODAY!"

> **The Challenge:** A weak, ineffective, or annoying voice, a voice that is uncertain and constantly shifting, one that saps your confidence, transmits disorganization, and undermines your credibility.
>
> **The Solution:** A deeper, more resonant voice, filled with power and certainty. Inflection that reassures rather than plants doubt in minds of listeners. A voice that commands respect rather than assaults the ear.
>
> **The Benefit:** Your improved presentation voice communicates rather than detracts from your message. It invests your message with *gravitas* and power with every word, sentence, paragraph. A powerful presentation voice can instill in your audience confidence and belief in you as a presenter.

In this chapter, I talk about two things – voice *quality* and *technique*. With respect to your voice, I want you quickly and dramatically to improve your voice for business presentations. To 1) make you aware of major flaws and 2) to correct these flaws, if you have them.

If you think of a musical instrument and the music it plays, you quickly grasp the concept. For you to play music that is sweet to the ear your instrument must be of fine quality and it must also be played well, with technique and finesse and feeling. Likewise, your voice is an instrument, and you must learn to play it well.

Quality and *technique* – you can improve both.

Every semester, I have two or three students in each class with amazingly facile and resonant voices. They possess magnificent voices crafted to speak in public.

Voices that are *far* better than mine. They resonate with raw power and range and depth.

Yet they often don't even recognize their talent, this *gift*. They must be told, and often they must be *sold*. Because it seems to be a characteristic of human nature to be blind to what we are most excellent in.

What about *my* voice?

I don't have the best of speaking voices. My voice doesn't resonate like the deep baritone of James Earl Jones, the voice of *Star Wars* villain Darth Vader, but I am occasionally complimented on it. I don't know why. Perhaps it's because I work hard to camouflage my limitations. I exercise my meager vocal cords, and I develop my tools to their sharpest, to their fullest potential.

This is what *you* must do to become a superior presenter.

Voice Quality – A Case of "Bad Voice"?

Like it or not, others judge us by our voices. Pleasant or unpleasant. Think of it this way: the quality of your voice is a part of how you communicate. Not just the words we use, but *how we articulate our sounds*.

You know the problem of "bad voice" when you hear it.

Fortune 500 speech coach Jeffrey Jacobi commissioned a survey of more than 1,000 speakers of English to determine "Which irritating or unpleasant voice annoys you the most?" Results of that survey appear below.[1]

Voice type	Percent most annoying
Whiney; complaining	44.0
High-pitched; squeaky	15.9
Loud and grating	12.1
Mumbling	11.1
Very fast talking	4.9
Weak and wimpy	3.6
Flat and monotonous	3.5
Heavy accent	2.4
Don't know; no response	2.6

1 Jeffrey Jacobi, *How to Say it with Your Voice* (New York: Prentice Hall, 1996), 61.

The average college student's natural response to a survey such as this often is to portray this state-of-affairs as "your problem, not mine."

"If you don't like my voice, that's tough. *Deal* with it."

If this is *your* response, recognize that such a precious attitude gets an "A" for arrogance and an "F" for common sense.

If you don't care how well you communicate with others and don't mind carrying the burden of an additional handicap, such as an unpleasant voice, then that's your choice. And you will find your opportunities limited and your influence greatly diminished in favor of others who are less prone to precious behavior. It indeed *may* be "tough" for *you*.

You may find that people – especially employers and customers – choose *not* to "deal" with it. Curiously and unfortunately for the current college generation, the "whiney, complaining" voice appears to be in vogue, and this is exactly the kind of voice that people, well, that people *hate*.

This is one of those issues where you may find yourself in what I call the Prison of Freedom. You have full opportunity and knowledge and ability to choose a course that gives you exactly what you want with respect to your voice, but you may hold yourself back with insecurity, ego, belligerence, stubbornness, or perhaps even laziness. Recognize that these self-limiting factors all influence the personal choices that we ultimately make, the consequences of which we must bear.

When you choose your path with regard to development of your voice, you choose with full knowledge of the consequences of your choice. Whichever path you take, I wish you well; I hope that you choose the course of continuous improvement. Let's proceed.

Take Your Voice for a Spin

Consider your own voice. Think of it. Try it out. Speak a few sentences. Say this sentence several times, and listen to the way you sound:

"The songs of Justin Bieber rival those of the greatest artists of all pop history."

Is your voice pinched? Do you use your chest as the resonating chamber it ought to be, or does your voice emanate from your throat alone? Do you swallow your voice in the back of your throat so that you produce a nasal twang? "The tone becomes rough and impure when the column of air passing over the vocal cords is not allowed free and unrestricted movement. The cure for impurity of tone is primarily a relaxed and open throat."[2]

Judging from what I hear in class, in the elevator, on the subway, and in the campus coffee shops, the odds are good that your voice is pinched and smaller than it ought to be. This is a result of many influences in our culture that, within the last decade or so have urged on us a plaintive, world-weary whine as voice-of-choice.

Thus, voice becomes a matter of style – not just in the slang we choose to use, but in the way our voices sound when we use that slang. High-pitched. Small. Weak. Unpleasant. Pinched. Nasal. Raspy. A voice from reality television. A *cartoon* voice.

The cartoon voice is more prevalent than you might imagine. Several reasonably known celebrities have cartoon voices, and they dwell in the wasteland of daytime television.

Cartoon Voice is Everywhere

One daytime cartoon voice belongs to someone called Kelly Ripa. Television serves up Ms. Ripa not for her voice, but for other attributes. She is worth watching, *once*, if only to hear Ms. Ripa's slam-on-the-brakes whine.

Two other champions of the squeaky, whiney cartoon voice are people who appear to have achieved a degree of questionable fame for all of the wrong reasons: Kim Kardashian and Meghan McCain, who appear on television for some reason unknown to all but the producers of the shows they inhabit. Commonly called "divas," their voices are barely serviceable for even routine communication. Granted, these young women are not delivering business presentations, but their negative influence has infected an entire generation of young people who *do* deliver presentations.[3]

These women embody all that is wrong with regard to delivering powerful presentations. If this sounds harsh, it is meant to be. They exhibit habitual pathologies of the worst sort. Where do these people learn to speak this way, in this self-doubting, self-referential, endlessly qualified grinding whine?

---

2 George Rowland Collins, *Platform Speaking* (New York and London: Harper & Brothers Publishers, 1923), 33.

3 For video and audio of more than a dozen women whose voices are archetypes of clear expression, see this website: "Female Presenters," My Corporate Face, http://www.mycorporateface.com/Female-Presenters/female-presenters.html (accessed June 20, 2012).

One culprit appears to be the Disney Channel, inculcating a new generation of young folks into the practice of weak-speak. Numerous other popular young adult shows occupy the lowest rung of this speech food chain, passing on lessons in weak voice and poor diction.

Most anywhere, you can hear people who talk this way. They surround us.

Next time you stand in line at the convenience store, listen to the people around you. Focus on the voices. Listen for the trapped nasal sound, the whine of precious self-indulgence. Or the sound of a voice rasping across vocal cords at the end of every sentence. A voice that has no force. No depth.

I often hear this cartoon voice in the elevator as I commute between my office and classrooms. Elevator conversations are often sourced from lazy, scratchy voices. These voices are ratcheted tight in the voice box with barely enough air passed across the vocal cords. What do I mean by this? Let's have an example.

I hear snippets of conversation daily, whether in line at the campus Starbucks at the 7-Eleven or on the subway. Young people chatter quite freely about their relationships with girlfriends and boyfriends, and they do so with refreshing abandon.

What is not so refreshing is the frequency of lazy raspy voices that I hear uttering the word "like" in rat-a-tat fashion. Everything apparently is always "like" something else instead of actually *it*. And apparently "totally" so. Ya know?

"*Like. Like. Like.* Totally! *Like. Like. Like.* Totally! It was *like...* ummmm... okay... *whatever.* Ya know what I mean?"

I'll always remember one young man's voice that sounded like a death rattle. His verbal stutter of "like" gave the impression that he was unsure of *anything* he was saying. His voice was a lab experiment of bad timbre. It cracked and creaked along.

The air barely passed over his vocal cords, just enough to rattle a pile of dry sticks. Not nearly enough air to vibrate and give pitch and tone. *No* resonance came from the chest. The voice rasped on the ears. *Every* sentence spoken was a question.

There are two major problems here. First, the cracking and grinding sound, which is at the very least, irritating. Second, the primitive infestation of what I call "dum-dums."

The Dum-Dum Disease

Dum-dums are moronic interjections slipped into every sentence like an infestation of termites.

"*Like*. Totally! Ya know? Ummm. *Like*. Totally! It was *like*, okay, you know — ya *know*? Ummm. *Like*, whatever."

Be honest and recognize that adults don't speak like this. If you choose to speak like this, you will never be taken seriously by anyone considering whether to give you responsibility. Folks who fill the empty air with cartoon voice peppered with dum-dums give the impression of having nothing worthwhile to say.

Dum-dums are the result of lazy thought and even lazier speech. It started on the west coast as an affectation called "Valley Speak" and has seeped into the popular culture as relentlessly as nicotine into the bloodstream. Exaggeration? No, it's a voice you hear every day.

Listen for it. Maybe it's *your* voice.

In the abstract, there is probably nothing wrong with any of this if your ambitions are of a lowest common denominator stripe. If you are guilty of this sort of thing, you can probably get by with laziness, imprecision, and endless qualifying in everyday discourse.

The problem comes when you move into the boardroom to express yourself in a professional way to a group of, say, influential skeptics who expect to be impressed by the power of your ideas and how well you express them. They want to hear powerful concepts, clearly stated in a voice that communicates surety and competence.

Cartoon voice infested with dum-dum words — this debilitating pathology destroys *all* business presentations. You *cannot* deliver a credible business presentation speaking this way. You're on the express train to failure with a first-class ticket.

Good News!

But the good news is that all of this is reasonably easy to correct — *if* you are willing to accept that your voice and diction *should* be changed.

If you recognize that you have cartoon voice and that you pepper your speech with dum-dums, ask yourself these questions: Why do I speak like this? Why can't I utter a simple declarative sentence without inserting dum-dums along the way? Why do all of my sentences sound like questions? Do I really want and need to sound like a ditz just because the people around me can't seem to express themselves except in staccato dum-dums with a cracking voice?

Deciding to change one's voice is a bold move that takes you out of your current cramped comfort zone, but you don't have to do it! Nope, don't change a thing.

If you recognize that you have cartoon voice and you are comfortable slathering your speech with dum-dums, and you see no reason to change just because someone recommends it, well then keep on keepin' on!

Sure, it's okay for your inner circle of chatterers. Relish it. Hang onto it, and don't even give a backward glance. Let 1,000 dum-dums flourish!

But do so with the clear-eyed recognition that dum-dums make you sound like a moron. You make a conscious choice. Dum-dums make you sound like a reality TV show lightweight who is unable to utter an original thought or even speak in complete sentences. Recognize that if you want to succeed in an intensely competitive business climate, consider leaving Disney Channel behind.

When you want to be taken seriously in a business presentation, speak like an adult.

Why Change?

Many people are fearful or resistant to adjusting their voices. It even angers some people. They think it's "cheating." Or "unnatural." They revere "spontaneity" and believe that their voices are, well, *natural*.

More than likely, they have neglected the development of their voices. For some reason they now revere this product of their benign neglect as natural. As if there is some far-off judge who weighs and measures the "naturalness" of voice. As if there is some kind of purity benchmark or standard.

But there is no such standard for "naturalness." Only pleasant voices, unpleasant voices, and lots of voices in-between. Moreover, the variety of voices, from bad to good, has been with us eternally.

Nasality, harshness, extremes of pitch, and other unnatural vocal quality distract the audience. They impede communication; they clog the speaker's transmission. They hinder the persuasion of any audience, be it one or one thousand.[4]

There is nothing holy or sacrosanct or "natural" about the way you speak now. It is not "natural" in any meaningful sense of the word, as if we are talking about breast augmentation versus the "natural" thing.

Your voice today is "natural" only in the sense that it is the product of many factors over time, most of them unintended – *negative* factors as well as positive. Factors you've probably never thought of.

So in that sense, why would you have any problem with changing your voice *intentionally*, the way that *you* want it changed?

Time for You to Take Control

Face it – some voices sound good and others sound bad; and there are all sorts of voices along the spectrum between those two extremes. You can improve your speaking voice to become a first-rate speaker, but you must *first* accept that you *can* and *should* improve it.

I train students to attend to the voice, to pay attention to it, to analyze it. It's the fundamental instrument of communication in the story you tell, and yet it's one of the most neglected. The voice is taken for granted.

Most likely, *you* take your voice for granted. Unless you have taken voice lessons, your voice has evolved over time, probably without instruction, without exercise, without thought. It's "natural." It simply *is*. You might even bristle at the notion that you ought to "change" your voice.

"What's *wrong* with my voice?" you could respond. "My voice is *fine*, and people can take my voice just the way it is."

You say this to me in a pinched, small voice, a voice with barely enough air passing across the vocal cords, a voice cracking and grating at the end of every sentence.

No, I've not heard you speak. I probably never will. But have *you* heard yourself? Have you listened to yourself? Try it.

If you want to become a good speaker, but you do not accept that you can and should improve your voice, it means that you are much like an un-coachable

---

4 George Rowland Collins, *Platform Speaking* (New York and London: Harper & Brothers Publishers, 1923), 21.

football player. Oh, you *want* to become a superb football player, but you refuse to listen to the coach.

The coach suggests that you develop your muscles and coordination in the gym, but you refuse. Instead, you respond that your body's musculature is "natural." You believe that you can become a great football player without "cheating" with weight training or cardio conditioning, or by modifying your "natural" physique by exercising and building your muscles.

I'm sure you see the absurdity in this.

The same is true when it comes to your voice. Voice is an extremely personal attribute, and people don't take criticism lightly, perhaps viewing it as a self-esteem issue or an attack on personhood. It's not.

Don't bristle at the notion that you should change your voice. This is naiveté and vanity and ego. You impose a handicap on yourself and an excuse for inaction. You hold yourself back. It is also a manifestation of fear. Most college students have *always* had this fear. *I* had this fear. Clare Tree Major observed this fear almost a century ago in college students of her time:

> People are exceedingly sensitive about changing their methods of speech for fear it will bring upon them the ridicule of their families and friends... Charm and grace and beauty will come only when speech is unconscious – not while you have to think of every word and tone. If a thing is right there can be no question of affectation. It is a greater affectation to do the wrong merely to pander to the less cultured tastes of others. If you know a thing is right, do it. If you have not this ideal and this courage, then it will waste your time to study correct speech.[5]

What *is* your voice but a means of communication? Does it have purposes other than speaking or singing? Other than communicating?

It's easy to see that clear communication depends upon the timbre of your voice. It *does* matter what others think of your voice, since you use it to communicate, and it is *others* who receive your messages. Doesn't it make sense, then, to cultivate the most effective voice you possibly can so that you might communicate most effectively? Put another way, doesn't it make sense

---

5 Clare Tree Major, *Your Personality and Your Speaking Voice* (New York: Grosset & Dunlap, 1920), 16–17.

to eliminate what is unpleasant, ineffectual, shrill, and dissonant from your voice, if possible?

A weak, raspy voice calls out weakness. It erodes the image of confidence that you want to project. You have several options to deal with this. You surely have the option to accept your voice as-is. You can accept it as the willy-nilly product of years of neglect and nonchalance. You can enshrine that product as somehow "natural" and superior to a voice that is well-trained to communicate clearly. Again, if you bristle at the notion that you should "change" your voice to suit the ear, then *don't* change it. It's that simple.

If you don't want to accept this advice, then don't. Leave yourself at a disadvantage *vis-à-vis* others who are more flexible. If you see this state of affairs as perfectly fine, then leave your voice unmodified. Celebrate your certitude and skip this chapter. And in doing so, you surrender incredible competitive advantage to others with less precious attitude.

But if you open yourself to the possibility of improvement, then read on.

Time to Improve

If nature has not endowed you with a good speaking voice, you can do much toward acquiring one. The organs of speech can be trained, like any other part of the body, by assiduous attention and practice.[6]

Let's consider two things you can do to improve your voice. Nothing extreme at all, and actually quite fun. We have two goals.

First, we want to rid your voice of the chronic crack and rasp. That crack and rasp is a symptom of meekness – no confidence. Do you have this crack and rasp? If not, congratulations and let's move along. But if you *do* "In addition to relaxing the throat muscles, the speaker should make a special effort to vocalize every particle of breath passing over the vocal cords. There should be no wheezy leakage of air."[7]

---

6 Grenville Kleiser, "How to Speak Well," *Radio Broadcasting* (New York: Funk & Wagnalls, 1935), 42–3.

7 George Rowland Collins, *Platform Speaking* (New York and London: Harper & Brothers Publishers, 1923), 33.

Second, we want to deepen your voice. Why? Like it or not, deeper voices are perceived as more credible.[8] A Stanford University study, one among many, gives the nod to deeper voices:

> Our studies show that directions from a female voice are perceived as less accurate than those from a male voice, even when the voices are reading the exact same directions. Deepness helps, too. It implies size, height and authority. Deeper voices are more credible.[9]

Now, should things be this way? Is it "fair" that deeper voices have some kind of advantage?

It's neither fair, nor unfair. It's simply the reality we are dealt. It's no less fair than the fact that some people are taller than others or larger or faster or score perfect marks on the SAT. If you want to devote your life fighting for "voice equality," you have my support.

If, on the other hand, you want to deepen your voice so that you gain personal competitive advantage, then let's analyze what the deep-voice reality means to us.

It means that a deeper voice is more desirable for presenting, regardless of who presents, male or female. It's been this way for centuries, in fact. Speaking master Charles Horner speaks to us across the years:

> I think, generally speaking, the voice should be pitched as low as possible, having in mind the speaker's vocal range and the distances voice must carry. Shrill tones are never pleasing, a strident voice worries those who listen to it. The lower registers of the voice should be developed as much as possible. Not only is the effect better, the tones pleasanter, but the speaker thus always has the opportunity for immediate emphasis, should occasion require him to raise his voice.[10]

Now, you are empowered by the very fact that you are armed with that information. When you decide to *act* on it, it adds to your personal competitive

---

8 J. K. Suter, "Der Eindruck vom Ausdruck – Einfluss paraverbaler Kommunikation auf die Wahrnehmung von Nachrichtensprechenden" [The impression of expression – The influence of paraverbal communication on the perception of newsreaders]. Unpublished master's thesis, University of Bern, Switzerland (2003).

9 Anne Eisenberg, "Mars and Venus, On the Net: Gender Stereotypes Prevail," *New York Times*, October 12, 2000. http://www.nytimes.com/2000/10/12/technology/12VOIC. html (accessed October 28, 2009).

10 Charles F. Horner, *The Speaker and the Audience* (Kansas City: Matthews & Churchill, 1922), 72.

advantage. If your voice is already deep, congratulations and move along. If not, and you'd like to add some depth, have a look at the next section.

The Basic Changes

Let's start by acknowledging that there are *many* things you can do to improve your voice – your articulation, your power and range, your force and tone. If you decide that you want to move to an advanced level of presentations and are drawn to improve your voice's quality through study and practice, many books and videos and recordings are published each year to help you along.

Much of the best writing on voice improvement was produced in the years when public speaking was considered an art – between 1840 and 1940 – and the advice contained therein is about as universal and timeless as it gets.

The reality is that the human voice is the same now as it was 100 years ago and responds to the proven techniques developed over centuries. At the end of this chapter, I suggest several sources for further improvement, should you pursue that worthy goal.

The quality of business presentations is generally so low in the United States that even minor improvements in your voice technique and quality yield major returns in personal competitive advantage.

What about *my* voice? Professor Ridgley's voice? Am I satisfied with it? Do I consider it "resonant" and top-notch? No, not by a long shot. So I work on it…

I begin each day with resonating exercises in the privacy of my home, where no one can hear me run the gamut of my not-so-deep register. I stretch and develop my vocal cords. Daily, I attempt to deepen my voice, to increase its resonance and pleasant qualities. And so should you.

The goal is to rid ourselves of the crack and rasp and to deepen the voice. We can achieve both of these goals with a single exercise.

The goal of this exercise is to move your voice down a bit in its routine pitch. Sure, you'll vary your pitch during your talks. Sometimes you speak higher and sometimes lower, sometimes faster, sometimes slower. But we want to move the "average" pitch down as much as we reasonably can. At the same time, this exercise helps us push more air across the vocal cords and eliminates the crack and rasp.

This exercise requires that you be somewhat familiar with the voice of James Earl Jones – the voice of Darth Vader in the original *Star Wars* trilogy from the 1970s and early 1980s. I do this exercise myself, and I conduct it *en masse* in my classes when I detect that students are expressing themselves less than enthusiastically. You, however, do this exercise alone.

Find a place where no one can hear you or see you. This is to get you into a stress-free mindset. Of course, you shouldn't worry what other people think of you, but *just in case*, move to a private area where you can express yourself freely. And loudly.

Now, stand up and envision yourself as Darth Vader. Spread your arms to either side and say this, in your best Darth Vader voice:

"I feel especially *powerful* today!"

It's okay. Go ahead and say it.

"I feel especially *powerful* today!"

Say it loudly, *but not only with your voice box*. You do not want to strain your vocal cords. Control your voice, and focus on using your chest as a resonating chamber. Push air from your abdomen. Say it in various ways. Say it with your voice emanating from your chest.

Boom it out. Deepen your voice as much as possible and picture it coming from deep inside your chest, from the deepest recesses of your very heart. Unleash the beast within you, clearly and forcefully. *Project* your voice.

"I feel *especially powerful* today!"

These are power words. They are no mistake, nor are they random. And it's not a joke. If you think it's a joke and "not worth my time," then move along. Others *will* learn, and they will be pleased that you abandon the task and drop by the wayside. The competition thins.

Power words.

Power words spoken honestly and with gusto help you to slough off the muck of your daily life. Like a Brillo pad, they scrub away the affectations and the hesitations that infest your inner core. Power words can shatter this crust.

Athletes use power words often, to invest themselves with confidence at crucial times in a contest. With these power words, *you* invest yourself with energy and confidence. With power words, you tap your inner *chi*, the strength that is generated within you. Too many external events in our lives can sap our strength and energy, our very life force. You can rejuvenate that strength. You can draw energy from others.

Several weeks of this simple exercise and you will feel your voice changing, gaining resonance and depth.

This is not the only thing you can do to improve your voice. You can work with a voice coach to improve your voice's quality in a number of ways. But most of us will never meet a voice coach, let alone work with one. In the absence of a coach we can make these minor adjustments that pay incredibly large dividends to us as presenters.

"I feel *especially powerful* today!"

Techniques

How you *use* your voice is equal in importance to your voice's quality. A Stradivarius violin is a marvelous instrument, but can only produce music of a rank with that of the player, whose use of technique and skill with the instrument combine with its quality to produce a masterpiece.

Think of your voice again as a musical instrument and your presentation as the piece of music you play. Music is invested with emotional power by the use of technique – *crescendo, decrescendo, andante, allegro, pianissimo*. You don't have to be a musician to appreciate the effects of technique. You can easily harness the emotional impact of techniques such as inflection, pitch and pace, pause, and purging.

Inflection

Inflection is the emphasis we place on words in a sentence to clarify meaning. How we inflect our voice can radically alter a sentence's meaning. For instance, take the simple seven-word sentence: "I didn't say he stole that car." This sentence, which seems clear and direct, takes on seven distinctly different meanings depending on the word emphasized. Read these sentences aloud, emphasizing the italicized word in each one.

I didn't say he stole that car.

I *didn't* say he stole that car.

I didn't *say* he stole that car.

I didn't say *he* stole that car.

I didn't say he *stole* that car.

I didn't say he stole *that* car.

I didn't say he stole that *car*.

Such is the power of inflection. It pays us to be conscious of the inflection we use, since the inflection changes the meaning of our words dramatically.

Most of us are conscious of inflection, and we get it right most of the time. But three common problems with inflection can get people in trouble. These are three "tics."

"Tics" are habits, usually unconscious habits. *Merriam-Webster* defines "tic" as: "a frequent usually unconscious quirk of behavior or speech ['you know' is a verbal tic]."

Yes, **you know** is the scourge of the land, along with his evil twin **like**. And we'll get to these abominations soon enough. But right now, the tics that plague at least 50 percent of all college student presenters are these:

1. The Verbal Up-Tic

2. The Verbal Down-Tic

3. The Verbal Grind

A goodly percentage of students carry the *Verbal Up-Tic*. It's one of those unfortunate verbal eccentricities that is performed unconsciously. It irritates the audience in an eerie way. It unsettles people. If the speaker engages in it for too long, the audience begins to squirm. It's simply this…

The voice rises slightly at the end of each sentence and phrase. As if a question is being asked, or as if something is to follow, the next item in a list. It is subtle and insidious. Voice coach Patsy Rodenburg calls this the "rising line" that occurs at the end of a sentence. Says Rodenburg:

> The end of a thought is forced up… and it puts a questioning stress on ideas that are not questions. This lift makes statements sound like questions, which gives the listener the sense that the speaker is unsure of what they are saying.[11]

This heinous habit was first identified as a major and growing problem in a 1993 *New York Times* column by James Gorman, in which he coined the term "uptalk."[12] Uptalk has been linked to something called "mallspeak," which

---

11 Patsy Rodenburg, *Power Presentations* (New York: Michael Joseph, Penguin Books, 2009), 116.

12 James Gorman, "On Language," *New York Times*, August 15, 1993.

also infests student business presentations and leeches them of all credibility. Says British writer Matt Seaton:

> [C]ommentators have likewise associated uptalk with other features of west coast "mallspeak," such as the slacker habit of self-interrupting sentences with "like," using the intensifier "totally," and responding to any actual question (as opposed to an uptalk interrogative) with "whatever."[13]

The effects of uptalk are cumulative and destructive. Uptalk grinds away like a whetstone on the nerves of listeners. This Verbal Up-Tic occurs repeatedly, sentence after sentence, sometimes four, five, *eight* sentences without a break. This cliff-hanger puts the audience unconsciously on the edge of the precipice, wondering if the speaker has a clue, waiting for the end of the thought. Waiting, anticipating, waiting, anxious, but the end doesn't come soon enough.

Certainly there is an appropriate time to use this technique, if you use it properly. But you must know that it *is* a device. It is a tool with a certain purpose. It's a verbal cue that keeps the audience hanging for the completion of a thought. You can control the anticipation of the listeners with the Verbal Up-Tic. You keep them waiting for more. You can keep them *expecting* more.

But if it's used habitually, blindly, relentlessly, unconsciously, it bewilders the audience. Your listeners grow uneasy, and then angry.

Moreover, as Patsy Rodenburg notes, "Because everything has an upward rhythm, this lift signals weakness and begs interruption. The rhythm is actually saying, 'I don't know what I think and I can't stand by what I say.'"[14]

This tic is hidden in plain view, yet it's buried so deeply in the shifting sands of our modern rhetoric, that most people who hear it are unaware of it. Listeners feel their nerves fraying, yet they cannot pinpoint the source of their discomfort – they just know it has something to do with *you*.

Five in ten college presenters suffer from the Verbal Up-Tic to some degree. Where do I get this statistic? From the dozens upon dozens of presentations I view each year. Are you one of them? Record yourself performing a five-minute presentation, then listen for this verbal tic on playback.

---

13 Matt Seaton, "Word Up," *Guardian*, September 21, 2001, http://www.guardian.co.uk/books/2001/sep/21/referenceandlanguages.mattseaton (accessed 26 July, 2012).
14 Patsy Rodenburg, *Power Presentation: Formal Speech in an Informal World* (New York: Michael Joseph, 2009), 116.

Can you identify it in your own speech? If you hear it, eliminate it ruthlessly.

You can eliminate it simply by consciously dropping your voice at the end of sentence, in finality. It signifies the completion of a thought. But don't go so far as to adopt the other verbal tic.

The Verbal Down-Tic

The *Verbal Down-Tic* can drain the life from your audience. In severe cases of verbal down-ticking, you can induce depression in your listeners.

Patsy Rodenburg calls this bad habit the "Falling Line," and it occurs at the end of a sentence. At the end of *every* sentence, after sentence, after sentence.[15] The final syllables at the end of a sentence are garbled and lost in an expulsion of air as the speaker inflects his voice downward in ultimate finality.

The Verbal Down-Tic – it is lifeless. It's world-weary. It makes us feel as if we are all on a death march to the end of your talk. It sucks the energy from the room.

The good news is that I encounter far fewer cases of verbal down-ticking than of verbal up-ticking. Who knows why this is? Perhaps it's because the up-tic is associated with uncertainty and hesitation, while the down-tic is associated with resignation and jaded cynicism.

The solution to a Verbal Down-Tic is to finish each sentence strongly, decisively, with closure and confidence. Do not swallow the last few syllables, nor puff them out in a tired expulsion of air.

Verbal tics such as the Rising Line and the Falling Line are affectations that we adopt for "public speaking." We don't usually talk like this, with these bad habits. We save it for our presentations. We "dress up" our speech for presenting, sometimes unconsciously. As with the up-tic, simple awareness of the down-tic problem is halfway to solving it.

The Verbal Grind

The Verbal Grind is a symptom of the pervasiveness of "Valley Girl" talk that arose in the 1980s like a scourge on the land. Its signature is the grinding of the voice at the end of almost every sentence that results from pinching off the flow of air and letting the vocal cords flop as they wish.

The grinding sound that results appears to be desirable in certain circles, indicating perhaps a world-weariness and "whatever" posture. Bill Clinton has an incurable case of verbal grinding that is part of his *persona*. He has

---

15 Ibid.

managed to turn this tic into a part of his personal brand; it is a negative, but his speaking skills across the range of other dimensions – stance, gesture, expression, movement, appearance, and passion – are so strong as to neutralize any negativity. You, unfortunately, do not have that luxury.

Meghan McCain, daughter of Senator John McCain, has an apparently incurable case of verbal grind. Tune in to her interviews on the web for a first-class lesson in bad voice. Actress Demi Moore grinds all the time, not just at the end of sentences. Listen for the verbal grind in others and in yourself and work to purge it from your voice. Purge it by pushing air across the vocal cords to the end of every sentence.

Pitch and pace

The slow death of many presenters is the monotone. The monotonous speaker combines the sins of unvaried pitch and pace in one horrific combination.

The dawning realization of an audience can be audible when it grasps that the monotonous drone of a keynote speaker will continue unabated for the duration of a talk. A monotonous speaker is a dark magician – he can make 15 minutes feel like an hour. An audience begins to signal its displeasure in a dozen different ways – coughing, whispers, shuffling of feet, clanking of silverware (if an after-dinner talk), occasionally audible sighs.

His voice neither rises nor falls to any significant degree. Nor does it speed up or slow down with any regularity or in any pattern connected to the words he speaks. Neither high nor low, nor fast nor slow.

Be conscious of your pace rather than run blithely at the mouth. Self-awareness is the cure for much of what ails us in our presentations, so take note of this tendency in your own speech.

Spice your talk with rapid-fire recitation juxtaposed with slow enunciation. Drop your voice in tone and slow down when you want to impart power. Just as well, make liberal use of the following technique...

Pause

Silence is your friend. In public speaking, it's called the *pause*.

The pause. The long, *calculated* silence. Most of us are uncomfortable with the absence of words or music filling the space between us. Something in our culture, perhaps something in our very natures causes us to feel discomfort with absence of sound in our interactions with others. In our conversations with others, long pauses can be uncomfortable.

In your own presentation, a long pause can be utterly excruciating. Such a pause can cripple you, because you haven't planned for it. Because you think it's unnatural in some way.

Maybe it's because your generation has grown up with constant aural stimulation, and you have been trained to expect constant sound. You expect snappy, snarky repartee with a constant barrage of percussion in the background. Its absence feels eerie.

Regardless of the reason, this discomfort is almost universal. This discomfort is universal *except* among the small group of people who recognize the opportunity in the absence of sound. This absence of sound is called a *pause*.

The masters of elocution knew the pause is an effective tool of emphasis. Princeton professor Robert Kidd put it this way 150 years ago:

> The rhetorical pause consists in suspending the voice either directly before or after the utterance of an important thought. The pause before the principal word awakens curiosity and excites expectation; after, it carries the mind back to what has already been said.[16]

Power of the pause

The correct pauses imbue your talk with incredible power. With proper timing and coupled with other techniques, the pause evokes strong emotions in your audience. A pause can project and communicate as much or *more* than mere words. The pause is part of your nonverbal repertoire and a superbly useful tool.

The comfortable pause communicates your power. It radiates confidence and telegraphs deep and serious thought. Grenville Kleiser put it this way: "Paradoxical though it may seem, there is an eloquence and a power in silence which every speaker should seek to cultivate."[17]

When you use the pause judiciously, you emphasize the point that comes immediately *after* the pause. You give the audience time to digest what you

---

16 Robert Kidd, *Vocal Culture and Elocution* (New York: Van Antwerp, Bragg & Co., 1857), 41.

17 Grenville Kleiser, *How to Develop Power and Personality in Speaking* (New York and London: Funk & Wagnalls Company, 1912), 179.

VOICE: "I FEEL ESPECIALLY *POWERFUL* TODAY!"   83

just said. You generate anticipation for what you are about to say. So save the pause for the moments just prior to each of your main points.

A truly effective pause can be coupled with a motionless stance, particularly if you have been pacing or moving about or gesturing vigorously. Link the pause with a sudden stop – go motionless, and look at your audience intently. Seize their complete attention.

Pause.

You can see that you shouldn't waste your pause on a minor point of your talk. In point of fact, you should time your pauses to emphasize the single most important point of your show and its handful of supporting points.

Voice coach Patsy Rodenburg says, "A pause is effective and very powerful if it is active and in the moment with your intentions and head and heart... a pause filled with breath and attention to what you are saying to your audience will give you and your audience a bridge of transitional energy from one idea to another."[18]

Purging

Purge the garbage and clutter from your presentations. Don't create a presentation landfill. *Rid* yourself of these abominations:

> *You know.*
>
> *Like.*
>
> *Totally.*
>
> *Basically.*
>
> *Whatever.*
>
> *Ummm. Uhhh.*
>
> *You know what I mean.*

Who can say where and when these barbarisms first poisoned our discourse?

Doubtless they crept into our speech slowly, like an infection, until the disease raged unchecked. Until almost all of us came under their sway. I am reminded of the horror disease-epidemic film *28 Days Later* – the fatal epidemic was out of control before anyone knew there *was* an epidemic. To carry the metaphor

---

18 Patsy Rodenburg, *Power Presentation: Formal Speech in an Informal World* (New York: Michael Joseph, 2009), 107.

to its logical end, unlike in that horror film, you *can* inoculate yourself against infection.

We all utilize verbal clutter to fill in the gaps of our talks. It's a common verbal tic. Verbal clutter creeps into our speech without our notice. The cure is simple – *purge* these barbarisms.

Be conscious of their use. Record yourself giving a short presentation. Then listen to yourself on playback, and be astonished at your use of clutter to fill space. Most of this can be purged from your speaking repertoire by virtue of awareness.

By listening for them, you raise these verbal tics from the status of unconscious habits to the status of audible irritants, and they are much more easily eliminated.

Conclusion

Your voice is obviously a key to a fabulous presentation, or a disastrous one. We take our voice for granted. Because we do, it can undermine us and destroy all of our hard work. But you *can* become quite a good speaker, a presenter whose voice exudes confidence and is welcomed by the ear.

It's time to recognize that your voice is not a sacred artifact, nor is it some precious extension of your very being. It is an instrument with which you communicate. You can sharpen your communication skills by improving your voice. Simply *thinking* of your voice in this way will improve its quality. *Working* to improve it with the exercise described in this chapter will improve its quality dramatically.

In this chapter, we learned of the debilitating effects a "bad voice" and "bad technique" can have on a presentation. Let's start working today to improve both.

Further reading on voice

This chapter can take you a considerable way along the road to improving your voice. We now move on to the next piece of the presentations puzzle. But if the idea of voice improvement fascinates you and you want to take your voice to new heights of power, passion, and projection, then the following resources can speed you on your way:

- Renee Grant-Williams, *Voice Power: Using Your Voice to Captivate, Persuade, and Command Attention* (2002)

- Jeffrey Jacobi, *How to Say it with Your Voice* (1996)

- Patsy Rodenburg, *Power Presentation: Formal Speech in an Informal World* (2009)

- Clare Tree Major, *Your Personality and Your Speaking Voice* (1920)

6

GESTURE

The Challenge: Meaningless hand and body gestures that distract both you and your audience and degrade your presentations.

The Solution: An understanding of how gesture enhances your show and generates power and persuasiveness. You adopt positive gestures that harness and project emotional energy.

The Benefit: Your show gains power from the added emotional emphasis that the proper gesture at the proper moment provides.

Professors may see a dozen presentations every week – I've seen as many as 16 in five days. As a result, we have the privilege and opportunity to identify bad habits, and one negative tendency that appears repeatedly is that of the "bad gesture."

Not long ago a student of mine – James – began his presentation with aplomb and confidence. But as he moved through his delivery, his voice began to tremble, and he accelerated his sentences.

No surprises there. The body can betray all of us at some point during our presentation careers. James probably thought he looked like a shambles, but I've no doubt that he felt much worse than he appeared. His presenting was serviceable.

But the thing I remember most was his dramatic use of the clicker to advance his slides. What we call the "clicker" is actually a hand-held "wireless remote control presenter," made and sold by companies such as Targus and Logitech. We need not hide behind a lectern or hover over our laptops, where we must click the mouse to advance our slides. The clicker gives us mobility and unhitches us from our laptops.

But in this case, James let the clicker take him over. What began as a minor gesture – a subtle aim of the clicker at the screen behind him – quickly spun out of control. He would pivot and lash at the screen with his invisible bullwhip to change a slide. He changed slide-after-slide with a flip of the wrist and a frenetic crack-of-the-whip.

Let's leave aside for a moment that a clicker has no connection whatsoever to the screen, and so you need not point the clicker at the screen to advance the slide. Wild clicker pointing has no effect. James's increasingly animated gesticulations at the screen illustrate a common problem plaguing modern business school presentations: bad gestures, inarticulate gestures, useless and irrelevant gestures.

Bad Gesture Goes Way Back

The problem of bad gestures is common to every generation of presenters. In 1924, Robert West noted that:

> An unusual or a constantly recurring gesture soon becomes so obvious that it clamors for attention and gets it at the expense of the idea the speaker is trying to deliver. It matters not how graceful the gesture is as an isolated movement, if it is a distraction it is worse than no gesture at all.[1]

I see finger-tugging, floppy wrists, grandiose gripping at the air, even balled fists. I see it all the time. I see it so often that I wonder if there isn't a school somewhere training people to behave this way. The problem is not just the oddness of the gestures. It's that the gestures have nothing to do with what's being said. I hope you can see that gestures uncoordinated with the words being spoken might present a serious comprehension problem for the audience. At best, it can be confusing. At its worst, it can induce laughter.

The problem *must* be corrected, and this can be difficult to do. It's so difficult because the "problem" is easy to talk about in the abstract, but is often intentionally invisible with respect to actual persons.

No one likes to be corrected, especially with regard to something as personal as how we gesture. This is human nature, and it complicates things tremendously; in this respect, human nature is an obstacle to improvement. But given that it's human nature and has been around for a long, long time, it might provide

1 Robert West, *Purposive Speaking* (New York: The Macmillan Company, 1924), 141.

some reassurance to the modern student to see how it was addressed almost 100 years ago. There is a familiar sameness in the following passage.

> The remedy for such meaningless action is simple but difficult, like having a tooth pulled. All there is to it is to get rid of it, but the process of riddance sometimes hurts. It is not pleasant to have a teacher or friend point out to you specifically and bluntly some of your idiosyncrasies. Such criticism comes close to one. It cuts to the quick... The student should be warned again and again that meaningless gesture is a serious handicap; it may be a handicap that cannot be compensated for in any way. It must be gotten rid of, even at the cost of great effort. Your teachers and friends should deal harshly with your mannerisms. The student who resents such treatment is putting stumbling blocks in his own path. If one's friends see that he is super-sensitive about such criticism, they are not going to give it, and the would-be speaker loses his opportunity.[2]

So, is it a serious problem with respect to delivering your business presentation? I mean, is it really so important? Is it worth worrying about? Aren't the words themselves the key to clinching a deal? Ah, if it were only so easy!

You can't separate sincerity from your appearance. You can't eliminate movement from your talk, from your volume, from your nuance. And you cannot separate your words from *gesture*. If you deliver the wrong gesture, a meaningless gesture, or a conflicting gesture, you damage your message and your credibility considerably.

Gesture is so important because gesture is rooted in human history. Long before the spoken word enabled us to communicate with each other, gestures did the job.

> Gesture, within its limitations, is an unmistakable language, and is understood by men of all races and tongues... Gesture is almost instinctive language; at least it goes back to the beginning of all communication when the race, still lacking articulate speech, could express only through the tones of inarticulate sounds and through movements. And because it is so deeply embedded in our primitive reactions, all men express themselves by gesture and all men understand gesture.[3]

Gesture can increase your talk's power, lending emphasis to your words. In fact, gesture is essential to take your presentation to a superior level, a level

2 Robert West, *Purposive Speaking* (New York: The Macmillan Company, 1924), 142.
3 James Albert Winans, *Public Speaking* (New York: The Century Company, 1915, 1917), 468–9.

far above the mundane. You limit yourself if you don't gesture effectively as you present. In fact, many speaking masters contend that great speaking is impossible without the incorporation of the appropriate gestures.

Students never find themselves as speakers, never escape the bonds of restraint, never become really direct and communicative, until they gesture. It is unnatural not to gesture in any wide-awake discourse. Any real speaker would be in distress if compelled to restrain gesture. One might as well run a race with one's hands tied.[4]

What's Gesture?

Because gesture has been integral to the public talk for as long as there has been public talk, its importance has been lauded and lauded still more over the entire course of presentation history. The issues of gesture have bedeviled generations, and yet the solution of *good* gesture is well within our grasp.

Gesture may be broadly defined as visible expression, that is, any posture or movement of the head, face, body, limbs or hands, which aids the speaker in conveying his message by appealing to the eye.[5]

The term *gesture* is broad enough to cover every action and posture expressive of thought or feeling… A speaker who is full of his subject and has a great deal to express will feel the need of every means of expressing himself… Gesture is often a quicker, plainer and stronger means of expression than spoken words, for its appeal is to the eye. In motion toward the door, a shrug, a lifted eyebrow – what words can equal these gestures?[6]

Gestures that can either enhance or destroy your presentation abound.

A lifted eyebrow

A wave of the hand

Crossed arms

A stride across the stage

A scratch of the chin

4 James A. Winans, *Public Speaking Principles and Practice* (Ithaca, NY: The Sewell Publishing Company, 1915), 121.
5 Joseph A. Mosher, *The Essentials of Effective Gesture* (New York: The Macmillan Company, 1928), 3.
6 James Albert Winans, *Public Speaking* (New York: The Century Company, 1915, 1917), 468.

Professional presentation coaches understand that most of the information transmitted in a show is visual. This is a result of the *presence* of the speaker. An audio recording of a talk is not nearly as powerful as a live presentation. Why? Because "at least 85 percent of what we communicate in speaking is non-verbal. It's what people see in our eyes, in our movements and in our actions."[7] Executive coach Lynda Paulson is spot-on when she notes the power of gestures to persuade an audience, or to alienate an audience.

Gestures provide emphasis, energy, and accent. They add power to our words. Throughout the history of public speaking, the finest communicators have known the importance of the proper gesture at the proper time. Entire books, in fact, have been written about gesture. Gesture is too important to leave to chance.[8] Certainly too important to dismiss with the airy "move around when you talk."

Let's understand exactly what gesture means.

Gesture in your presentation should be natural. It should flow from the meaning of your words and the meaning you wish to convey with your words. We never gesture without a reason or point to make. Typically, the emotion and energy in a talk leads us to gesture. Without emotion, gesture is mechanical. It is false. It feels and *looks* artificial.

> In a normal, natural, genuine function of life like public speaking, where everything is real, and where complete sincerity is the great virtue, you cannot plaster Art on from the outside and expect it to conceal the fact that it is Art... The speaker must have something to say. He must feel the urge to say it. And then he must yield not merely his voice but his whole body to the task of saying it.[9]

What is gesture, and why do we worry about it at all? It's nothing more than an add-on, right? Something perhaps *nice* to have, but unessential to the point of our presentation.

Gesture is part of our repertoire of non-verbal communication. You have many arrows in the quiver of gesture from which to choose, and they can imbue your presentation with power. On rare occasion, gesture can imbue your presentation with majesty of epic proportions. Yes, I said "majesty of epic proportions." For if you do not begin to think in grand, expansive terms about yourself, your career and your presentations, you will remain mired in the mud, stuck at the bottom.

---

7 Lynda R. Paulson, *The Executive Persuader* (Napa, CA: SSI Publishing, 1991), 26.
8 Edward Amherst Ott, *How to Gesture* (New York: Hinds & Noble, 1892, 1902).
9 John Dolman, Jr., *A Handbook of Public Speaking* (New York: Harcourt, Brace, & Company, 1922), 113.

The Power of Gesture

We gesture to add force to your points. To demonstrate honesty, decisiveness, humility, boldness, even fear. A motion toward the door, a shrug, a lifted eyebrow – what words can equal these gestures? While its range is limited, gesture can carry powerful meaning. It *should* carry powerful meaning; this form of nonverbal language predates spoken language.

Imagine the powerful communication you attain when, at the proper moment, your voice, your gestures, your movement, and your expressions combine and align to fill your audience with emotion and energy. "Gesture is probably the most important factor in action on the platform. Energetic, emotional speaking is not often possible without it."[10]

The Foundation

Your gestures should be natural. You already know how to gesture. You do it all the time in your sincere moments. When you feel at ease with others, when you let your guard down, when you make yourself vulnerable to others because you trust them. Your task is to develop that ease of gesture all the time. It's akin to the ease we feel when walking.

When we actually think too much about the mechanics of walking, we impair our ability to walk. We become conscious of each step and all of the subsidiary movements that go into it. Our arms swinging, where we place each foot, the action of the legs. It becomes impossible to take a step without over-thinking it and interfering with the natural process.

At our best, we act in bold and dashing ways without thinking through our actions. But over time, we have given in to bad habits. And if we originally learned bad habits, we doubtless have those habits ingrained in us and must unlearn them. We do them without thinking. This means that we have to go through the difficult process of unlearning bad habits and then learning good ones.

The pay-off for you is this – what seems to come so naturally to that rare breed of speakers we admire will *also* come naturally to *you*.

Be mindful of gestures to eliminate. Rid yourself of useless distractions. One of our public speaking masters called such fiddling "scribble" movements.

---

10 George Rowland Collins, *Platform Speaking* (New York and London: Harper & Brothers Publishers, 1923), 56.

Don't be, physically, a scribbler. Here are some of the scribbling that listeners particularly dislike:

Weight-shifting

Body-swaying

Toe-teetering

Arm-swinging

Finger-fidgeting

Hand-hiding

Clothing-adjusting

Shoe-shuffling

Erase these meaningless mannerisms from your platform behavior.[11]

Your Repertoire of Gestures

In Chapter 4, we constructed your ready position. Either the basic stance or the classic stance is acceptable. Let's build on your ready position.

Remember your ready position. To summarize, your shoulders are squared, and your weight is distributed evenly over your feet in your Basic Stance or 80–20 back–front in your classic stance. Your toes are pointed slightly outward. Arms are loosely at your sides. Now, recall that we made one addition to your ready position.

You placed your left hand in your pants pocket, out of the way. This position is your default position. In your ready stance, you have your left hand out of harm's way in your pocket or tucked partially behind your back.

Your goal at this point is to maintain a solid physical foundation. You want to project an image of confidence to the audience and to imbue yourself with confidence in point of fact. You begin to do this with your stance – solid and confident.

You cannot go wrong with this rock-solid position. This position carries a multitude of positives and no negatives. It imbues you with confidence. To your audience, it projects competence, confidence, reassurance, and sobriety.

---

11 Richard C. Borden, *Public Speaking – As Listeners Like It!* (New York and London: Harper & Brothers Publishers, 1935), 98.

This is your *ready position*. Everything else you do flows from this position.

Let's now add your default gesture. This gesture will be your steady friend for years to come. It's called the John Kennedy Thumb Press.

You close your right hand in what looks to be a fist, but your thumb does not grip your fingers as in a fist; move your thumb up and let it rest upon the top of your clenched fingers as you see in the photo. Your arm is bent at a 90° angle at the elbow. This is your default ready position.

Now, you are ready to gesture. Here are the five gestures you must do in a business presentation.

John Kennedy Thumb Press. This is the workhorse of your gestures and part of your default ready position. It emphasizes without being too sharp or aggressive. You can always safely return to this gesture. It is so benign that it's almost invisible to the audience.

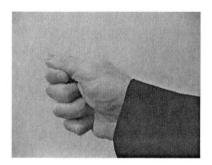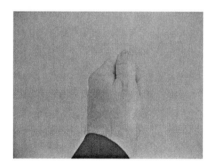

Obama Lint Pick. This is a favorite of President Barack Obama and is best used to indicate precision. Start with the Kennedy Thumb Press and simply touch your thumb and forefinger together like you're picking a piece of lint off your coat.

Magic Dust. This is nothing more than the Kennedy Thumb Press with the last three fingers extended, as if casting dust into the audience. It can be used to indicate "you people" off to either side, typically with the words "Over here… and over there."

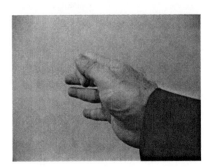 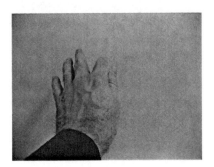

This Many. At some point in your presentation, you will likely have to tick off a series of numbers, preferably no more than three. As in "My first point, my second point, my third and final point."

The best way to do this is to use your thumb for your first point. Hold your left hand up, in a fist with your palm facing you. For "Number one," you extend your thumb. This looks very much like you're hitching a ride. "Number two," and you extend your index finger. "Number three," and you extend your middle finger.

Two-Fisted Passion. This is a powerful technique to use sparingly for emphasis. It consists of two balled fists held in front of you about four inches apart, as if you are clutching vertical parallel bars. Don't extend your elbows to either side; your elbows remain touching your sides.

The power of these gestures comes from their use in combination. *Any* gesture becomes monotonous if overused. A habitual gesture can quickly become a distraction and pass over into the bizarre, even the gestures suggested here.

Your best gesture friend is the John Kennedy Thumb Press. It is so blunt and unobtrusive; it can be used 70 percent of the time without distress. As you diverge from the thumb press and utilize the other gestures suggested here, your talk gains emphasis, power, and momentum. The more sparingly you use them, the more power they add to your words. Conversely, if you latch on to a single gesture and overuse it, it has a numbing effect on the audience.

Your Attitude

You already have an approach to presentations. You already look at them a certain way. We all do. Your approach or attitude is an important component of every presentation you deliver. Whether you are conscious of it or not, your approach colors tremendously the quality of your presentation. Perhaps this bothers you, perhaps it does not. But at the very least, be aware of your approach and its impact.

Here's why. Your approach and attitude can lead to utilizing great gestures, or they can lead to gesturing that degrades your performance.

For instance, many young presenters view the presentation session with dread, almost hate. In fact, I hear the phrase "I hate presentations" so often that it's almost a cliché. With such an attitude, your prime motivation is to just get through it somehow.

You cobble something together that lasts for the assigned 3–4 minutes, prep your PowerPoint slide crutch to help you hobble through it, produce some jargon that sounds like what the professor says and is marginally connected to the course content, and assume a defensive posture. You believe that if you're lucky, you can step close to the audience and turn your back to them and read from the slides. This is the ultimate cop-out, and you see it all the time. You pretend that the presentation is not about you. You pretend that the presentation is up on the screen, and you're just another member of the audience with the duty of reading the slides aloud.

If this is your attitude, or anything close to it, think seriously on this for a minute. Of what use to anyone is such an attitude and performance? Why would anyone pay you a salary to do that? And yet, this is the attitude displayed by a majority of the business students I've seen, as if the presentation is simply an unpleasant and temporary phase of school. This attitude can lead to all sorts of unconscious gesture pathologies that you should eliminate immediately.

Under no circumstances engage in "finger play." This is a habit many people develop unconsciously as they try to discover what to do with their hands. You *know* you should do something with your appendages, but no one has told you what. So you develop these unconscious motions. Many different activities come under the heading of "finger play." Examples include:

- *Tugging at your fingers.* I suspect that we all carry a "finger-tugging" gene embedded deep in our DNA that is suppressed only with difficulty.

- *Bending your fingers back in odd manner.* This is a ubiquitous movement, universally practiced. It consists of grasping the fingers and bending them back as if counting something, and then holding them there for a spell. It's almost a finger-tug, but more pronounced.

- *Waving your hands around with floppy wrist movement.* This is not only distracting, but destructive as well. The wobbly wrist action creates a perception of weakness.

Conclusion

In all of this, remember that someday, someone will pay you to deliver presentations, and it's a good idea to adopt a positive attitude now. Realize that your attitude informs your entire presentation and that a positive attitude infuses your gestures with life and power.

Your gestures in your presentation should flow from your words and message, lending emphasis to your show. Rid yourself of unconscious bad habits and develop new ones that enhance your stature.

Further reading on gesture

- Carol Kinsey Goman, *The Nonverbal Advantage: Secrets and Science of Body Language at Work* (2008)

- Tonya Reiman, *The Power of Body Language* (2003)

EXPRESSION

> **The Challenge:** Facial expression and expressiveness that falls short of communicating your message, and which sometimes conflicts with the message that you want to send.
>
> **The Solution:** Conscious awareness of the power of your expression and expressiveness so that you develop a consonance between what you want to communicate and how you express it. You carefully attune your expression to the message in a way that touches and moves the audience.
>
> **The Benefit:** Your presentation takes on a sincerity and authenticity and even warmth that delivers added persuasive power.

Do you ever consider how you appear to people with regard to your facial expressions? What do people actually *see* when they look at your face?

Your facial expressions can reinforce your message, confuse your audience, or detract from your message. Yes there exists something called bad expression, and at its worst, it can generate hostility in your audience.

Expression is sometimes discussed in conjunction with gesture, and indeed there is a connection. The power of expression has always been recognized as a vital communication tool, reinforcing words and even, at times, standing on its own.

In your business presentation, you communicate far more with your face than you probably realize. But many folks disregard their own facial expressions or are oblivious to them.

This chapter explains how facial expression and expressiveness in general have been recognized and cultivated for centuries as a powerful communicative device. Improper expression can actually detract from your message, and so it is necessary to utilize the tools of your expression to synchronize message and expression to produce the most powerful impact possible.

Bad Expression

Bad expression has plagued presentations for centuries, but there is no *ipso facto* bad expression – instead, there is only unsynchronized, out of place, thoughtless, random, and inappropriate expression.

It's the context of your presentation and the subject matter of your presentation that dictate your use of expression. Beware of incongruity.

Your expression should reflect your words, your feelings, your passion. When there is a disjuncture between your expression and your words, it creates confusion in your listeners. Unless you are striving for confusion – say, for a moment or two to make an instructive point – you quickly engender the indifference of your audience with bad expression. The incongruity unsettles the audience as your message diffuses, confuses and loses focus. Carry on too long with this, and you generate hostility.

The problem of bad expression has nettled speakers as long as there have been speakers. Some of our earliest writers on oratory lamented the poor expressive skills of the great mass of folks who took to the stage to speak.

Lost Ancient Secrets

Quintilian was a great Roman teacher of oratory in his time, and he has influenced countless generations of public speakers up to the present day.

Quintilian published his monumental *Institutes of Oratory* at the end of the first century AD, and it continues as a powerfully influential treatise on presentations today, rich with insight and practical instruction. Take this passage on expression:

> [The teacher] will have to take care that the face of his pupil, while speaking, look straight forward; that his lips be not distorted; that no opening of the mouth in moderately distend his jaws; that his face be not turned up, or his eyes cast down too much, or his head inclined to either side. The face offends in various ways; I have seen many speakers, whose eyebrows were raised at every effort of the voice; those of others

I have seen contracted; and those of some even disagreeing, as they turned up one towards the top of the head, while with the other the eye itself was almost concealed. To all these matters, as we shall hereafter show, a vast deal of importance is to be attached; for nothing can please which is unbecoming.[1]

I wish that our modern instructors of presentations would take a moment to share even the modest insights offered by great orators such as Quintilian. After 1,900 years, he remains relevant to us in the need for coordinated and thoughtful expression as well as in a great many other timeless techniques.

Quintilian has staying power. And a heckuva personal brand.

As he notes with respect to expression, "nothing can please which is unbecoming." Your facial expression should reflect your spirit, your heart, and your soul, and if it does, you will be in no danger of appearing "unbecoming." Your face should transmit sincerity and earnestness that match your words.

Joseph Mosher was one of the giants of the early twentieth century public speech instruction, and he ventured into territory rarely visited by today's sterile teachers of "business communication." Mosher actually addressed the *personality* of the speaker. These are the qualities that bring success:

[T]here is no one element of gesture which furnishes as unmistakable and effective an indication of the speaker's thought and feeling as does the expression of the mouth and eyes. The firm-set mouth and flashing eye speak more clearly than a torrent of words; the smile is as good as, or better than, a sentence in indicating good humor; the sneering lip, the upraised brow, or the scowl need no verbal commentary.[2]

A Curl of the Lip...

Consider these expressions: A curl of the lip to indicate disapproval, or even contempt. The raising of one eyebrow to indicate doubt, or skepticism. Sincere furrows in the brow to indicate sincerity, or great concern.

These expressions, coupled with the appropriate words, have a tremendous impact on your audience. They increase the power of your message. They

---

1 *Quintilian's Institutes of Oratory*, trans. J. S. Watson (London: George Bell & Sons, 1910), 89–90.
2 Joseph A. Mosher, *The Essentials of Effective Gesture* (New York: The Macmillan Company, 1928), 21.

ensure that your message is clear. Facial expressions erase ambiguity and leave no doubt in the minds of your listeners what you are communicating. The appropriate facial expression can arouse emotion and elicit sympathy for your point of view.

In their more subtle use, expressions can be used to convey irony. Take for example the lifting of a skeptical eyebrow and the turning up of the mouth into a wry smile when making an apparently serious statement, thus calling into question your own words, or someone else's. For instance, let's look at the following example:

"Mr Jones insists that his product is the equal to ours in terms of quality, features, longevity, and price."

Read the previous sentence aloud in an expressionless voice. Keep your face immobile for the most part. In this reading, you merely convey information.

Now read this sentence again, only this time do it this way: consciously raise one eyebrow as you speak and smile tightly as if you question the veracity of your own words:

"Mr Jones insists that his product is the equal to ours in terms of quality, features, longevity, and price."

You will hear and feel the difference in your voice as your very expressions modify your delivery of that single sentence.

Our expressions can enhance our presentation, or cripple it. Thorough knowledge of how our expressions can lift our talk or derail it is essential to becoming a powerful business presenter.

Earnestness

"Earnestness" is a word that we don't hear much these days. We don't use it, either. That's a shame, because the word captures much of what makes for an excellent presentation and the development of an expressive face.

Later in this book, I relate earnestness to another important principle – passion. And in fact, earnestness has a great deal to do with investing your business presentation with passion.

But here we look at the quality of earnestness as crucial to utilizing facial and physical expression as powerful presenting tools. Some even consider earnestness as one of the core values without which you cannot deliver a presentation imbued with authenticity: "Earnestness is the soul of oratory. It manifests itself in speech by animation, wide-awakeness, strength, force, power, as opposed to listlessness, timidity, half-heartedness, uncertainty, feebleness."[3]

Today, maybe you frown at the notion of "earnestness." Maybe it's somehow "uncool." Or a defense mechanism. After all, if you appear *too* interested in something, and then you fail, the penalty in your own mind might be too heavy to bear. If you somehow are perceived as having failed, then your presentation "defeat" is doubly ignominious.

As a result, the default student attitude is to affect an air of cool nonchalance, so that no defeat is too damaging. And you save your best – your *earnestness* – for something else.

I see this in numerous student presentations, this nonchalance. I don't believe it to be genuine nonchalance in the sense that students really don't care. Of course, students care much about their grades. *You* care much about your grades.

But I believe that a self-defense mechanism can kick-in during public speaking or a business presentation. It's a mechanism that protects our dignity, or what we perceive to be our dignity. It protects us from embarrassment in that we can always say "I know it wasn't good, but I really didn't try," or "I couldn't get interested in the topic."

Instead of attacking your presentation and investing it with earnestness, you enter the presentation with a desire to limit the damage to yourself. You deliver your presentation with one goal in mind – survival.

Consequently, you present with the idea *not* to communicate your subject, but with the idea of *not to make a mistake*. Not to be adventurous. Not to call attention to yourself. Certainly not to show earnestness about the subject.

These are modest goals. They are, in fact, negative goals, and I'm being generous. With such meager goals in mind, you can doubtlessly achieve them. But this also means that every one of your successes is necessarily small. Meager effort yields acceptable results in areas where only meager effort is required. You not only deliver dry, uninteresting presentations, but your expression conveys your nonchalance. This attitude leeches away positive expression.

Now think for a moment what this means to the audience. The audience receives the message that you don't care. The audience *sees* this in your resulting

3 Edwin Dubois Shurter, *Public Speaking: A Treatise on Delivery* (Boston and Chicago: Allyn & Bacon, 1903), 102.

expression. If you subscribe to this, you can expect your career to stagnate accordingly. Don't let this happen to you.

Do not underestimate the power of earnestness when conveyed through expression to your audience: "When communicated to the audience, earnestness is, after all is said and done, the touchstone of success in public speaking, as it is in other things in life."[4]

Let your earnestness for the subject infuse your presentation with power and inform your expression. Wrap your material in *you*. How can we do this? By using the tools of expression.

Eyes, Mouth, Brow – Your Secret Weapons

Your eyes, mouth, brow, and head all act together to provide you with a magnificently versatile expressive tool.

Your eyes can convey sincerity and warmth, or deception and dishonesty.

Your mouth can dismiss with a sneer, or it can affirm with a smile.

Your brow can question, show skepticism, display anger, or deliver earnestness.

Your head can emphasize any of the above with its various positions – bowed in respect, up in thought, turned away in disgust, cocked to one side in interest.

Smile

For some reason, I have detected in the latest generation of business students a disinclination to smile. This no-smile rule seems only in play during business classes or where business subjects are concerned.

Most folks have great smiles in their unguarded moments, but deadpan looks otherwise, especially when strolling the campus. And even *more* deadpan in delivering a presentation. Perhaps it's because business courses are *supposed* to be dull and unenjoyable? Perhaps because passion is absent.

The simple smile is one of the most powerful tools that a person possesses. And yet most people are oblivious to its potential, especially for imbuing business presentations with credibility and accessibility. This combination of simplicity, power and a public obliviousness to its potential qualifies the smile as a *secret weapon*.

---

4 Ibid.

It's not really secret, of course. Everyone smiles on occasion. At a joke, at a loved one.

But the conscious use of the smile as a tool of persuasion in a business presentation is a rarity. Perhaps this is because we, as business people, believe that *business is serious business*. How can we possibly smile while reviewing figures from an income statement, or while delivering an industry analysis?

So we assume what we believe to be a serious demeanor and affix a deadpan expression to our faces. And when we do this, we forfeit the overwhelming advantage that the well-placed smile can bring us. The smile can be a deal-clincher when utilized properly.

Eyes and brow

Your eyes and your brow should be used for one overriding purpose, and that is to convey sincerity. Do not underestimate what your eyes say, even without your conscious direction. Your eyes are like powerful projectors, so take hold of what is being projected. "The eye is the window of the soul. Out of it the soul seems to shine, and the heart can be read by peeping in the eyes."[5]

Widen your eyes right now. Go ahead, open them up and pay special attention to your brow.

Look in the mirror; see and feel how your brow is furrowed? Try it again, only this time, think of a friend in the hospital and show concern. See how your brow furrows and peaks? This is a display of earnestness and concern. It indicates a seriousness of purpose, dedication and belief in what you are saying.

One eyebrow cocked communicates disbelief or healthy skepticism. With a slight adjustment, it can also indicate interest. How might you use this in your own presentation? You can use this device to cast doubt on what you, yourself, are saying. This is handy when quoting someone else of doubtful veracity or citing statistics about a competitor that seem too good to be true.

In short, this is one occasion when words and expressions *can* conflict and enhance your point. This ironic juxtaposition between what is said and what is seen during a presentation also confirms the generally held notion that nonverbal communication is more powerful than simple words. If you deliver a verbal message while contradicting it with an ironic and questioning expression, the audience accepts your *facial expression* as the actual message.

---

5 Edward Brooks, *A Manual of Elocution and Reading* (Philadelphia: Eldredge & Brother, 1885), 83.

Here I've provided you with a basic tool of expression that you can use to good end, but your tool chest of facial expressions is large and full of many other tools that can add subtlety and nuance to your business presentation. When you believe yourself adept at utilizing your eyes to send your message, try progressing to these additional techniques. Brooks provides us with this excellent description:

> The eyes bend downward in grief, perplexity, diffidence, shame, and humility; they are raised upward in joy, delight, hope, and admiration; they look straight forward in expressing courage and determination; they are averted in disgust, aversion, and listening; they roll in rage, jealousy, and despair; they glare in madness; they are vacant and despair, flash and anger or malice, and are wide and fixed in fear and terror.[6]

Frown

Rarely should you frown in a business presentation, if at all. It's a powerful negative tool that has more potential to harm our message than help it. A frown conveys much more negativity than we imagine we display.

Frown only when talking about something repulsive that is outside of our firm or topic, or something that is an obstacle to our progress, our mission, our vision. But it should be something *universally* considered negative. And your frown should last not more than a few seconds.

This handful of techniques can enhance the power of your presentation when used in conjunction with the techniques of the other six secrets of stance, voice, movement, gesture, appearance and passion. These techniques derive most of their punch, in fact, from their use in combination. Be aware of this unique power that is yours for the taking and use it judiciously.

I urge you in your presentations to smile often, frown sparingly, stare never, question occasionally, and show sincerity throughout.

How to Develop Earnestness

Most of the problems of poor or inadequate expression arise from the lack of earnestness. How do you go about developing earnestness for the subject of your presentation?

---

6 Ibid.

If there is a single word that encompasses what you must do, I believe that word is "embrace." You must embrace your subject. You can no longer think of the subject as something outside yourself; it must become part of you so that you *care*.

The embrace is a subjective measure of how close you get to your material. How intimately you know your subject. Do you *embrace* the material, or do you keep your distance? It is the difference between surfing the wave and deep-sea diving. Do you immerse yourself in the material of your presentation or do you dive for the treasure?

If you do not embrace your subject to the extent that you become excited about it, to the extent that you want to do your best to make the subject *yours*, to the extent that you cannot wait to wax eloquent about it to your audience, then you will remain part of that great *hoi polloi* of folks who sleepwalk through their business presentations. Ineffectively, Monotonously, ignominiously.

Embracing your topic means giving a presentation that no one else can give, that no one else can copy, because it arises from your essence, your core. It means demonstrating genuine enthusiasm for your subject and recognizing that the subject of your presentation could well be the love of someone's life – you should make it yours when you present.

Drama

On a final note of expression and expressiveness, I touch on drama. I do not mean the phony excitement and angst of "relationships" gone wrong, the anxiety of the "drama queen." I mean the "dramatic situation" that you can use to your advantage with regard to expressing ideas in the most powerful way. You have drama inherent in any situation where there is conflict or the potential for conflict. Business cases are chock full of dramatic situations – conflict, suspense, turning points, great decisions. You simply must learn to recognize them and to bring them out. It does *not* mean exaggerated behavior during your presentation.

> This is not a recommendation of paroxysms of feeling, wild gesticulation, tearing and combing of the hair with the fingers, violent pacing up and down the platform, and other manifestations of old-style oratory, happily now obsolete, but rather to suggest a power which, when properly used, will give life, variety, intensity, and color to the spoken message.[7]

---

7 Grenville Kleiser, *How to Develop Power and Personality in Speaking* (New York: Funk & Wagnalls Company, 1908), 104.

Life. Variety. Intensity. Color.

It means incorporating the notion of drama into your presentation, and setting up situations that allow you to utilize expression to its fullest potential. This is a notion that may seem foreign to you. It surely seems foreign to many business faculty colleagues, steeped in financial analysis and disdainful of anything that smacks of "soft skills."

A professor came into my classroom at the end of my class. He was a colleague of mine and a smart man. He has my respect for his knowledge and substance of finance.

He waited patiently as I finished chatting with several students, and he listened-in as I gave the final feedback for the group that had just presented a case to my class. He heard the last words of advice on the "rising line" or the "Verbal Up-Tic," as I call it. And I was giving a demonstration of this voice pathology, so that my students could avoid it in future. The students left, and my colleague approached.

He said to me: "Well! All this drama! It sounds like drama class."

I don't think that I imagined the almost accusatory tone in his voice. As if an unspoken prohibition against "drama" had been violated. I took the challenge.

"Yes Bill, there's lots of drama. It's putting on a show. It's why I call my presentations "shows" and my students my "show-people. Some of the most dramatic situations in life occur in the boardroom, on the factory floor, in training sessions. Why ignore them?" Bill just smiled, unconvinced, I'm sure.

It's no accident that I use the word "show." A presentation *is* an expressive show, because that, in essence, is what visual and verbal communication is all about – "showing."

This is what we do when we give a presentation, when we present. We don't deliver a presentation – we *present*. The presentation is *not* something behind you on a screen. The presentation is not on a whiteboard or butcher paper. It's not on a flip chart. The presentation is *you*.

This theatrical aspect of presenting can, in theory, surely be overdone. But given the staid status of business presenting, the danger of overdoing the drama in business presentations is nil. You can harness dramatic techniques to your business presenting style, and a number of books delve into this. One of the finest books available on the subject is Ken Howard's *Act Natural*.[8]

---

8 Ken Howard, *Act Natural* (New York: Random House, 2003).

Conclusion

It's a bane of business school that seems often to train us to leech expressiveness from our faces and voices when we present. The injunction of "just the facts" has the unfortunate side-consequence of stiffening us up. It's time to loosen the facial muscles and use them to your expressive advantage.

An expressive face that offers authentic and judicious reinforcement of a sincere message can help construct an especially powerful presentation.

Further reading on expression

- J. Berg Esenwein, *How to Attract and Hold an Audience* (1902)

- Deb Gottesman and Buzz Mauro, *Taking Center Stage: Masterful Public Speaking Using Acting Skills* (2001)

- Ken Howard, *Act Natural: How to Speak to Any Audience* (2003)

- James Albert Winans, *Public Speaking: Principles and Practice* (1915)

- Nathan Sheppard, *Before an Audience: The Use of the Will in Public Speaking* (1886)

MOVEMENT: NO MORE STICK-PUPPET PRESENTING

> **The Challenge:** Aimless wandering movement that distracts from your show, or no movement at all that sacrifices the inherent power that can arise from planned movement.
>
> **The Solution:** Understanding of how movement can increase your presenting power and of what specific movements you should engage in to accomplish your presenting goals.
>
> **The Benefit:** A richer and deeper three-dimensional presenting experience that multiplies the force of your presentation by harnessing the power of conscious directed movement.

You're well on your way to mastering your voice and to speaking like a powerful motivator, with concise and effective gestures, and with skilled expression.

But you *know* there's more to it than just talking. What must you actually *do* during your talk? Where to do it? How to do it? Why should you do it, and when?

Movement – the *right type* of movement – invests your presentation with dynamism and depth. Again, the *right type* of purposeful movement.

Unfortunately, knowledge on the right type of movement is far from universal. In fact, bad advice in this regard seems to take on a life of its own, entering the lexicon of presenting as some kind of sage wisdom. But it does more harm than good. Take the example that follows, for instance.

A student in one of my classes once observed to me that: "I follow good presentation principles, and I stand in one spot during my presentations, but another professor told me to move around when I talk."

I replied, "Did he tell you how?"

"Tell me what?"

"Did he tell you *how* to 'move around when you talk'? Did he tell you what it would accomplish?"

"No, he just said to 'move around when you talk.'"

"Just 'move around'?"

"Yes."

Ponder that for a moment.

It's awful advice, and here's why. Aimless pacing around the stage is worse than no movement at all. Aimless movement indicates indecision, the sign of a disorganized mind. It's usually accompanied by aimless thoughts and thoughtless words. Is this the message that you want to communicate to a potential customer? To the CEO of your company?

"Move around when you talk."

It's not the worst piece of advice a professor has ever given a student, and at first, the advice seems innocent enough. Even sage. Aren't we *supposed* to move around when we talk? Don't we see powerful presenters "move around" when they talk? Didn't Steve Jobs "move around" when he was presenting?

Yes, we see them "move around" quite well.

But do you know *why* they "move" and to what end? Do you understand how they orchestrate their words and gestures to achieve maximum effect? Do you recognize their skilled use of the stage as they appeal to first one segment of the audience, and then another? Do you think that Bill Clinton or Barack Obama just "move around" when they talk?

If I tell you to "move around when you talk," just what will you actually *do*?

Think about it for a moment, how you might actually follow through with that sort of vague advice. Will you flap your arms? Pace side-to-side on the stage as would a jungle cat? Shake your fist at the crowd?

Move, you say? How? Where? When? Why? How much?

Don't Mimic Steve Jobs

Never just "move around" the stage. Steve Jobs, the late CEO of Apple, Inc., had a deserved reputation as a visionary. He was one of a handful of powerful entrepreneurs to have effected incredible change in the world's technology, helping to ignite a tech revolution whose end is still not yet in sight. But Jobs also had an undeserved reputation as a superior presenter.

Steve Jobs was an above-average presenter who had improved quite a bit.

One of his flaws – in fact, his trademark flaw – was his aimless wandering around the stage as he delivered news of Apple's latest tech gadgetry. Jobs's enthusiastic audiences forgave him for it, because they weren't there to hear him or see him. They were in that audience because they are Apple fanatics who ached to get the first look at the latest generation of Apple products. It was a set-up and not a typical business presentation. Jobs's meandering around the stage served to detract from his message, but the message and his props were so powerful and the audience so self-selective that it didn't matter. For you, however, it does matter a great deal.

"Move around when you talk." We will never know how much damage such well-meaning *naiveté* has done to our presentation discourse. Like many things, it carries a kernel of truth, but it's really worse than no advice at all. Movement must *mean* something.

Centuries of practice and delivery advise us on this technique of movement:

> Every movement that a speaker makes means – or *should* mean – something. Hence avoid indulging in movements which are purely habit and which mean nothing. Do not constantly be moving; it makes the audience also restless. Do not walk back and forth along the edge of the platform like a caged lion. Do not shrug your shoulders, or twist your mouth, or make faces.[1]

Remember that *everything* you do and don't do should contribute to your message. Movement on-stage is an important component to your message. It's a powerful weapon in your arsenal of communication.

Movements can and should contribute force and emphasis to your show. But just as there can always be too much of a good thing, like pecan pie, so it is with movement during your presentation. Some people move *too much*.

Just as there are those who are rooted to one spot and *cannot* move, there are those who cannot *stop* moving. They prowl the stage like a wild beast constantly pacing, as if dodging imaginary bullets, afraid to cease moving lest their feet put down roots.

---

1 E. D. Shurter, *Public Speaking* (New York: Allyn & Bacon, 1903), 117.

Like the professor urged, they just "move around" because they don't know better. Why *should* they know better, when some professor urged them to start pacing?

From Stick Puppets... to 3D Presenting

If experience is any guide for us, I think it's safe to say that 80 to 90 percent of our business presentations are delivered in 2D fashion. No, I don't mean this literally in the sense that people become stick figures. I mean that typical business presenters strip the presentation of depth and breadth. They strip it of humanity. It is systematically stripped of the qualities that make it interesting, stimulating, and persuasive.

The potential richness, energy, vigor, and power provided by purposive movement are absent. We are left with cutout figures, like stick puppets.

You've seen stick puppets – crude, flat little figures pasted onto sticks and then used in a child's display to convey a story. This is truly an ineffective form of entertainment, as rudimentary as it gets. The puppets shake and move up and down as someone voices dialogue from somewhere offstage. Today's business presentations are sometimes no better than a stick-puppet show delivered in 2D fashion. Think of this as "stick-puppet presenting."

Stick-puppet presenting is characterized by a zombie-like figure who is crouched behind a lectern, gripping its sides. Or by a speaker who reads from a laptop computer and alternately looks at a projection screen behind him, reading verbatim. If any movement occurs, it's unconscious swaying, rocking, or nervous happy-feet dancing. Perhaps there is a bit of pacing back-and-forth to fulfill some ancient advice mumbled to the speaker years earlier: "Move *around* when you talk!" And so the stick-puppet presenter aimlessly wanders the stage.

But we want to move from 2D to 3D presenting. One powerful step in that direction is the addition of proper movement. The addition of proper movement to your presentation can imbue it with energy, depth, richness, and enhanced meaning. So let's analyze this movement component on the stage in support of your presentation.

The Four Spaces

Remember your ready position? When we move, we always start from that position. And we always return to it.

It's time to step out of your ready stance and begin purposeful movement that adds value to your presentation. Before you take that first step, let's learn about "distance" and how you can use it to your advantage. And how you can prevent yourself from inadvertently abusing distance.

Many speakers are unaware of the effect that distance-from-audience can have on their talk. You achieve four distinct effects by varying the distance that you maintain between you and your audience.

The formal term for how these different distances affect the relationship between speaker and audience is called *proxemics*. The distinguished anthropologist, Edward T. Hall, developed the concept of how these four distances communicate vastly different messages from speaker to audience.[2]

First, the most common space is public space, and this is a distance of more than 12 feet from your audience. Obviously, this space is necessary when you deliver a lecture to a large audience of, say, 200 persons or more.

The second space is social space. The speaker who wants to connect in a personal way with his audience occupies this space. It's the space from four feet to 12 feet from your audience. Think of a seminar of 12 students with a professor in close proximity. Here, eye contact is frequent and effective. A conversational style is possible and desirable. In fact, conversational and relaxed style is essential in this scenario.

The third space is personal space. This space begins at 18 inches from a person and extends out to approximately four feet. It is conversational space and is generally not utilized in public speaking.

The fourth space is intimate space. This space is highly personal and you must be invited into this space. Without an invitation, you invade this space at your own risk. You make others feel uncomfortable, and they may respond in any number of ways, few of which will please you.

Now that you know the four spaces and their utility, think of yourself on the stage and in the command position directly in front of your audience.

The command position is yours to take and make your own. The command position is located in front of a lectern or to the side of the lectern and four to eight feet from your audience. It extends approximately four feet to either side of you. You are not a visitor in this space. As a presenter or speaker, this is your home. You own this space, so make it yours. You must always perform

---

2 Edward T. Hall, *The Hidden Dimension* (New York: Anchor Books, 1966, 1990).

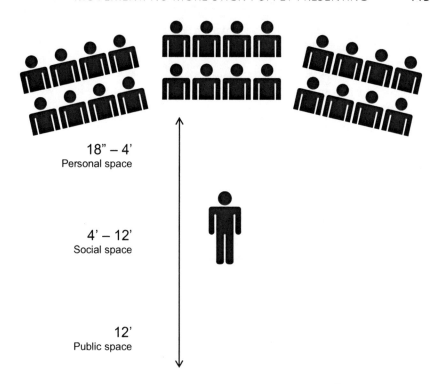

18" – 4'
Personal space

4' – 12'
Social space

12'
Public space

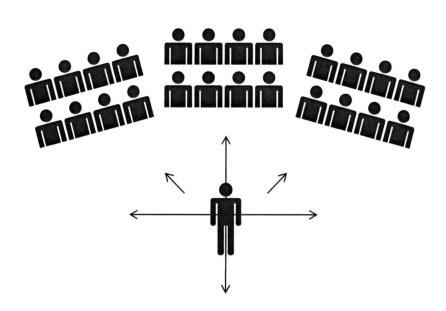

as if you *belong* there. So *act* like you own the space. Don't behave like a visitor who cannot wait to depart.

Make the space yours. Learn to be comfortable in it and to utilize all of the space at your disposal. It is *your* space, so you employ it to add power and depth to your presentation. At the same time, apply the principles found in this chapter. Do not move *just* to be moving.

Broad Movement

Let's try our first staged movement. We can call it a series movement. Yes, it's scripted, but you can move out of the script after you learn the purpose of the movement and begin to feel comfortable doing it.

Your purpose in moving is to emphasize or deemphasize portions of your talk. Movement can also act as a cue to the audience that you are moving from one major point to another and to another.

Coordinate your movements with major segments of your talk. For instance, follow the script below. The boldfaced statements describe the actions you take.

SPEAKER: "My talk has three major points. As I share these points with you tonight, I want you to consider how each of these powerful issues affects you, personally. The first major point?"

<<Bow head and walk slowly to the left. Take ready stance. Look up at audience.>>

SPEAKER: "The first major point is humility. In this we are the same as our earliest fathers and mothers."

<<Look to your right and walk slowly, meeting the eyes of several audience members in turn. Stop in ready position.>>

SPEAKER: "The second major point is confidence. Surely there is not one among us who has not felt the fear of failure, of being judged unworthy."

<<Look to the center and walk slowly to center-stage. Stop and assume ready position. Gesture with both hands in supplication.>>

SPEAKER: "The third and most important point is this – understanding of a kind that passes beyond…"

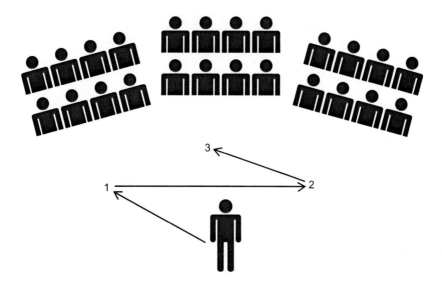

The movements are displayed in the diagram. This type of broad movement accentuates the major points of your talk. You anchor each point at a different part of the stage:

Point 1 to the *left*

Point 2 to the *right*

Point 3 to the *center*

This simple movement series is a highly visual reinforcement to the segmentation and organization of your talk.

Coupled with the proper hand gestures and expressiveness of face and voice, this series movement invests your message with immediacy and dimensionality and increases its impact immeasurably. The combined effect of movement, position, and spoken message *connects* you firmly with your audience; appropriate movement deepens the connection and moves you from 2D presenting to 3D presenting.

Again, think.

When you are ready to make a point crucial to your thesis, when you are ready to shift subjects or major ideas, *then*...

Step to the left while addressing the people on the left flank. Talk to them. Then step to the right and address those on your right. Hold open your hands, palms up. Walk toward your audience a step or two. Look them in the eyes. Speak to individuals.

Then, move back to the center and retake your ready position. Let your movements emphasize your points. When you gesture to a portion of the audience, step toward them in a kind of supplication. And remember these injunctions against unnecessary movement:

> There are two sorts of action that become distractions: actions that are meaningless, and actions that mean something not at all connected with the idea under discussion. Most of us have little mannerisms of movement, a shrug of the shoulders, a twist of the head, playing with the button on one's coat, constant walking about or what not... Our friends are apt to be very unkind to us in regard to these mannerisms in that they refuse to tell us of them. They do not want to hurt our feelings, and in refraining from doing so, they do us a still greater hurt. They lead us to believe that our mannerisms do not exist.[3]

Avoid Visual Monotony

We are all familiar with the droning voice of the numbing speaker who rarely varies pitch, tone, or pace of a talk and who quickly loses us in monotony. In similar fashion, it is possible to be visually monotonous.

Visual monotony – either of repetitive constant movement or of no movement whatsoever.

We know well the "rocker" and the "swayer." We know "Mr Busy-Hands" and the "foxtrotter," who quicksteps in a tight little dance.

But before you begin hopping about the stage willy-nilly, recognize that you should incorporate movement into your presentation *for specific reasons.* Your movements should contribute to your presentation by reinforcing your message. At the risk over over-alliterating, you should mesh your movements with your message.

Remember that every single thing you do onstage derives its power by its *contrast* with every other thing you do. If you move all the time, like a constant pacing jungle cat, it becomes the equivalent of white noise, and your movements then contribute no meaning whatever to your presentation. In fact, your movements become a distraction, leeching energy and attention from your message. It's a form of visual monotony.

Likewise, if you remain stationary 100 percent of the time, the result is visual monotony. You lull your audience into inattention, especially if you combine verbal and visual monotony in a single presentation – the kiss of death.

3 E. D. Shurter, *Public Speaking* (New York: Allyn & Bacon, 1903), 117.

Those in theater know this principle well: "Your best tool to avoid this dangerous state is variety. Three lines of loud need soft. Three lines of quick need slow. A big dose of movement needs still. Or change your tactics."[4]

Conclusion

Movement serves a far greater purpose than as a mere garnish for your presentation. Well-considered movement can propel your presentation from the realm of 2D stick-puppet presenting to a higher level, richer and more powerful than the vast majority of conventional presentations. Proper movement deepens and broadens your stage presence and helps you capture and keep the audience's attention.

We see how it is not enough to "move around when you talk." In fact, aimless movement can quickly erode a presentation by distracting the audience from your message. For it to be positive and effective, movement should always be purposeful, goal-directed, and intentional – never aimless or the product of nervous habit.

This chapter has focused on appropriate movement and has provided you a framework within which to develop the proper use of movement. Proper movement is a powerful component in your message delivery, and a powerful personal differentiator.

The coordination of your movements with your message generates synergy, a system effect expressed in the adage "The whole is greater than the sum of its parts." A simpler definition is the equation: $2+2 = 5$. This means that the parts of a system working together can generate an outcome greater than those parts acting in uncoordinated and singular fashion.

So, think of movement as one more tool in your repertoire to evoke feeling from your audience and to convey a powerful and persuasive message.

---

4 Jon Jory, *Tips for Actors* (Lyme, NH: Smith & Krause, 2000), 74.

9

APPEARANCE

> **The Challenge:** Thoughtless dressing and grooming that result from a nonchalant attitude, which can delegitimize any presentation. People *do* judge a book by its cover, they just won't tell you so.
>
> **The Solution:** Care and attention to your appearance in your presentation, based on your audience, your subject, your venue, and whom you represent.
>
> **The Benefit:** The appropriate appearance reinforces all the other aspects of your presentation in powerfully subtle ways and contributes to the persuasiveness of your message.

Oftentimes, we don't consider that our physical appearance transmits messages to those around us. Most certainly, the appearance of a speaker before an audience conveys non-verbal signals. This happens whether you are conscious of it or not.

What message does *your* appearance send to people? That you don't care? That you're confident? That you are attentive to detail? That you care about your dignity, your physique? Is your appearance one big flip-off to the world because you fancy yourself an ageless rebel, shaking your fist at the "man" and refusing to "conform" to the "rules?"

If so, then you are paying a dear price for so meager a prize. That price comes in the form of ceding competitive advantage to your peers, who may want to spend their personal capital for more luxurious rewards.

Perhaps you had no idea of the impact of your appearance on an audience and how it can help or hinder your career? If so, it may be because the signals sent to you in college can be contradictory.

College Cues

You often receive improper cues on appearance from places and people
who ought to know better. While many business professors understand the
importance of self-respect and appearance in communication and set an
appropriate example, others do exactly the opposite.

Some faculty members, particularly in the liberal arts, are the most unkempt
folks who you'd never want to emulate. Even professors in the business school –
folks who ought to know better – fall short. Some of them believe it's their
God-given right to dress poorly, a perquisite of tenure. Others just don't get
it. Some save on their dry-cleaning bill. Still others dress for a part they believe
they're playing.

There is even a lobby for professors who want to be boring, listless, unenthusiastic
about their subject, and poorly dressed. Or, perhaps, who look for excuses to
not take presenting seriously enough to do their best in the classroom. Take
this example, for instance. In a comment on an article by well-known academic
Stanley Fish, an anonymous faculty member from East Lansing calling himself
"Dr Bob" claimed that professors, to succeed in the classroom and gain good
student evaluations, should:

> 1. Project enthusiasm (even if you don't have any) by continually saying
> how interested and passionate you are and waving your arms around, 2.
> Call on your students by name and praise them for every little thing they
> do, 3. Dress sharp![1]

The most obvious facts are that professors *ought* to: 1. Project enthusiasm for
the subject they teach (or they shouldn't be teaching it), 2. Call on students by
name as a demonstration of basic respect, and 3. Dress appropriately to set the
example for students who desire success in the world of business.

But beyond this is the seeming obliviousness to the notion that your appearance
is essential to the message conveyed in class. The professoriate does the
profession and students a disservice in sending the message that it's okay to
dress like a vagabond, or perpetuating the fallacy that what "really matters" is
only the substance, not the "form" or "style."

---

1 Stanley Fish, "Student Evaluations, Part II," *New York Times,* June 28, 2010, http://
opinionator.blogs.nytimes.com/2010/06/28/student-evaluations-part-two (accessed July
26, 2012).

Dress for Success

The fact is that you cannot dress for lazy comfort and nonchalance and expect to send a message that conveys seriousness, competence, and confidence. You simply can't, and this is non-negotiable. It is not a matter of opinion or "personal choice."

This attitude and resulting lazy mode of dress is self-indulgent, of course, and self-indulgence carries a high price – lost credibility, scorn, and lowered estimation, among other unpleasantness.

This is a call for you to recognize opportunity. Here is your chance to create a memorable and positive professional presence for yourself that lifts you above your peers, but not in an overt or obnoxious manner. And, in so doing, your presentation message gains power and credibility.

Throughout your presentation, you send messages to your audience. Your words, your actions, your visuals all communicate. But your general appearance transmits a message as well. That message should be consistent with your overall intent.

There are two sources for your powerful appearance – internal and external. Let's look at external sources first.

External Factors of Professional Appearance

Many young speakers seem unaware of the messages that their appearance conveys. Or worse, they attempt to rationalize the message, arguing what the audience "ought" to pay attention to and what it "ought" to ignore.

Your appearance sends a message to your audience, and you cannot decide *not* to send a message with your appearance. You cannot tell an audience to disregard the message your appearance transmits, and you can't dictate to an audience the message it receives.

This is the lesson that so many fail to grasp, even on into the middle management years.

"I'm a rebel and exude confidence and independence!" you think as you suit up in the current campus fad. The message received is likely much different: "You're a slob with no sense of proportion or clue how to dress, and I will never hire you."

The best public speakers understand the power of appearance and mesh their dress with their message. Take President Barack Obama, for example. He is a superb dresser, as are all presidents. On occasion, you will see the President speaking as he wears an open-collared shirt, his sleeves rolled up in "let's get the job done" fashion. That's usually the message he's trying to convey by his style of dress: "Let's get the job done – let's work together."

You will never see a president address the nation from the Oval Office on a matter of gravity with his jacket off and his sleeves rolled-up. The messages must mesh. The lesson here is that your dress ought to reinforce your message, not offer conflicting signals.

Moreover, don't believe that the little things are unimportant. Details matter a great deal. Shined shoes, properly knotted tie, buttons buttoned. Colors matching. Nothing bizarre or distracting. People examine you while you speak, their eyes searching. They size you up, much as you evaluate other people when you first meet. So why not transmit the powerful message you choose rather than allow it to evolve on its own or be dictated by a peer group, oftentimes to your detriment.

Always dress a half step above your group. Just a half step. If T-shirts are standard, wear a collared polo shirt. If tennis shoes are standard, wear comfortable leather loafers.

Just a half step. Nothing conspicuous, but enough to look sharp by comparison. Enough to gain you a subtle reputation for being "well-dressed."

Think about it. Isn't it better than the alternatives? Who wants to be thought-of as "rumpled" or "slob?"

Adapting to Your Audience's Expectations

There is a physical element to appearance. Vigor, health, fitness.

How you look externally can affect how you feel internally, for better or worse. This is another important reason why we strive not only for a sharp clothing ensemble, but for a pleasing physical appearance as well.

Evaluate yourself, and take a personal test now. Answer this question: What do excess weight, haggard, slumped shoulders, haphazard attitude, lazy posture indicate to your listeners? Am I guilty of any of these?

Regardless of the various pop-therapy movements that infest our society, movements that offer validation and encouragement for almost anything you want to do in the interest of self-esteem, I offer no such thing. The fact is that if you are overweight and you want to be a powerful presenter, you have handicapped yourself in a host of ways. It is *not* okay, and I won't tell you here that it is okay.

You can point to any exception you like – it doesn't matter. Exceptions are exceptions for a reason. And the fact is that for every exception, you will find a host of compensating situational factors or qualities that explain the exception. Factors that you probably don't have.

Your health and your success largely depend upon your appearance and your carriage, and any powerful speaker worth his or her mettle is always striving to improve across all seven dimensions of presenting.

Regardless of your physical state now, if you are improving weekly through steady practice, exercise, proper diet, *that* is the important contribution to your state of mind and your skill level. *And* to your eventual success as you climb into the ranks of the top one percent of executive presenters in America.

It is not a matter of becoming something we are not. It is a matter of not squandering the gifts of life and health with bad choices.

If you want to be a successful presenter, you must be in a state of constant improvement and learning, both mental *and* physical.

Internal Factors of Professional Appearance

While much of our external appearance during a presentation is dictated by fashion convention and common sense, there is an internal element as well. So much has been written about the fear of public speaking, it has become almost a necessary mantra to tip our hats to it.

After your reading of the symptoms and hearing of the handwringing, if you weren't fearful of public speaking earlier, you certainly are now.

It's called "stage fright," and it attacks everyone at some point in a presentation career. Many people *do* fear speaking before an audience. It's so universal and it is so pervasive that we must come to grips with it.

This fear has made its way down through the ages. It has afflicted and paralyzed hundreds of speakers and presenters who have come before you.

> The very first problem that faces the average man in speech-making is the problem of nervousness. To stand up before an audience without a scrap of paper or a note of any kind, to feel the eyes of dozens and even hundreds of people upon you, to sense the awful silence that awaits your own words, to know that you must depend upon yourself and yourself alone to hold the audience's attention is as trying a task as it is possible

to undertake. Most men find the task too great and shun it religiously. Those who do attempt it, voluntarily, or involuntarily, testify to the severity of the physical and mental suffering it involves.[2]

So you see that the fear of speaking has been around as long as there has been public speaking, ever since the first business presentation at the dawn of commerce, when men and women first began trading with each other.

The Solution to the Fear

There *is* a solution. And the solution now is the same as it always has been. It addresses the root *cause* of your fear and nervousness, not the fear itself. In short, almost all physical manifestation of nerves can be traced to one thing – the unknown.

When we are uncertain of ourselves at a time of great trial, our body prepares us for the crisis as it goes into a fight-or-flight response. Our adrenaline spikes and we become keenly alert; our hearts race and breathing speeds up. Within us, we feel the acute urge to run or to strike. Our bodies dictate that we flee the sensed danger, or that we lash out and eliminate the threat, as if our very survival were at stake.

But this is a completely unnecessary biological response.

Our survival is *not* at stake. We are not on the cusp of grappling with a wild beast, nor are we going into battle. We are delivering a talk to an audience that probably wants very much to hear what we have to say, whether the local Rotary Club, the CEO of our firm, or a group of prospective clients or venture capitalists.

So how do we rid ourselves of this false response? The key to controlling the body's response is to reduce the uncertainty as much as we can, so that what remains is manageable. I have tracked nervousness among my students for several years, and I find inevitable commonalities among them. The source of extreme nervousness before a talk can be traced to three factors:

1. You are not prepared

2. You don't know what you're talking about

3. You haven't practiced

---

2 George Rowland Collins, *Platform Speaking* (New York and London: Harper & Brothers Publishers, 1923), 7.

All of these factors usually spring from one source: *You simply don't know what to do when giving a presentation, because no one has told you or shown you how.*

You can't prepare, because you don't know how to prepare. You don't know what you're talking about, because you don't know how to shave your talk down to the barest essentials and then deliver critical points in powerful fashion. You can't practice because you don't know how or what to practice.

The solution, then, is the three Ps that we reviewed in Chapter 3 – principles, preparation, practice. Through judicious pursuit of these three factors, you achieve self-confidence.

Self-Confidence *versus* Self-Consciousness

Confidence is one of those elusive qualities. It's almost paradoxical.

When we have it, it's invisible. When we don't have it, it's all too apparent to us. Confidence in public speaking is hard to come by. Or so we think.

Let's back into this thing called confidence.

Take the trip test. Have you ever stumbled on the sidewalk, your toe catching an impossibly small defect in the concrete, enough to trip you up? You stumble and stagger a bit. And then…

…and then do you glance quickly around to see who might be looking? Do you feel shame of some sort? If not shame, then *something* that causes you to mildly fear the judgment of others? Even strangers?

Recognize this "trip test" as a measure of your self-confidence, your conception of yourself. Recognize that you don't need the validation of others in what you do.

This does not mean you should act in immature and self-indulgent ways. It means charting your own course with your internal moral and professional compass and having the strength of mind and purpose not to yield to kibitzers, naysayers, and kneejerk critics.

Now, bring that strength of mind and purpose to the realm of business presentations. For many, the audience is your bogeyman. For some reason you fear your audience. But understand that they are not gathered there to harm you; they are gathered to hear what you have to say. And 99.9 percent of them mean you well. They *want* you to succeed so that they can benefit in some way.

Yes, even your fellow students want you to succeed. They want to be entertained. They are open to whatever new insight you can provide. And they know, for a fact, that *they* will be in your same place many times during their careers. They are fellow-travelers in the business school presentation journey. So confidence is yours for the taking.

Confidence is not a thing. It cannot be grasped or packaged or bought. It's a state of mind, isn't it? It's a feeling. When we get right down to it, it really is just the mental context within which we perform. What does it really mean to be confident? Can you answer that direct question? Think about it a moment.

See? We can't even think of confidence outside of doing something, of performing an action. Our confidence – or lack of confidence – provides us the context of our activities.

Is it certitude? Is it knowledge? Is it bravery? Is it surety? Think of the times when you are confident. You might be confident at playing a certain sport or playing a musical instrument. It could be an activity.

Think. Why are you confident?

Paradoxically, it is the absence of uncertainty. You *know* what to do, and you *know* what you are doing when you do it. For it is uncertainty that makes us fearful. That, and the dread of some consequence like embarrassment, ridicule.

You are in possession of the facts. You are prepared. You know what to expect because you have been there before. And because you practice. You rehearse. There is still, of course, an element of uncertainty. There is uncertainty because you cannot control everything or everybody, and this causes a tinge of anxiety, but that's fuel for your creative engine.

The key for you is to control what you can and to dismiss your fear of the rest. Recognize that this fear is what makes you human, and it is this humanity that gives us commonality with all the public speakers and presenters who have come before us. Hear this advice from speaking master J. Berg Eserwein from more than 100 years ago:

> Even when you are quaking in your boots with the ague of fear, and your teeth fain would beat "retreat," you must assume a boldness you do not feel. For doing this there is nothing like deep stately breathing, a firm look at the dreaded audience… But do not fear them. They want you to succeed, and always honor an exhibition of pluck. They are fair and

know you are only one man against a thousand… Look at your audience squarely, earnestly, expressively.[3]

Think of the soldier told to walk through a minefield. For those unmilitarily inclined, a minefield can be an open space of ground or road in which explosive devices called mines are buried. They explode if someone steps on it or a truck drives over it. They are dangerous.

If you are forced to walk through a minefield, you are nervous. You sweat. You feel real fear. And you gingerly take careful step after careful step until you make it through and the path through the danger is clear.

After the path is clear, how then do you walk through the field? You stride confidently, perhaps even whistling a tune. The absence of uncertainty. Ambiguity is swept away. Fear dissolves into an effervescence of confidence.

Suddenly, we realize that we can freely walk the precipice. Suddenly, we realize we are hurtling along the interstate sitting astride a chunk of metal with no protection. Suddenly we realize we are precariously hurtling through the air five miles high. And it is exhilarating.

A man who reads thoughtfully and sees things with real discernment, whether they be children's games, factories, sunsets, crowds before shop windows, or forests in winter is laying a foundation for self-confidence in speaking, because he is acquiring a store of thoughts and experiences upon which such confidence is most securely built.[4]

Conclusion

The upshot of all of this is that your appearance matters a great deal, like it or not, and it is up to us to dress and groom appropriate to the occasion and tailored to our personal brand and the message we want to send.

"Slob cool" may fly in college – and I stress *may* – but it garners only contempt outside the friendly confines of the local student activities center and fraternity house.

Is that "fair?" It certainly *is* fair. You may not like it. It may clang upon your youthful sensibilities.

3 J. Berg Esenwein, *How to Attract and Hold an Audience* (New York: Hinds & Noble, 1902), 157.
4 Joseph A. Mosher, *The Essentials of Extempore Speaking* (New York: The Macmillan Company, 1935), 139.

APPEARANCE

You're on display in front of a group of buyers. They want to know if your message is credible. Your appearance conveys important cues to your audience. It conveys one of two chief messages, with very little room to maneuver between them.

First, your appearance telegraphs to your audience that you are: sharp, focused, detailed, careful, bold, competent, prudent, innovative, loyal, energetic,

or...

Your appearance telegraphs to your audience that you are: slow, sloppy, careless, inefficient, incompetent, weak, mercenary, stupid.

Moreover, you may never know when you are actually auditioning for your next job. That presentation you decided to "wing" with half-baked preparation and delivered in a wrinkled suit might have held in the audience a human resource professional recommended to you by a friend. But you blew the deal, without even knowing it.

Think. How many powerful people mentally cross you off their list because of your haphazard, careless appearance? How many opportunities pass you by? How many great connections do you forfeit?

Granted, it's up to your discretion to dress in the first wrinkled shirt you pull from the laundry basket, but recognize that you may be paying a price.

Remember that beyond your presentation, you are *always* on-stage. You are always auditioning. And you are creating your personal brand one wrinkled shirt at a time, one exposed pair of boxers at a time. Or you are creating a brand that is clean, professional, sober, serious, decisive, thoughtful, and bold.

Your choice.

Further reading on image and appearance

- Susan Bixler and Nancy Nix-Rice, *The New Professional Image: Dress Your Best For Every Business Situation* (2005)

- Susan Bixler and Lisa Scherrer Dugan, *5 Steps To Professional Presence: How to Project Confidence, Competence, and Credibility at Work* (2000)

- Veronique Henderson and Pat Henshaw, *Image Matters For Men: How to Dress for Success!* (2007)

- Edith Hyams and Joe Hyams, *Success* (2009)

PASSION: EVOKING EMOTION, DISPLAYING EARNESTNESS

True emotional freedom is the only door by which you may enter the hearts of your hearers.

—Brees and Kelley, 1931[1]

Earnestness is the secret of success in any department of life. It is only the earnest man who wins his cause.

—S. S. Curry, 1895[2]

The Challenge: The presenter lacks energy, enthusiasm, and dynamism on stage, and this leeches interest from the presentation, as the audience perceives a sleepwalking performance.

The Solution: Embrace the topic and engage the emotions, develop an earnestness that is infectious. Realize the importance of passion to a superior presentation and learn the techniques that invest the presentation with vigor.

The Benefit: Enhanced audience interest and engagement with an animated and breathless presentation that excites and inspires.

Do you have passion in your life? What is it you long to do? What is it that fills you with the thrill of discovery, the adrenaline of newness? What can compare

---

1 Paul R. Brees and G. Vernon Kelley, *Modern Speaking* (Chicago: Follett Publishing Company, 1931), 118.
2 S. S. Curry, *Lessons in Vocal Expression* (Boston: The Expression Company, 1895), 253.

with the natural high of applying yourself to a task that excites you? What generates those endorphins? What brings a smile to your face involuntarily? What furrows your brow? Is it "world hunger?" Or European soccer? Is it social injustice? Is it political theory? Is it comic book collecting? Chess? Numismatics? Tennis?

What's your passion? Can you generate passion? Of course you can. Will it be "artificial" passion? Of course not!

Passion Is Passion Is Passion

In the world of business presenting, unless you have passion for a subject and *demonstrate* that passion, you will always be at a disadvantage with respect to those who do. You cannot ignore this dictum, and you cannot wish it away.

If you compete with several other teams pitching a product or service to a company for millions of dollars – and there is no difference in the quality or price of the service – then how does the potential customer decide?

Passion!

If he sees a real passion for the work in one team, if he feels the energy of a team driven to success and truly excited about the offering, don't you think he'll be inclined to the team that stirs his emotions? The team that makes him see possibilities. The team that helps him visualize a glorious future.

Recognize in yourself the capacity for passion. Recognize that you have the wherewithal to embrace even the most staid material, the "dullest" project. Remember always that it is *you* who makes it better. *You* who invests it with excitement. *You* are the presentation alchemist.

Many times you hear an "interesting" presentation about an "interesting" topic. It is well-done, and it engaged you. You sometimes wonder why *you* never seem to get the "interesting" projects.

Have you ever admitted to yourself that *you* might be the missing ingredient? That maybe it's *your* task to invest a project with interest and zest? That what makes a project "interesting" is the interaction between material and presenter?

Ultimately, it *is* your task to transform a "case" or business situation into an interesting and cogent presentation. It's *your* task to find the key elements of strategic significance and then to dramatize those elements in such a way that the audience is moved in powerful and significant ways.

Yes, you can do this, and you don't need an "interesting" case to do it. You just need passion. And the components of passion are emotion and earnestness.

The Twin Pillars of Passion – Emotion and Earnestness

We sometimes hear the phrase "he's too emotional" used in a pejorative sense, as if, *de facto*, the display of emotion is a bad thing. Conversely, we sometimes hear that you ought to keep your emotions in check at all times, particularly in business situations. As the master James Winans noted, what is unacceptable is not "emotions" but the display of *excessive* emotion, or *sentimentality*.[3]

Like most generalizations, this injunction against emotional display is based upon a minor truth that has been overextended to cover situations where it is not appropriate. Yes, there *is* a kernel of truth that leads some to equate "emotional" behavior with a lack of discipline or with "out of control" behavior. But this is simply not the case more generally. In fact, if you deny yourself the power that emotion can bring to your presentation, you handicap yourself. You deny yourself one of the most powerful weapons of persuasion in your arsenal.

Some folks may believe that the use of techniques to create excitement in an audience is somehow, well, somehow *unfair* or *manipulative*. There are always folks in every generation who believe this. Speaking master J. Berg Esenwein comments from more than a century ago:

> This excitation of the emotions for oratorical purposes may be cultivated. *Artificiality!* sneers someone. *Trickery!* complains another. "Stale indignation, and fervor a week old!" laughs Sydney Smith. All wrong. It is physical earnestness. It is a legitimate calling upon the body to be what it was created to be: the instrument of the soul, responsive to its moods and tenses.[4]

When I think of emotion and the power it bestows on our public performances, I cannot but think of Sheridan Knowles. Knowles is a near-forgotten playwright from the early 1800s. I remember him for one thing. I remember him not for obscure plays such as *Virginius* or *William Tell*, but for this spectacular observation on the power of emotion:

> Emotion is the thing. One flash of passion on the cheek, one beam of feeling from the eye, one thrilling note of sensibility from the tongue – have a thousand times more value than any exemplification of mere rules, where feeling is absent.[5]

---

3 James Albert Winans, *Public Speaking: Principles and Practice*, (Ithaca, NY: The Sewell Publishing Company, 1915), 108.

4 J. Berg Esenwein, *How to Attract and Hold an Audience* (New York: Hinds & Noble, 1902), 157.

5 James Sheridan Knowles, quoted in Ebenezer Porter, *Analysis of the Principles of Rhetorical Delivery as Applied in Reading and Speaking* (Boston: M. Newman, 1827).

Does this seem too "over the top" for you? Of course it does! That's because you have likely been conditioned to look askance at this kind of rich, lusty pronouncement. *That* is a major part of the business school presentation problem.

When was the last time a business professor criticized you for showing too much emotion in your presentation? Have you ever heard *anyone* criticized for it? For giving a presentation with *too much* feeling? Or for being *too* interesting? For actually making you care? For actually being memorable for more than a few moments?

A World of Business Automatons?

Sometimes it may seem as if you are expected to purge all emotion from your presentations, especially your *business* presentations. It's as if you are instructed to behave like a robot under the guise of looking "professional" or "business-like." We often respond too readily to these negative cues. And our presentations suffer for it.

In a world where business presentations are homogenized, it's too easy to imitate what is bad. If we are told that stilted delivery is acceptable, then who can blame us if we believe that this is how to deliver a quality presentation?

Worse, think of the arrogant VP who shows up at your business school to give a talk and who relies totally upon his corporate position to awe you. When he gives a sloppy presentation that he has obviously not practiced, who can blame you for taking your cues from him?

Is this always the case? No, but it happens too often that it gives *faux* legitimacy to the haphazard and unprepared presentation that is delivered listlessly and without passion.

How many monotoned, lifeless efforts make it onto the guest speaker list and into the classroom before we actually begin to believe that *this is how it's supposed to be?* We must realize that emotion and professionalism are *not* exclusive of each other. Conversely, indifference is your enemy.

> The opposite of earnestness is indifference. An indifferent man cares no more for one thing than for another. All things to him are the same; he does not care whether men around him are better or worse… There are other opposites to earnestness besides indifference. Doubt of any kind, uncertainty as to the thought or to the truth, a lack of conviction, all these tend to destroy earnestness.[6]

---

6 S. S. Curry, *Lessons in Vocal Expression* (Boston: The Expression Company, 1895), 254–5.

You know of the indifferent man or woman, delivering a presentation that obviously means nothing to him or her. Perhaps you've done this yourself. Haven't we all at one time or another? Unknowing of emotion, believing that we *cannot* show we care?

Understand from this moment that this is *wrong*. No, it is not a matter of opinion; it is not a "gray area." It is incontrovertibly *wrong*.

Seize the Power

We do pay occasional homage to emotion and to "passion." But more often than not, it's only lip service. We don't truly believe it. Our fear of others' judgments can push out any thoughts of investing our talks with *anything* interesting. We separate our "real" selves from our work and from our "formal" exposition in front of an audience. We save our passion for our sports teams and our politics and our religion.

Maybe we construct a barrier for the audience to prevent an audience from seeing our vulnerabilities. We affect an air of nonchalance as a defensive mechanism. Regardless of the reason, by not investing ourselves in our presentation and in our narrative, we render ourselves less persuasive, less effective, perhaps even *in*effective.

Emotion is a source of speaker power. You can seize it, master it, and use it to great effect. And you can learn to do this more easily than you imagine.

> A speaker should feel what he says, not only to be sincere, but also to be effective. It is one of the oldest of truisms that if we wish to make others feel, we *ourselves* must feel... We know we do not respond with enthusiasm to an advocate who lacks enthusiasm. And quite apart from response, we do not like speakers who do not seem to care. We like the man who means what he says.[7]

Do *you* mean what you say? Do you even care? Or do you sleepwalk through your assignments? Do you read from a note card, read from the slides behind you, oblivious to why you are up there? Do you just go through the motions?

I understand why you might cop this attitude. Layer upon layer of negative incentives weigh down the college student. Adding to your burden is the peer pressure of *blasé*. It is perceived as somehow "uncool" to appear to care about anything, to actually do your best.

---

7 James Albert Winans, *Public Speaking: Principles and Practice* (Ithaca, NY: The Sewell Publishing Company, 1915), 109–10.

Now, one purpose in all of this counsel is not simply for you to display powerful emotions in service to a cause. You are not simply "being emotional" for its own sake. You want to evoke emotions in your audience. You want them to think, yes, but you also want them *feel*. You want to establish a visceral connection with your audience. You want to do this, because the more you can evoke the appropriate emotion in your audience, the more connected they feel to your message, and the more persuasive your message becomes.

Alexander Melville Bell, father of the more famous Alexander Graham, was an elocutionist of the first rank. Many presentation masters have argued the case for emotion, but certainly none more eloquently than the elder Bell:

> Every orator aims either to instruct, to persuade, or to a means; and he cannot do the one or the other without a manner suited to the end in view. A miser cannot teach benevolence, or a drunkard temperance; a bigot cannot inculcate toleration, or a hypochondriac infuse mirth or cheerfulness; neither can a speaker produce the effect he aims at, on his auditors, if he is not himself correspondingly affected first. He must "assume the virtue if you have it not."[8]

You retain detachment and indifference at your own risk. That risk is the destruction of your presentation or, at the very least, another edition of the listless, pointless exercises that infest corporate America today – just another unpersuasive and forgettable presentation bore.

Let us seriously consider emotion as a tool for our passion, a tool to engage the senses and feelings of our listeners. But before we can talk further about emotions and how their judicious use can lift your presentation quality to new heights, let's discover exactly what we mean by "emotion."

The Emotions

Several American psychologists have independently developed the theory that there are eight basic emotions. These emotions – which can exist at various levels of intensity – are anger, fear, joy, sadness, acceptance, disgust, surprise, and interest or curiosity. They combine to form all other emotions.

But isn't a blatantly emotional appeal anathema in the business world, where supposedly hard facts rule the day? It seems that most *anything* blatant is anathema. Frontal assaults are frowned upon in arenas where everyone seeks credit. It is time to break through this moribund conventionalism to reveal a gem of a thought:

The emotional appeal is as legitimate as any other.

---

8 Alexander Melville Bell, *Elocution* (New York: Edgar S. Werner, 1886), 153.

This point is so important that we should linger on it. The emotional appeal is as legitimate as any other, and it is far more powerful. In fact, you would be hard-pressed to find a more effective persuasive technique. If you harness this power, and other presenters ignore it, think of the competitive advantage you gain.

Experts from antiquity to the present have recognized the power of a presentation fueled with emotion and passion.

> You can wreck a communication process with lousy logic or unsupported facts, but you can't complete it without emotion. Logic is not enough. If all it took was logic, no one would smoke cigarettes. No one would be afraid to fly on airplanes. And every smart proposal would be adopted. No, you don't win with logic. Logic is essential, but without emotion, you're not playing with a full deck.[9]

We live in a world where emotions interact with rationality constantly. So to pretend that we can turn off emotions, or excise them from a portion of our day, is arrogance of the worst sort.

People react to you emotionally, whether you want them to or not. Don't pretend otherwise. To pretend means that we open ourselves to whatever emotions rush in to fill the void that we leave with our mistakenly emotionless pitch.

Isn't it better to attach cues to our message that signal to our audience the emotions we wish to evoke – joy, elation, optimism, zest – rather than allow unwelcome emotions to sprout willy-nilly – anger, frustration, irritation, scorn, fear, indifference?

Now, crafting definitions of emotion is one thing, but grasping the power of emotion is something altogether different. We want to recognize emotive power, harness it, and then channel this emotive power to achieve our communication goal. We want our audience members to *feel* along with us.

We have several ways to coax emotion, to plant the seed and then prompt its growth. One of the best ways, if not *the* best method to use to evoke emotion in the audience is storytelling. Three later chapters in this book speak directly to storytelling as a powerful presenting tool and as the best means to stir your audience emotionally.

The first pillar of passion is emotion. The other pillar of passion is *earnestness*.

---

9 Seth Godin, *Really Bad PowerPoint*, eBook (2001), http://www.sethgodin.com/freeprize/ reallybad-1.pdf (accessed July 26, 2012).

Earnestness

Prior to the advent of television, computers, cell phones, Internet, and the other bells and whistles, the word "earnestness" was one way to characterize the passion invested in a talk.

Today, we might use the word "enthusiasm," but I think that "earnestness" carries a deeper and richer connotation. For brilliant speakers, earnestness encompasses the "embrace" of the material that I so often refer-to in this book. "Earnestness" captures a welter of drivers that generate and propel our excitement, that make our excitement infectious to any audience.

It comes from a root meaning "to excite." Earnestness means an eager desire of the heart for the cause of truth; the deep longing that other men shall accept a truth that is realized by the speaker. The earnest man feels so intensely the importance of a truth that he longs to share it.[10]

Earnestness is the natural language of sincerity and high purpose. It manifests itself in *voice, look,* and *gesture*. It is the result of deep conviction, sympathy, self-abandonment and a heartfelt desire to share the truth with others.[11]

How do you gain passion, or earnestness? What does the earnest speaker look like on the stage? How does an earnest presenter carry himself? Again, the masters of an earlier age transmit their wisdom:

> Earnestness comes, if it comes at all, from a thorough knowledge of your subject, from a sincere faith in that subject, and from a determination to implant in others that knowledge and that faith. Earnestness manifests itself in speech by animation, wide-awakeness, strength, force, power, as opposed to listlessness, timidity, half-heartedness, uncertainty, feebleness.[12]

Earnestness comes when you embrace the topic of your presentation rather than remain aloof from it. You gain earnestness when you pledge yourself to become an expert on the narrow slice of life that is the topic of your presentation. When you become that expert, understanding the nuances and intricacies of your topic, your confidence increases and you become infinitely more believable. You begin to develop that most highly sought quality in the public speaker – charisma.

---

10 S. S. Curry, *Lessons in Vocal Expression* (Boston: The Expression Company, 1895), 253.

11 Grenville Kleiser, *How to Speak in Public* (New York: Funk & Wagnalls, 1906), 166–7.

12 E. D. Shurter, *Public Speaking* (New York: Allyn & Bacon, 1903), 102.

Let's not mistake passion *for the subject* with passion for *speaking on the subject*. Many topics in life do not interest me. I don't give them a minute's thought. I certainly have no special regard, special feelings, or burning passion for these many topics outside my experience. *But...*

If I find myself in a situation where I am responsible for communicating an unfamiliar topic to a group of people, I embrace the task at hand. It becomes a mighty challenge. I surely don't whine that: "I never get an interesting topic."

In learning of a new topic, defining the task, getting your arms around the entire problem, distilling the issue to its core essence, you discover the most compelling and powerful method to convey this topic.

Then you stand before a group of people, steeped in this new knowledge and prepared to deliver an impassioned presentation that grips the audience and calls your listeners to action. That is the way to invest your talk with emotion and earnestness and to exude passion. *Not* to approach the task with a groan and a negative attitude that guarantees a substandard product.

When you acquire and exude earnestness about your topic, you set yourself above the norm. In fact, demonstration of earnestness is so rare and valuable that it can establish for you a tremendous advantage – it widens the gulf between you and the great mass of presenters who simply go through the motions.

Conclusion

Passion is not a tangible quality, and yet we know it when we see it. Paradoxically, while you cannot fake it, a certain degree of artifice is necessary to carry it off. If you are not passionate about the subject of your presentation, you must *become* passionate about it, or suffer horrendous consequences as you stumble through a presentation that interests few and persuades none.

The key to developing passion is the *embrace*. By embracing a topic and by immersing yourself in the process of learning, in the process of developing your talk, in the process of becoming the world's greatest expert on your assigned slice of life, you consciously engage emotion and earnestness, and through this process, you develop passion.

PART III

THE STORY

Story telling has ever been a medium of culture, a teacher of history, literature and ethics. It has been a maker of standards and builder of ideals, not only in one century or country, but during every age and in every land whose achievements have been chronicled.

—Katherine Cather, 1925[1]

Introduction

Business presenters generally don't tell stories. I don't know why not, since storytelling has been shown to be the most powerful medium of communication we have. And business presentations offer a grand opportunity to tell some of the most powerful and dramatic true stories conceivable.

But such is the state of business presentations that any hint of drama, energy, imagination, and *joie de vivre* is purged. When stories *do* find their way into a presentation, they can fire an audience like you've never before seen. An audience hungers for *anything* to relieve the mind-numbing effects of the average presentation.

Effective use of stories in business presentations is so rare that the bar is low with respect to your competition. A great story well-told – *that* is powerful. And storytelling is as old as civilization itself.

> The telling of a story is an event so usual that no latitude and no century can have been without it; wherever there were children to listen or tribesmen to shout or maidens to weep, there must have been the child's story, or the saga, or the romance.[2]

1 Katherine D. Cather, *Religious Education through Storytelling* (New York: The Abington Press, 1925).
2 Arthur Burrell, *A Guide to Storytelling* (London: Sir Isaac Pitman & Sons, Ltd, 1926), 5.

Perhaps the reason we don't use stories in our presentations is that we simply don't know how. Most of us think we're sharp – we all think we know what a story is, don't we? But do we really?

What *Is* A Story?

Defining "story" is like trying to define "culture." Most folks offer up definitions to suit the points they try to make. Here's my definition of a story, and it's honed from a series of definitions that by their nature are slippery.

> *A story is a narrative of events, either true or untrue, that appeals to the emotions more-so than the intellect and which features a character's struggles to overcome obstacles and reach an important goal.*

This definition of a story captures what we do in business. In the world of commerce, we struggle against mighty challenges, both internal and external to us. Entrepreneurs – *especially* entrepreneurs – struggle to convince others that their innovative ideas can transform lives. Mighty corporations engage in titanic struggles against each other and against market forces that lash them mercilessly. Companies rise and fall. Executives rocket to fame and plummet ignominiously.

Yet most of the drama, conflict and emotion is purged from our presentations in a misguided attempt to make them "businesslike."

But don't we all somewhat believe, maybe, that stories are important in presenting? Sure, but when it comes down to "serious" presenting, many folks back off what they profess and offer up the usual tofu.

Who knows why, but that's what happens. Maybe it's the all-pervasive myth that presenting is a "soft skill" that must yield to something else.

Facts, numbers, hard data – *you* choose the weak substitute for a good story, well told.

These substitutes offer false precision. They offer *faux* comfort. They have achieved status as somehow being superior to stories. But it turns out that this status is unearned and may be outright false.

The Science behind Storytelling

Kendall Haven's 2007 book *Story Proof: The Science Behind the Startling Power of Story* exalts the power of story and yields evidence that storytelling is the most powerful means of communication available.

Haven compiles a wealth of sociological studies that inform us exactly what is meant by "story," and the source of its power. He then makes a compelling case that stories work so well because our brains are hardwired to learn most effectively from story-based narratives.

The results of this compendium of research are compelling. More than 120 direct studies encompassing research in more than 800 additional scientific studies point to this conclusion: "Stories are a more efficient and effective vehicle for communicating factual, conceptual, emotional, and tacit information" than any other method.[3]

More powerful than just the facts, just the numbers, just the hard data.

The bad news for business is that most folks remain ignorant of this power not through any fault of their own, but because of the impetus in modern business thought that has erected barriers against story narrative.

The good news is the same point. You gain incredible power and advantage by embracing the power of story in your own presentations. Storytelling is so powerful, in fact, that anti-business factions actually fear that we in business might adopt storytelling as a weapon in the world of commerce. One writer actually views storytelling in the corporate world as "insidious" and a "means of oppression."[4] We need no more powerful lesson than that the enemies of commerce fear the power that storytelling can confer.

It's time to understand and harness that power for your business presentations. The chapters in this section show you how.

---

3 Kendall Haven, *Story Proof: The Science Behind the Startling Power of Story* (Westport: Libraries Unlimited, 2007), 122.
4 Christian Salmon, *Storytelling: Bewitching the Modern Mind* (London: Verso, 2010).

STORYTELLING I: THE SECRET WEAPON

I divide the topic of "storytelling" into several chapters, because you may be impatient. Some impatient students just want barebones technique and not an elaborate explanation of why something works. *"Just tell me how to do it."*

That's a superficial approach, and I find it unsatisfactory. But I accept that there may be good reason for it. It's surely possible to tell a good and satisfying story without knowing the history behind storytelling.

Although I find it helpful to understand the source of the magic, you need not learn the reasons *why* stories are so powerful. So if the thought of this bores you, then move along to the next chapter on "how-to." But move on with this warning.

Your Caveat

If you don't know *why* good stories are powerful, then how can you possibly tell a powerful story? You'll always doubt what you do. You'll doubt its emotive power. You'll doubt its efficacy. You won't even try. You'll tell half-hearted stories that persuade no one. And then you will mutter to yourself: *"Aha!* I knew it was too good to be true. I *knew* that telling a story was just too simple. I'll drop this story nonsense and go back to—"

Go back to what? Go back to the comfort of boring presentations where you read from slides and talk in a monotone? Exciting no one? Persuading no one? Energizing no one? Sedating everyone?

So, I recommend that you read this chapter, because stories have power and you need to know why. Once you understand the ability of a story to evoke emotions, once you understand its subtle and insistent force to establish a connection with an audience, and once you know the most powerful story themes to convey your message and you adopt the fundamental presentation techniques revealed here, you can begin to position yourself in the top one percent of presenters in America.

Read this chapter to acquire certitude and understanding. Read it to understand *why* we tell stories and how stories affect other people. Read it to prepare yourself to wholeheartedly embrace the next chapter on storytelling.

The Single Most Powerful Story

Joseph Campbell was this country's greatest authority on the role of myth in history and on myth in storytelling, and he contended that he had found The Story.

Over years of research, Campbell discovered that there is one story that runs throughout history. It is a story that you find in every culture, in every time and every place on the planet.

It's the story of the *hero's journey*.

Think of Ulysses and his homeward trek following the Trojan War. Homer's *Iliad* and *Odyssey* inspire us today with Ulysses' 10-year journey home serving as the archetype of the most universal story ever told, in all cultures and in all times. In what is modern-day India the Sanskrit heroic epic, the *Mahabharata*, carries a sweep and majesty that has carried it across two millennia. Socrates told stories through the use of dialogues. Plato as well, who scattered tales throughout his own dialogues. Confucius leavened his philosophy with stories. Buddha, Mohammed, and Christ all communicated morality through tales and parables.

Stories communicate in ways that straight factual exposition cannot. And in harsher times than ours, they have been used to mitigate a dangerous situation in which unlucky messengers would be killed if they brought bad news. In 600 BC India, legend has it that the game of chess was invented as a way to tell a story so as not to anger the monarch into murderous frenzy.

In what we know as the dark ages in medieval Europe, Charlemagne became the first Holy Roman Emperor in 771 AD and showed evidence of being an enlightened despot. He established schools for the passing on of history, tales of heroes of Gaul, Italy, Greece, and the Orient. The emperor's early schools served as foundation for what would later become the University of Paris.

Toward the end of the dark ages, storytelling bards provided ballads and epics; they were the castle entertainers.[1] Their only "multimedia" accompaniment was the harp. In different lands, these men were known by different names. In Britain and Ireland these storytellers were called minstrels; in Germany, *minnesingers*, and in France, *trouveres*, or troubadours. But always they were teachers, men with a mission and a message. Not until the beginning of modern times was history taught in any other way than by the lips of storytellers.[2]

Why Tell Stories?

We live in the twenty-first century age of dazzling kaleidoscopic multimedia. Right now, a kindergartener has at his disposal more computing power in a laptop than did Neil Armstrong in his lunar module when he landed on the moon in 1969. In such an age, why do we even speak of an anachronism like "storytelling?"

Because stories still serve as our main form of entertainment – we see and hear stories every day from many sources. Newspapers are filled with "stories." Films, television shows, novels, even technical manuals regale us with stories. *You* tell stories all the time.

Stories are as old as man and still hold fascination for us. In an age of cinematic special effects that depict events with a richness and grandeur unavailable to past generations, film producers have found that without a strong story populated with sharply drawn and sympathetic characters, multimillion dollar computer-generated graphics cannot carry a film to success.

Some stories are more interesting than others, of course, but even the most pedestrian of tales keep our attention far better than dry exposition of facts delivered in a monotone. Unlike straight expositions, stories appeal to the *emotions*. This is the secret of their incredible power. If you search for a verity in the human condition, a key that unlocks the power of persuasion, then this is it – the appeal to emotion through storytelling.

Katherine Cather was a superior storyteller of her generation, and her masterpiece written in 1925 captures the universal appeal of this mode of communication. We seem to have left behind its enduring truth in favor of

---

1 Katherine D. Cather, *Religious Education through Storytelling* (New York: The Abington Press, 1925), 22.
2 Ibid., 23.

cynicism and wry gimcrackery at one end of the scale and a barren "newspeak" at the other end.

> Human emotions are fundamentally the same in every country and in every period of history, regardless of the degree of culture or the color of the skin. Love and hate lie dormant in the human heart; likewise gratitude, and all the other feelings that move mortals to action. They manifest themselves according to the state of civilization or enlightenment of those in whose souls they surge, but the elemental urge, the motive that actuates men to right or wrong doing, is the same now as it was at the beginning of time. The story has power to nurture any one of the emotions... What is the secret of the power of either the spoken or written tale to shape ideals and fix standards? Because it touches the heart. It arouses the emotions and makes people feel with the characters whose acts make the plot. Mirth, anger, pity, desire, disdain, approval, and dislike are aroused, because the characters who move through the tale experience these emotions."[3]

Six Powerful Words for Presentations

"Let me tell you a story" are six of the most powerful words you can utter in a presentation. If your goal is to grip your audience, entertain them, persuade them, and move them to action, you *always* generate interest with these default words: *Let me tell you a story.*

"Let me tell you a secret" is just as compelling, but when you think about it, it's really the same storytelling device worded in slightly different fashion. The story puts incredible power in your hands, on your lips. This power of story has been known for ages. Stories are "windows that let the light in."[4]

> Because the story has power to awaken the emotions and to enlarge the range of experience, it is a tool of universal adaptability. Its appeal is like that of music, sculpture, or painting.[5]

> Probably everyone has experienced the universal interest and attention which results in a dull and abstract lecture when the speaker says, "That reminds me of a story." Like a dog at the back door waiting for a bone,

---

3 Ibid., 23–5.
4 Grenville Kleiser, *How to Develop Power and Personality in Speaking* (New York: Funk & Wagnalls, 1908), 130.
5 Cather, *Religious Education through Storytelling*, 26.

an audience will prick up its ears at the approach of the speaker with a story or illustration that arouses mental imagery. Why? Because such stories are concrete, the opposite of abstract, and tend to arouse pictures which vivify an idea, setting it out in relief with bold colors against a background of drab and hazy abstractions.[6]

Despite rising interest in storytelling as a novelty, corporations don't utilize the power of stories. They leave this incredible potential untapped, because it is in the nature of modern business to embrace the hard and fast and to view anything that is not quantifiable with suspicion.

But just as storytelling can confer personal competitive advantage on you, it can also yield competitive advantages to firms that embrace story as part of the strategic arsenal. Smart corporations utilize the power of stories.

One multinational biotherapy firm I've dealt with incorporates storytelling at the highest levels of its management training. This corporation is unique in many ways – in its management philosophy and in its commitment to core values. It is unique in its devotion to storytelling and the inculcation of this skill in its managers.

Every year, approximately 25 chosen senior managers gather in a location to participate in a global leadership program. The time is divided into halves – 50 percent of the program is devoted to "competencies" such as finance, operations, personnel, and such like. The other half – *50 percent of the entire program* – is given over to storytelling.

"We teach them how to tell the story of their journey," says one professional with the company. A "fireside" atmosphere is encouraged as well. The executives who come out of this program have acquired a powerful tool, for both internal communication and for marketing the company externally.

I have witnessed one company president's superb storytelling skill, and his personal presence and power confer on his company an advantage that cannot be directly connected to a balance sheet, and yet is tangible nonetheless.

Our Definition of Story

We all think we know what a story *is*. But do we really? Remember this definition of story, and ponder how it encompasses our business experience.

---

6 J. K. Horner, *Elements of Public Speech* (New York: D. C. Heath & Company, 1929), 160.

A story is a narrative of events, either true or untrue, that appeals to the emotions more-so than the intellect and which features a character's struggles to overcome obstacles and reach an important goal.

One key point is that it appeals primarily to the *emotions*. Stories engage the audience in ways that mere exposition of facts and numbers cannot.

Let's look at an example of powerful storytelling from one of the great films of the last 20 years – the 1996 legal thriller *A Time to Kill*. This film adaptation of John Grisham's first novel is a superb storytelling vehicle that exemplifies how a deep appeal to emotion and to the heart can overcome an appeal to logic and reason.

A Time to Kill is the story of the rape of a little girl and the subsequent killing of her rapists by a heartsick father and his trial for murder. The story takes place in racially divided Mississippi. The interracial struggle for justice and understanding is the centerpiece of the narrative. It is really several stories – a young lawyer's struggle for his client, a father's struggle for his life, and a town's struggle for its soul.

At the end of the film, the young lawyer, Jake tells the father, Carl Lee that he's going to lose the case. That he should bargain with the prosecutor for a lesser charge to gain life in prison rather than the death penalty.

But Carl Lee is on trial for his life, and he rebukes Jake.

He urges Jake to "think like the jury."

"Jake, you're one of the bad guys," Carl Lee says. "You can't help it, it's the way you was raised. That's why I *picked* you. You're one of them white folk. You *think* like them. That's why *you* can set me free. Throw out all your 'points of law' and talk to them like *one* of them."[7]

Jake is shocked at this revelation of a point of view that he'd never considered. Carl Lee is giving Jake the time-honored advice that we all must follow. This is the sage wisdom to know your audience. Know your audience and craft your message accordingly.

How does Jake respond? He responds with the power of a story. Literally.

Jake prepares a closing argument without his "points of law," and he appeals to the emotions of the jury instead of their logic or sense of duty to the laws of man. He calls out to their humanity, and to do this, he must tell a story. It must be the most compelling story of his young legal career.

7 *A Time to Kill*, DVD, directed by Joel Schumacher (1996; Burbank, CA: Warner Home Video, 1997).

Jake first apologizes to the jury for his ineptitude due to his inexperience. He waves away any appeal to "points of law." He pauses. Jake then places his hand in his pocket, and he approaches the jury box. He gestures with his other hand, gently but firmly. Simultaneously, he utters the magic words.

"Now I'm gonna tell you a story."

The response is phenomenal and real. Everyone in the film leans forward. The prosecutor. The defendant. The members of the jury. *All* of them. *You* feel yourself lean forward. Perhaps you even shift in your seat with expectation.

Why?

Because everyone loves a story.

A story touches emotions where simple exposition cannot. A story can make people laugh, can make them angry. In this case, Jake tells a tragic and heinous story that makes them cry. But why does he do this? Couldn't he have given a straight closing argument and touched on the "points of law" that might have freed his client? Of course he could have and he probably would have lost the case. In this instance, all that was left was an appeal to emotion. And stories touch the emotions in ways that straight exposition cannot.

The scene of Jake pleading for his client's life is a masterful demonstration of story power. The armor we wear against fact and logic is porous and vulnerable to the gentle probing of a story. As Jake weaves his spellbinding story of rape and trauma, the stolid men and women of the jury begin to crumble. Eyes glisten. Adam's apples bob with hard swallowing. Even the most callous and racist man on the jury is moved by Jake's tale.

"Let me tell you a story."

How Can We Use Stories?

You already tell stories. You tell them all the time. You tell them to your friends, to your family, and to the people you run into in line at the grocery store, at the church fellowship on Sundays, and at the bar during Friday happy hour. We tell stories because they convey information in a dramatic way that stirs us far more so than mere data.

But oddly enough, we seem to purge stories from our professional lives. It's as if they aren't "serious" enough for the gravity of business. It's as if this powerful device, that is capable of stirring the soul and moving the heart, is banned from communicating business concepts or scientific ideas.

This is the medium used by author John Grisham, by director Quentin Tarantino, and by the most callow of journalists. Is this powerful tool somehow beneath the minimum acceptable standard in a professional venue where the *gravitas* of high finance or of corporate analysis is at issue? I think not.

But instead of moving stories in our presentations, we're faced with presentations cloned from annual reports and delivered with the *panache* of a Puritan and with the spice of tofu.

It's the same regardless of the industry or the level of business unit. Presentations all look unsurprisingly the same. Drones in business suits and well-coiffed styles making monotone points with staid factual accuracy. Nary a story is told, unless it's inadvertent. Just "facts," busy slides, and stiff presentation – the standard template.

It remains a mystery why this should be so. Who says it has to be this way? Is there some central clearinghouse that has decreed that business presentations, to be taken seriously, must bore? It's a serious problem and has been a problem plaguing business for more than a century. Grenville Kleiser's lament is as true today as it was in 1908:

> Abstract philosophy and close argument if long continued in speech, become wearisome to an audience. They demand some relief. A good illustration, skillfully introduced, rests the mind of the listener, lends variety and vivacity to the speaker's style, and drives home his message with increased effectiveness.[8]

Folks, primarily in the non-profit arena, often use storytelling *against* corporate America. Greenpeace, PETA, the Animal Rights Movement, and many far less visible social activist organizations have used the emotional power of stories to devastating effect against business.

But the moguls of corporate America are steeped in the conservative ethos and convicted in their belief in the power of facts and logical argument. They are earnest in their own defense, but they relegate "storytelling," "poetry," and "emotion" to another realm that is populated by idealists from the humanities and the traditional liberal arts.

Sure there are some "hip" businesses like Apple and Google, but the majority of businessmen of the buttoned-up corporation reject emotional appeals. They often cannot understand the public attraction to emotional arguments when, many times, those arguments don't have the weight of fact on their side. But such emotional

---

8 Kleiser, *How to Develop Power and Personality in Speaking*, 130–31.

arguments win in the public arena. The same acumen that makes many CEOs successful can cripple them when it comes to powerful communication.

This is the secret weapon that anti-business activists use against corporate America, for good or bad. That weapon is the power of a good story. Stories appeal explicitly to the emotions. They stir the heart, and they simplify complex issues, sometimes to the detriment of the truth. And they win over the public in the face of superior arguments.

It's the tale of the economist in the three-piece suit who explains the benefits of free trade to us all. But he's pitted against the unemployed autoworker with five children and a mortgage, a man thrown out of work by a downsizing American corporation. You already know who wins *that* debate, and it's not the economist.

Who is not moved by the plight of the man who has lost his job? Who *cannot* but be angered by the impersonal and uncontrolled forces called "globalization," whose victims are so visible and whose beneficiaries so nameless and scattered? And who could possibly be convinced by the cold emotionless economist reciting the hard numbers that indicate that free trade "benefits us all" in the end? The scenario above is a version of the *Underdog* story, and there is a reason why the cliché says that everyone loves an underdog.

The economist may be correct. The facts may be on his side. His arguments may be air-tight. But oftentimes the human heart overrides the mind. In fact, people often search for reasons to override relentless logic so that they may convince themselves what their hearts tell them is "right."

Irrational they may sometimes be, but stories can carry the day. In their emotive power and power to persuade, stories are just as rational as any other tool. It depends on how you define rational or how you tabulate the calculus of human need – whether by unfortunate individuals or whether by fortunate aggregations. Regardless, the emotional power of story has battered business far too long.

Story is a legitimate and powerful tool in the presenter's toolbox. We should use it prudently, both inside the firm and to the outside public.

Fine, but how do I craft my stories? Where do I find stories that persuade? What constitutes a good story?

The next chapters show you how.

STORYTELLING II: WHAT KINDS OF STORIES?

Stories are so underused in business that even a simple fable can become a bestselling book. *Who Moved My Cheese?* was a 2002 business book and is nothing more than an allegory that illustrates an important business issue, dealing with change. It might seem like an incredibly unserious book, but it sold more than 10 million copies and became an international bestseller, reaching on the top of the *New York Times, USA Today, Wall Street Journal,* and *Business Week* bestseller lists.

Cheese launched a new genre of business book – the business fable – that conveys lessons in an almost childlike way. *Our Iceberg is Melting* is another business fable book, published in 2006.

Do you still think stories are unserious? The ground is so fertile and the well so untapped, that you can stride like a giant upon the stage by telling even the most minor of tales. The stage is set for you. In fact, the occasion for using stories in your presentations could not be more opportune.

Don't hesitate on the cusp of telling your first business story, because it seems grandiose and outside the reasonable limits of the topic at hand. It's not difficult, and it needn't be long. Moreover, this is a measure of whether you are prepared to step into the upper echelon of business presenting or not.

Look at the contrast – corporate America is swamped with PowerPoint presentations that numb the mind and deaden the spirit. The appearance of a tale with even a hint of imagination roils the waters in incredibly positive ways. This is why simple fables and tales impact the corporate environs so dramatically.

What kinds of fables are available for you? Have a look at Aesop's *Fables*. A fable can form the framework of your story, and there's no need for lengthy tale-telling. You relate a powerful story in three sentences. For instance:

A hungry fox saw some fine bunches of plump grapes hanging from a vine that was trained along a high trellis and strained to reach them, leaping high as he could into the air. But it was in vain, for they were just out of reach. So he gave up and walked away with an air of dignity, remarking, "I thought those grapes were ripe, but I see now they are quite sour."[1]

Aesop's *Fables* are packed with powerful morals and lessons and directives useful for business. "The Fox and the Grapes" fable above captures the human tendency to disparage what we want but cannot have. You can utilize it as it reads, or you can modify it to suit your situation. A major advantage in using a fable is its quality of familiarity – a familiar story resonates with your audience.

Another advantage is that it gets your audience in the frame of mind to agree with you. If your listeners agree with the moral of the fable, and they most assuredly will, then the direct link to the topic of your presentation can start them on the road to acceptance of your argument.

In fact, the juxtaposition of a short ancient fable with a modern business presentation would be a daring move on your part. Are you capable of such a feat?

It's Great And All – But How Can I Use It?

Perhaps you scratch your head or fidget with impatience. Storytelling is interesting in a fun sort of way, and it may even be ennobling, but how does it relate to your business school presenting?

Just like this: Once you understand the power of a story to evoke emotions, once you understand its subtle and insistent force to establish a connection with an audience, once you know the most powerful story themes to send your message, and if you adopt the fundamental presentation techniques revealed in this book, you begin moving toward the top one percent of presenters in America.

It's not enough to know the power of story. It's necessary to select the right story, to choose the right perspective, to anoint the right hero, and then to tell your story with relish – in such a way that moves your audience to action.

---

1 *Aesop's Fables* (New York: Barnes & Noble, 2005), 1.

I'm tempted to say that a bad story is better than no story, but this is not the case. A pointless story or a story that trails off without conclusion can be worse than no story at all, because the audience will feel cheated. And rightly so. They will feel cheated, because the best stories must satisfy the reader or the listener.

And whatever else you do, do *not* cheat the audience. That's part of the unwritten pact between storyteller and listeners. The listeners must receive a payoff. And no matter how well-intentioned, no matter how well-told, a pointless story leaves your listeners feeling hollow.

They feel led astray, betrayed. They feel cheated and angry.

You *don't* want an angry audience – an audience that is, at best, unreceptive to your message; at worst, hostile to whatever else you have to say. Do not cheat your audience with a pointless story, a story with no payoff.

Story Punch

So now you select the right story and tell it in such a way that captures the emotions of your audience.

I assume that you have read the previous chapter on why storytelling is so powerful. But even if you have not, I prepared this chapter as a "how-to" standalone.

Perhaps you don't want to know how and why storytelling adds so much power to your presentations. You just want "the facts."

"Just tell me how to do it."

Okay, but I guarantee that if you understand why the right kinds of stories are so powerful, you enrich your own presentation immeasurably and squeeze the absolute maximum of power and persuasiveness from your story. So if you skipped to this chapter, go back and read the last chapter right now.

Story Structure

You know how to tell a story already. You tell them all the time. They're probably pretty good stories. When you *care*, you tell good stories. You know they're better than stories you tell on subjects you're indifferent to.

In addition to caring about the subject matter, you also must bring some sort of structure to your story. Think of how you structure your stories. You don't tell the ending first – that much you know.

But beyond that, do you start talking aimlessly? Do you string sentences together randomly? Do you tell endless narratives that disappear into oblivion like my mother used to do, bless her heart?

The masters knew what makes for good story structure. Listen to this fellow, a maestro from a century ago – Edward Porter St John:

> Every good story must have a beginning that rouses interest, a succession of events that is orderly and complete, a climax that forms the story's point, and an end that leaves the mind at rest. Or, to put it another way, the story has a hero, action, a plot, and a solution.[2]

Every story consists of a hero, plot, action and a solution. Every story is constructed from these same four elements. The magic ingredient for all of this is transformation. In the process of solving a story problem, the hero and other characters are transformed into something more than they were before. So...

Hero, Plot, Action, Solution

Let's look at each:

Hero refers to a character who, in the face of danger and adversity, shows courage and willingness to sacrifice to achieve some greater good – the very definition of heroism.

Plot is a term for the events of our story as they relate to one another through cause and effect or even coincidence, creating a problem that must be solved. We are interested in how our events can affect our audience and tie into their emotions. The plot provides our story with a structure, a simple framework – a beginning, middle and end.

Action is what a character does in the story, with characters interacting in ways that move the story along to a satisfying conclusion.

Solution resolves the problem in the story in a way that is satisfying to the audience.

These four components of our story provide us with four main questions we must answer:

1, With regard to **HERO** – who is in my story and what roles do they play?

2. With regard to **PLOT** – what is the most important point of my story and what story theme best expresses that point?

---

2 Edward Porter St John, *Stories and Storytelling* (Philadelphia: American Baptist Publication Society, 1910), 13.

3. With regard to **ACTION** – what actually *happens* in my story?

4. With regard to **SOLUTION** – how do I tell and resolve my story?

Put People in the Story

Your first task is to populate your story with people. *Humanize* your story. People make your story real, make it breathe, make it come alive. Real names, descriptions, emotions.

Ultimately, your *audience* determines the worth of your story, and you don't tell the same story for every audience. In fact, your story *should* differ substantially depending on the needs of your audience.

Your audience could be the CEO of your client company, the CEO of your own company, the C-suite cadre of your company, the marketing department of a potential client, a group of line employees – you could tell a story to each of these audiences with substantially the same points, but change the focus.

And the Hero Is...

But this is not enough. Your story *must* have a hero. That hero must be in the audience. Every audience member ought to visualize himself or herself as the hero. You *change the hero* of your story as your audience changes from talk-to-talk. Each audience demands its own hero.

If your audience is the **CEO** and his senior staff, then *he* is the hero, aided by his trusted colleagues – he is Napoleon, she is Joan of Arc.

If your audience is the **shareholders**, then *they* are the heroes of your story. It is through their guidance and wisdom that the company is successful.

If your audience is your **subordinates**, then *they* are the heroes for keeping the machinery of the company running under even the worst conditions.

If your audience is your **students**, then *they* are the heroes of the subject matter as they take it, own it, and arm themselves to slay corporate dragons. You are but the armorer, and perhaps a former warrior.

My Arsenal of Stories

For purposes of your presentations, you have several story options you can use as the occasion warrants.

First is your *personal story*, a story that you tell repeatedly in various scenarios, most usefully in your job interview but also when it fits into a public presentation.

Second are *story moments*, the short stories and anecdotes you select to make major points in your presentation. These are minor stories, either whole or in part, which you tell to illustrate or emphasize one or two major points in your presentation.

Third is your *theme story*. This is an overarching story that provides a structure for your presentation. Ideally, the theme story should be well known or a version of a well-known tale, so that the audience identifies with it, either consciously or subconsciously.

Your personal story

This story changes only at the margins as you grow and experience new challenges. It is a heartfelt rendering of what motivates you. It should convey what is uniquely *you*, and it tells your listeners that *here* is a sincere person.

Think about your personal story and where you might find it. You can find your stories both great and small in your *resume*. The best thing about these stories is that all of them are *yours*. One of the confounding things about college students and recent graduates is that they believe that other folks' stories are always more interesting than their own. Of course, that's only a matter of perception, self-abnegation, and an over-cultivated modesty.

Humility is a fine virtue, but like anything else, you should practice it in moderation. The fact is that it takes practice and a keen eye to see our own special story within our breadth of experiences. It takes practice to look at the motion picture of our own lives and see something special and sparkling that we might otherwise dismiss as mundane.

> The stories of your own life are a personal treasure. They are your personal sacred bundle. Those sacred bundle stories represent the best of who you are, as well as the wisdom that you have accumulated over the years of your life.[3]

You can massage the most pedestrian activity to sound grandiose, suffused with meaning, bathed in moonlight, and kissed by the morning dew. The beauty of

---

3 Peg C. Neuhauser, *Corporate Legends & Lore: The Power of Storytelling as a Management Tool* (New York: McGraw-Hill, 1993), 68.

it is that you *are* sincere and truly believe your own grandiosity. You *believe* it, because in fact it's real.

This belief in your story invests it with *gravitas*, and all sorts of collateral benefits flow from this. The stakes must be sufficiently high to generate interest. If not, then the emotions should be engaged in suitable *pathos*. Regardless, gather your personal information and fit it into the story template that accommodates it best.

This personal story serves you in many situations, particularly the job interview. And if you feel reluctance to talk about yourself in glowing terms, then be indirect about your many virtues. Tell a story about *what I learned* in difficult circumstances.

Story moments

Incorporate story moments throughout your presentation. The story moment may be no more than two sentences that breathe life into a staid exposition of facts. Or it can extend to a one-paragraph allegory that plunges your audience into the meat of your show.

This is the key to your story's power – you select a story the audience already knows, and you populate it with sympathetic characters.

Speaking coach Suzanne Bates provides an excellent example of this type of story moment. She relates the example of a speech given by UPS chairman Mike Eskew to his employees. The occasion of the speech was a change of the company logo.

Many CEOs erroneously believe that employees want to hear a story of the CEO's vision and leadership. Eskew instead seized the opportunity to showcase the striving of his employees and gave a masterful show, demonstrating how a CEO can connect with the sympathies of his people. In reaching out to his employees, Eskew crafted his message to make the UPS rank-and-file employees the heroes of the UPS story, not himself.

> Our brand is all about our people and keeping the UPS promise. Just as Marty Peters… Marty's the longest-tenured active employee at UPS – out of 360,000 around the world. Marty is a fifty-seven year veteran of UPS. That's right; he started with us in 1946…and guess what…he still shows up at the job every day as a shifter and a customer-counter clerk in Detroit.

> And there's someone else we've brought to New York for this special day… Ron Sowder, a Kentucky District feeder driver. Ron's been with the company forty-two years. In fact, he started in 1961…the year of

our last logo change. When Ron started with the company...he wasn't old enough to drive. But today he carries the distinction of having the most years of safe driving among active employees in the company. In my book, Ron and Marty are UPS heroes. They not only represent the brand... like you – they live the brand every day.[4]

This is a superb example of the speaker *transforming* the audience with a powerful story. One moment they are employees assembled to hear a speech by the CEO on the company logo; the next moment, they are the heroes in an adventure story that spans decades! Here Mike Eskew does it explicitly and deftly. He outright calls them heroes. It isn't a bald bid for flattery. That kind of thing falls flat quickly. It was sincere.

The good news is two-fold. First, injecting a story moment is not difficult to do. Second, it is guaranteed to work. By *work*, I mean that it transforms your presentation into something magical. Think of it this way. A story is magic dust.

When the president calls for national action in time of need, he doesn't just inform us – he *inspires* us. He alludes to the wisdom and fortitude, the strength and durability, the innovation and drive of the American people. He sometimes refers to the greatest generation, the generation that fought and won World War II.

He may talk of hardy pioneers to dramatize the American sense of adventure. He may use story moments of American inventors to make his points about innovation – Thomas Edison, Alexander Graham Bell, Steve Jobs. He ties us to these powerful stories and he makes *us* the hero, not himself. President Ronald Reagan was a master of the story moments, calling on them to craft powerful speeches.

But you need not pull out the heavy artillery every time. You can utilize short punchy stories to launch your show or to illustrate minor points. A great source for this kind of storytelling is Aesop's *Fables*.

Aesop's *Fables* are narratives that can convey your point quickly and crisply. They are short, familiar, freighted with morals, and most of them carry heavy business relevance.

Goose and golden egg

You can find a fable to illustrate most any business point. Take the familiar fable of "The Goose that Laid the Golden Egg," which teaches, "much wants more and then loses all."

---

4 Suzanne Bates, *Speak Like a CEO* (New York: McGraw-Hill, 2005), 94–5.

But the Goose fable also captures deeper lessons about discovering the true sources of wealth and nurturing – the processes that create wealth. Fables can run the gamut of lessons, from betrayal to bigotry, from deceit to damnation.

Theme Story

This is the overarching story that provides the framework of your presentation, and it has the tremendous advantage of marshaling culture as your ally. It puts culture on your side.

When you prepare your presentation around a story that transcends generations, a story that is deeply embedded in your culture, you play a subtle trump card. You harness strong cultural forces for your show that give you incredible persuasive power. As a consequence, you gain a strong competitive advantage that might not even be recognized consciously by those listening to you. Transcendence is not a word we hear often in business presentations, but the word is appropriate here.

You can use a lengthy tale to serve as the theme of your entire presentation, framing your subject matter in ways the audience can understand. They understand and begin to accept the major points of your presentation because the broad story theme is already familiar to them, if even only subconsciously. Your **big story** packages your entire presentation in a memorable vessel. The appropriate theme story marshals incredible unseen cultural forces in service to your presentation.

Your story provides the take-off point and the end-point – the bookends for your presentation. By connecting your issues, company, and arguments to a tale that is well-known to the audience, you move them along the road of agreement with you. You make it easy for them to remember your points. They understand, because what you say – even if completely new – is already somehow familiar to them.

Some story themes

Those of us in business and in business school need only a handful of story themes for our presentations. These well-known story themes provide the basis for near-infinite variation, and this is just a sample handful. We're already familiar with all of them, because they provide the basis for most of our popular culture films and novels.

- Rags to riches
- The lost cause

- The underdog
- The accidental hero
- The lesson learned
- Failure and redemption

Story themes provide a template for you, and most of our own adventures in business, in the military, in academia, in sports fit one of the grand themes that run through history. The common thread of all of these themes is "transformation."

Transformation means that the plot and the action take the hero through a process that changes him in some fundamental way that is resolved at the end in a satisfying conclusion. Let's now look more closely at these familiar themes.

Rags to riches

This is a theme that resonates with most Americans and hearkens back to the American Dream, pulling yourself up by the bootstraps. It's Horatio Alger. It's a story of **transformation through hard work**. Think of the movies that play out this theme. *The Godfather*, *The Great Gatsby*.

The lost cause

This is a transcendent theme that takes us into the world of honor, courage and martial values. What compels us to struggle in the face of insurmountable odds? This is the heart of the lost cause theme, and it is as old as antiquity. It is **transformation through the acting out of courage**. King Leonidas and his 300 Spartans at the pass of Thermopylae exemplify the warrior spirit in the face of defeat.

The underdog

We all like to see the little guy pull off the big upset, and the underdog theme inspires us, especially when the underdog is gutsy and good. Think of the film *Rocky*, and the dream of a man with a million-to-one shot to prove he's not a loser. Think of the Bible and David and Goliath. This is a story of **transformation of the spirit through hope and belief**.

The accidental hero

A reluctant hero is a person thrown into the hero's role by accident and circumstance. Do *I* have what it takes to be a hero if I were thrust into such a situation? This is a story of **transformation by accident and realization**. Think of the classic film *The Magnificent Seven*, the futuristic action film *The Matrix*, or the Clint Eastwood film *Gran Torino*.

The lesson learned

Life throws challenges at us, and only the foolish refuse to meet those challenges and learn their hard lessons. The film *Remember the Titans* gives us a true story of conflict, drama, self-discovery, and transformation. From an earlier generation, *It's a Wonderful Life* is a film that does the same, with Jimmy Stewart starring in what the American Film Institute calls the most inspirational American film ever made. This is a story of **transformation through self-discovery**.

Failure and redemption

How we respond to failure can be a test of character. Coming back from failure can be a powerful story. Think of the film *Rocky III*. Rocky first loses and then finds renewed strength within himself to gain the final triumph. Think of the film *The Bird Man of Alcatraz*. A man finds redemption and his life's calling while in prison for murder. This is a story of **transformation by fire.**

These story themes embody human values of hope, of redemption, of compassion, and of great deeds. All the stuff of business. These are superb story themes, but if you have a choice and the opportunity and the occasion and material match, there is one overarching story you should almost *always* use. – the hero's quest.

The hero's quest

The hero's quest has animated societies in all parts of the world throughout recorded history. It's a story as old as time, stretching back into the mists of myth. It is the most widespread and inspiring of tales, according to America's late, great mythologist Joseph Campbell. Every man and woman knows this story and is moved by it. "The ultimate aim of the quest must be neither release nor ecstasy for oneself, but the wisdom and the power to serve others," Campbell said.[5]

The hero's quest is the story of Prometheus stealing fire, of Ulysses' quest for home after the Trojan War, Jason and the Golden Fleece, King Arthur's Knights of the Round Table and the quest for the Holy Grail. Of the real world stories that captivate, such as Davy Crockett at the Alamo, Teddy Roosevelt and his

---

5 Joseph Campbell with Bill Moyers, *The Power of Myth* (New York: Doubleday, 1988), xv.

charge up Kettle Hill. Of modern movie heroes like Luke Skywalker. Of the restless wanderers from the film *Easy Rider*. Of the seemingly endless spate of films and television shows that feature the voyages of the Starship Enterprise, whose very existence and purpose is a heroic journey "to seek out new life and new civilizations."[6]

In this adventure, the hero finds the strength within himself to conquer all obstacles no matter how impossible. It is epic. It is **transformation through triumph**.

This may sound grandiose and far from your world, but it is much closer than you imagine. Your life is filled with heroes and villains, conflict and conquest, failure and triumph. Your story is what you contrive, and the ease of it is that your story elements are all decided for you – its characters, its impersonal forces, its plot, the villain, the conflict, the climax, and the identity of the hero.

That's wonderful, you say, but how does this information help *me*? What does a hero's journey have to do with profit-and-loss, with declining market share, or price-cutting competitors?

You needn't become a scholar of mythology to put Campbell's discovery to work for you. The hero's journey is an epic. It's grandiose. When done well, it can infuse most any presentation with high-toned power and purpose.

It provides you with the framework – the beginning, middle, and end. The hero's quest ends with the ship in homeport, the knight saving his princess, the journey brought to successful conclusion. Perhaps its biggest advantage is that it resonates with people – the story sounds familiar. They may not even realize it while they are hearing it, but they find comfort in the familiarity.

Conclusion

In this chapter, you learned about the three levels of business storytelling – personal, story moments, and theme and the components of hero, plot, action, and solution. You learned how to choose a familiar story theme as a blueprint that structures your particular presentation story and to populate it your characters of the moment. Characters in your story must change in some way, must be transformed by the action and the plot. And in your presentation, this must be a positive, growing experience.

---

6 *Star Trek*, episode no. 1, first broadcast September 8, 1966 by NBC. Created by Gene Roddenbery.

In the next chapter, you learn refined techniques, how to meld your story's Most Important Point – your MIP – with the appropriate theme and to then color and flesh out that story so that it comes alive for the audience.

Further reading on storytelling

As with any other presentation technique the telling of the right story in a powerful and compelling manner takes practice. It also takes boldness, since storytelling is not the norm in business school presentations. The literature on business storytelling is not extensive, but you can find superb resources on the subject. As well, books on the art of storytelling can dramatically improve your professional presence and general storytelling effectiveness. Have a look at these books:

- Lucille N. Breneman and Bren Breneman, *Once Upon a Time: A Storytelling Handbook* (1983)

- Joseph Campbell, *The Hero with a Thousand Faces* (1949)

- Joseph Campbell, *The Power of Myth* (1988)

- Evelyn Clark, *Around the Corporate Campfire* (2004)

- Stephen Denning, *The Leader's Guide to Storytelling: Mastering the Art and Discipline of Business Narrative* (2005)

- Sandy Dunlop, *Business Heroes* (1997)

- Doug Lipman, *Improving your Storytelling* (1999)

- Ryan Mathews and Watts Wacker, *What's your Story?* (2007)

- Bill Mooney and David Holt, *The Storytellers Guide* (1996)

- Peg C. Neuhauser, *Corporate Legends and Lore: The Power of Storytelling as a Management Tool* (1993)

- Annette Simmons, *The Story Factor* (2001)

- Annette Simmons, *Whoever Tells the Best Story Wins* (2007)

STORYTELLING III:
HOW DO WE TELL A STORY?

We have discussed the components of the story – hero, plot, action, and solution – and several types of story vehicles that are most useful to the business presenter – the personal story, story moments, and theme story.

In this chapter, we move to a more advanced level of storytelling, deepening and enriching our stories with additional techniques. We bring to bear our personal style on our stories and combine them with the lessons of master storytellers.

Your own "style" is a result of honestly embracing the seven presentation techniques and making them yours. A good story, well-chosen and told passionately, is a powerful weapon in your presentation arsenal.

Here, we examine the techniques of *sensory involvement*, *WIIFY*, *focus on your Most Important Point*, *imagery*, and *concreteness*.

This is where story and storyteller join together to spark the magic of a great presentation. Here is where you combine the Seven Secrets you learned in Part II of this book with the powerful storytelling techniques of Part III.

Position the Audience with Sensory Involvement

The first technique, and probably the most important with regard to drawing in your audience to feel your message, is *sensory involvement*. This is a powerful technique that imbues your story with sensuality.

You engage the senses of your listeners so that they *experience* the story rather than simply *hear* it. Where possible, you incorporate the audience's senses. Ideally, you want to engage all five senses. The more senses you involve, the better.

This sensory technique positions the listener *inside* the story. You invite the audience into the story to become part of the action. This is a fiction-writing technique that draws the reader into the story by stimulating the audience's sight, smell, hearing, touch, and taste.

Likewise, if you use color, aromas, tastes, and powerful sound and visual imagery to good effect, your presentation evokes the emotions of your listeners, captures their interest, and conveys a more compelling message and call to action than if you recite only facts and figures. This use of multiple sensory stimulation affects your listeners in ways that they are really unaware of. They find themselves deep in your story and feeling what you want them to feel and they respond to your message.

Engage as many senses as you can. The audience should *hear* your presentation. They should *taste* your presentation. They should *see* your presentation. *Smell* it. *Feel* it.

The sensory technique paints a mind picture. It makes that picture vivid and powerful. It's powerful because it pulls the listener inside the story as a living, breathing, vicarious participant. You have *positioned* your listeners inside the story rather than allowing them to loiter outside the story as bystanders.

Use imagery. Stimulate the senses! The 1999 supernatural film *The Sixth Sense* illustrates the point. In this film, the Bruce Willis character – in spirit form – moves about within the story among living people, able to observe and, in a sense, *participate* in the various dramas that play out around him. Think of Bruce Willis as the audience of your presentation; you want to position the audience inside the story. Willis feels and senses the angst, joy, anger, sadness of those around him, and yet he is not an actual participant.

Bruce Willis is positioned as close as possible to the dramas around him without actually *being* there. Likewise, your story's vivid and emotive sensory stimulation engages your audience in a powerful way. You invite them into the story, much as the Bruce Willis character is placed into the mini-dramas that unfold around him.

Engaging the Senses

Dean Koontz is a master thriller writer, and advocates involving as many of the reader's senses as possible in a story. Koontz does this himself in his own taut novels.

Koontz engages smells, colors, sounds to enliven his descriptions, and he does this in unexpected ways. Not only does Koontz involve all the senses, but he also combines surprising descriptions, crossing from one sense to another.

For example, he describes the glow of a bulb as a "sour yellow light." In this way, Koontz combines taste with color to evoke a startling and memorable image. This is the same technique that serves powerful presenters well. It can serve *you* well.

Here are some descriptive samples of the technique in use as you involve all of your listeners' senses – taste, touch, smell, sight, and hearing:

- Don't just refer to "sandpaper." Say: "The scrape of scratchy sandpaper on skin."

- Don't just refer to a garbage truck. Say: "The roar of a garbage-truck compactor."

- Don't just refer to a "bus." Say: "Garish primary red on the side of a dirty bus."

- Don't just refer to a "cigarette." Say: "The nicotine-stained fingers and hacking death-cough of a lifetime smoker."

- Don't just refer to an old banana. Say: "The pungent scent of rotting banana."

- Don't just refer to the open field. Say: "The wetness of summer dew in a field of canary-yellow flowers."

- Don't just say "the sturdy building." Say: "The strength of a concrete tower ribbed with steel girders."

If you evoke the image of 1863 Battle of Gettysburg, your listeners should hear the distant rumble of the big guns and feel the earth tremble with their salvos; you should sting their nostrils with the smell of burnt gunpowder. Their dry throats should thirst for refreshment. Hundreds of battle pennants streaming in the slight breeze should fill their minds and move their hearts. You should evoke tragedy, honor, courage, and despair.

Don't believe for a second that such powerful imagery is the exclusive province of great and historic events or of fiction. Or that only other, more dynamic speakers may use them. Powerful imagery *is* at your call. In fact, you should use your imagination to conjure vivid images. How can you describe what you cannot imagine? Make it a habit to groom your imagination in ways prescribed by the masters:

A public speaker should cultivate the habit of making vivid mental pictures of what he sees and reads. This is one of the best remedies for self-consciousness. It also develops the power of concentration, gives freshness and reality to a speaker's utterance, and greatly increases the interest of the audience.[1]

In similar fashion, you can unlock the emotional power involved in the drama of business decisions. You can paint the powerful image of tense and critical business negotiations. In doing so, you can use cross-sensory stimulation in unique and surprising ways.

For instance, use a *taste* adjective to describe a *visual* image: "The old fluorescent tubing lit the room, but just barely. The tubes, stained with age, lit the room with a tart yellow fluorescence that hung heavy on those men and women arguing critical points of the negotiations."

The previous sentence combines taste and visual color – *tart yellow* – to stimulate an image in the listener's mind. It evokes a mood and a sense of presence by engaging the listener's emotions. It transports the listener to the time and place of the "final negotiations" far more effectively than a recitation about the "meeting."

Is there such a thing as *too much* emotion or description? Sure, but I wager that this isn't your problem. If you find yourself plagued with investing "too much emotion" in your own presentations, what an incredibly superb "problem" to have.

Powerful descriptive techniques can rivet audience attention on the main points of your presentation. The vividness of your descriptions sharpens their sense of context and ignites their imaginations with possibilities.

Emotion and sharply drawn scenes cannot replace facts or substitute for substance. The evocation of audience emotion should complement, deepen, and set off the factual and numerical data and your analytical conclusions and recommendations that are the guts of a great presentation.

WIIFY – What's In It For You?

What's in it for you?

Always ask yourself this question with regard to your audience and *from the point-of-view* of your audience. This strikes at the heart of a powerful and

---

1 Grenville Kleiser, *How to Develop Power and Personality in Speaking* (New York and London: Funk & Wagnalls Company, 1912), 95.

well-received presentation:

> The young speaker can do nothing better for himself than to fix firmly in
> mind that public speaking is a dialogue and to emphasize constantly the
> part of the audience, anticipating and watching for its response.[2]

This speaking basic also runs under the tag of "Know Your Audience."

To achieve its greatest effect, your story *must* center on the needs and interests
of your audience. At its best, your presentation should focus on the deepest
desires of the audience, but do so subtly and with great skill. Your story should
fulfill a need in the audience with regard to the story's topic.

Ask yourself these questions: Why have they come? What is it that motivates
these persons to gather in one place to hear me? How can I speak to the
audience as a group, and yet speak to each person individually? How can
I make the persons in the audience feel like a hero?

We know that the hero of your story must be in the audience. The CEO. The
stockholders. The employees. The people who are praised, instructed, lifted,
motivated, excited *must* be the heroes of your story. Aim your story at them to
make them feel good about themselves.

Speak with them as individual people, not as a group. They do not attend your
talk as a group, so do not address them as a group. They attend your talk as
individuals, because they have goals and aspirations and hopes. They hope that
your talk will benefit them in some way as an individual person.

Moreover, you must *understand* your audience. You must understand their
wants and needs, interests and desires. Discover what motivates them. Find
what shames them. Find the common thread among them, then speak to that
common thread as individuals. Build your story with that in mind.

Here is a powerful example of *know your audience* that we visited earlier.

The film *A Time to Kill*, based on the novel by John Grisham, is a motion
picture textbook of storytelling tips. "Know your audience" is demonstrated in
life-or-death fashion by Carl Lee Hailey, a black man on trial in Mississippi for
the murder of two white men who raped his 9-year-old daughter.

The night before the trial's closing arguments, Carl Lee's lawyer Jake visits
Carl Lee in his cell. Jake confides to Carl Lee that he expects to lose the case.

---

2 James A. Winans, *Public Speaking Principles and Practice* (Ithaca, NY: The Sewell Publishing
   Company, 1915), 19.

Jake wants Carl to plead guilty to a lesser charge in a deal with the prosecutor. The guilty plea will save Carl Lee from death row, but it will put him in prison for the rest of his life.

"No!" Carl Lee says. He will have none of it. Carl Lee Hailey then gives Jake a masterful lesson in analyzing and knowing the audience – the jury. He recognizes that Jake is not utilizing his strengths in the courtroom. Jake doesn't see what motivates and what shames his audience of 12 jurors. And because of this, he has not broken through to them. Unless Jake speaks to the deepest prejudices of the jury instead of pretending their prejudices do not exist, Carl Lee has no chance at freedom.

In this case, Jake's analysis of his audience results in a summation targeted at the emotions of the jury. His summation is harsh and gentle simultaneously – it aims at the heart and plays on the feelings both of compassion and of shame. Compassion for a little girl brutalized by thugs, and shame that they might treat the case differently if that little black girl had been white.

In this case, Jake offers the members of the jury the one thing we all crave at some point in our lives – a chance to be a hero. Jake offers the jury members a chance at humanity. He forces them to face their own prejudices. He shames them. At the same time, he shames himself. And then, he offers each of them a chance at redemption. Jake offers each juror a chance to be the hero, a chance to salvage their souls. He crafts a story and leaves the ending – the verdict – up to them.

It is a masterful display of audience analysis and presentation development based on WIIFY. The presentation that Jake develops also serves as the archetype example of the use of story to persuade.

What is *Your* Story?

If you don't have your personal signature story yet, then allot time to weave it. Or rather, make time to *discover* it. And then you can use it in multiple scenarios to good effect. Take a job interview, for instance.

One student asked me this question about job interviews: "How do I say great things about myself without it sounding like I'm bragging about myself? Touting my own accomplishments isn't really humble."

A job interview is not the best time to demonstrate extreme humility, but neither is it the time for arrogance. Of *course* you don't make a straight-up claim about your fine skills and outstanding personality. The solution is a middle course, and it can be done just this way. You tell a story. *Your* story.

Since your story likely emerges from your business school experience, it's appropriate that you spin a story for your interviewer that shares the marvelous things you learn as you grow and develop as a dedicated member of a team. You learn tremendous things about yourself. You face challenges that threaten to take you under, but instead you overcome the odds. You learn skills, you acquire experience, you gain wisdom, you learn to work with others, and you learn to understand them.

You say: "I learned things about myself. I grew in the process. I learned how to work in teams with people of different backgrounds. I learned the important application of knowledge as it meshes with the personalities of the folks I was teamed with. I gained tremendous experience with regard to following through and evaluating and evaluating still *again*."

You share specific interactions you had with someone from a different culture and you involve the sensory perceptions of the listener, weaving all five senses into your story. In short, you involve the interviewer in your personal drama. In doing this, you evoke emotions in them. They become a part of your story. They're along for the ride, and they *feel* your story. This is so much more effective and memorable and *believable* than a straight exposition of your character and skill traits.

Your goal, of course, is to connect with this person and to humanize yourself. Your resume doesn't sell you – it gets you in the door. Firms don't hire resumes, HR persons hire people. They hire people who will work in the next office for the next five years. Because of this, they want to know that you're a *good* person as well as a person qualified.

Your personal story can serve you on the platform as well. When you're searching to connect with an audience in a business presentation, humanizing yourself with a personal story to make a business point is always powerful. It must fit the occasion, of course, but you have enough personal vignettes in your arsenal of experience to fit most occasions.

The Most Important Point – Your MIP

In telling a story, we sometimes veer off-course. We get so enamored with our own words that they build a momentum of their own, and they draw us along with their impetus. It's imperative that we stay tethered to our main point – our Most Important Point.

Christopher Witt is a competent coach for today's executives, and he makes a powerful point about story focus. He calls it the Big Idea:

> A good movie tells one simple, powerful story. If you can't sum it up in a sentence or two, it's not a good story – and it won't make a good

movie. The same is true for a speech. A movie tells one story. A speech develops one idea. But it's got to be a good idea – a policy, a direction, an insight, a prescription. Something that provides clarity and meaning, something that's both intellectually and emotionally engaging. It's got to be what I call a Big Idea.[3]

What's your Big Idea for your presentation? Storyteller Doug Lipman calls this the "Most Important Thing" of a story. We'll call it the Most Important Point – the MIP.[4] And that's what we'll call it from now on.

Decide early on your MIP as you prepare your presentation and weave your story. Decide and make *that* point the focus of your story. Rivet your attention on that salient feature. Let this MIP be core of your story and build around it.

I urge you to focus on one point, because our tendency as business people is to include everything initially, or to add-on *infinitum* until the story collapses under its own weight. The military calls this "mission creep," and we can call it "story creep." Simple awareness of story creep is usually sufficient guard against it.

Your MIP should run through your story, both directly and indirectly. It informs your story and keeps you on-track as you prepare your presentation. At each stage of your presentation preparation, ask yourself and members of your group if the material at hand supports your MIP. If it doesn't, then it doesn't belong in your story.

Telling a story does not mean reliance upon emotion only – you must have substance. There must be a significant conclusion with each supporting point substantiated by research and fact and analytical rigor. Ralph Waldo Emerson stresses this point much better than I can:

Eloquence must be grounded on the plainest narrative. Afterward it may warm itself until it exhales symbols of every kind and color, and speaks only through the most poetic forms; but, first and last, it must still be at bottom a statement of fact. The orator is thereby an orator, that he keeps his feet ever on a fact. Thus only is he invincible. No gifts, no graces, no power of wit or learning or illustration will make any amends for want of this.[5]

3 Christopher Witt, *Real Leaders Don't Do PowerPoint* (New York: Crown Business, 2009), 81.
4 Doug Lipman, *Improving Your Storytelling* (Little Rock: August House, 1999), 87.
5 Ralph W. Emerson, quoted in Grenville Kleiser, *Helpful Hints on Public Speaking* (New York: Funk & Wagnalls Company, 1910), 29.

Imagery – It's Time to Word-Paint Your MIP

We learned the importance of stimulating the senses in our audience to give them a feeling of immediacy, to invite them into your story. With this technique, you create images in your listener's mind. This is one of the major animating objectives of storytelling that gives stories their power.

It's helpful here to think of your audience as one person. One listener, not a gaggle of people with different tastes and preferences. Just one. You address that one person.

When you talk to that person, you want to captivate him, interest him. If you do not interest him, you do not communicate with him. He tunes you out. He checks his cell phone. He thinks of his next meeting. You must capture his interest, and you must hold it.

Capturing attention is easier than you think, and yet the technique is rarely utilized. This is for two reasons: 1) people do not know of it, and 2) many people cannot engage in it comfortably.

Here's how you do it. When you tell your story, you create compelling images. Real images that people can visualize. Abstractions are almost useless in presentations. Theories don't play well in aural settings. No one can visualize a theory. You cannot *see* an abstraction. You cannot visualize "love," but everyone can picture two lovers holding hands, strolling along a beach, the steady sea breeze tossing a young woman's blonde hair.

No one can see "anger," but everyone can visualize a rock-throwing protester shouting political slogans at advancing black-uniformed riot police, their batons thumping a cadence against their Plexiglas shields. You can *feel* anger. You can *feel* love.

You must populate your presentation with people and things. *Real* images that people can visualize. *Images.* You must describe these people and things with gusto and relish and color and sound and light and flavor and smell.

Let's return to the excellent storytelling film *A Time to Kill.* Jake Brigans' summation to the jury at the end of the film is masterful in both form and content. Jake's delivery is sincere, poised, appropriate. He tells a story populated with real people. He knows that the *only way* he can move the jury is to appeal to emotion. Emotion is the only thing that will save his client, Carl Lee Hailey.

Jake's opponent Rufus Buckley is just as determined to prosecute Carl Lee Hailey. Buckley has given the jury a cold "points of law" summation and has appealed to the sense of the jury's "civic duty." He has appealed to their intellect.

Jake knows that he cannot save his client on "points of law." He *cannot*. He must overcome not only that his client is actually guilty of the deeds, but also that this Mississippi jury is largely prejudiced against African-Americans.

So with the knowledge that he cannot move the jury with fact and exposition, Jake risks everything on an appeal to emotions. He intends to make us feel pain, compassion and anger. He wants us to *feel* the rage and helplessness that his client felt, so that we might place ourselves in Carl Lee Hailey's moment of truth. So that we might see things through *his* eyes at that moment.

Jakes talks of "sweat" and "drunken breath." He talks about a little girl "soaked in their urine, soaked in their semen, soaked in her blood."[6]

He evokes powerful imagery, and drills the story into the minds and hearts of the jury. He asks the jury time and again: "Can you see her?"

"Can you see her?"

This is an extreme example of the power of story, and the same technique is can be used in almost any business presentation. Yes, you *can* do this with your presentation. It is powerful and moving, and people in your audience actually *want* to hear what you say. You gain incredible satisfaction doing it.

Concreteness

The technique of *concreteness* means specificity. Relish details. Stay away from the vague, and be explicit with what you say. "The story is not to be turned into an abstraction; its concreteness is the secret of its power to please and to move."[7]

Bringing details and specificity to our stories is not as easy as it sounds. Bad habits work against us when we speak. Nowadays, details suffer in the rush to be quick and sassy. We engage in *faux* communication daily. Some communication experts estimate that we generally use only 250 unique words per day in our conversations with others. Instead of rich, full-bodied and meaningful sentences, we talk in *cliché* and shorthand with nary a slip of originality.

---

6 *A Time to Kill*, DVD, directed by Joel Schumacher (1996; Burbank, CA: Warner Home Video, 1997).
7 Angela M. Keyes, *Stories and Story-Telling* (New York and London: D. Appleton & Company, 1916), 20.

Our conversation, especially among young people, tends toward using the hippest phraseology as often as possible. I won't even attempt to reprint examples of that vernacular, because it changes so rapidly. It would be out of date before these words saw print.

But you know of what I speak. You use it yourself. You use it because it's safe. It marks us as nonthreatening as a member of the group. A subscriber to the group ethos, whether politically based, ethnically based, socially based, or based on some other chosen affinity.

Reducing our vocabulary to the lowest common denominator of slang homogenizes us and molds us like everyone else in our chosen circle, as someone who will not upset the apple cart of our fragile psyches. It's part of the script in the play you're performing. It's also stale and unimaginative, and it limits you. But why is this bad? Isn't it just harmless slang?

Abstract slang substitutes for original idea and creative expression. It's mental graffiti. It marks you as "hip" and as someone who does not force others to think too much about what you say. It relieves you of the burden of crafting anything genuine or original. It relieves your buddies of the burden of hearing something unfamiliar, fresh, and new. It's the ejaculation of blunt, low-level feeling that becomes part of our repertoire of saying without saying.

This type of ersatz communication thrives because we live in a world where imprecision is often rewarded, where ambiguity protects us. It's a world where prominent businessman J. Pierpont Morgan's philosophy has been quoted as "Think much, say little, write nothing."[8] Abdication of responsibility rules the day.

Yes, slang *is* harmless. And it's useless. *Faux* thought. If your goal as a speaker is to appear "harmless" and unoriginal then you have achieved your goal.

Perhaps there is something to be said for such a philosophy, but it needn't compel you to be uninteresting. It doesn't dictate that you bore your listeners. Discard the slang and strive for something real. Concrete. Specific.

This principle has informed successful speakers for centuries. It's a principle that has weathered storm and ephemeral trend. Concreteness provides tangible grist for your listener's mill. It evokes an image in the mind. Take this from 1886:

> Concrete ideas render a composition beautiful by filling the mind with pictures. The abstract is dry and devoid of power over the imagination.

---

8 Peter Austin, review of *The World of Private Banking* by Youssef Cassis and Philip Cottrell (eds), published by EH.NET (June 2010), http://eh.net/book_reviews/world-private-banking (accessed July 26, 2012).

Concrete ideas have form and sometimes color, and so appeal to the mind through material objects which are their symbols. Such a use of language is sometimes called 'word-painting.'[9]

Let's take an example. Let's look only at the notion of "imagery" now. Later, we'll combine this into the notion of telling a story. But for now, visualize your slice of a group presentation and the concrete images you want to evoke in your listeners. Let's look at something quite practical, almost mundane – deodorant.

Marketing Deodorant

Let's say that your product is Axe Deodorant, and your section of the presentation is on marketing. The usual approach is to assemble facts and figures from a written report and to cram them onto three PowerPoint slides. You believe that the "Four Ps" of marketing should figure prominently in this section and a SWOT analysis, and a finance analysis. Sure, but at this point, let's break the task down.

Assess your portion of the story. Is it market share? Market growth? Marketing strategy? Market expansion overseas? A new product?

That's your MIP. In illustrating your MIP, there should be movement in your story, a change of some sort.

Market share: Is it growing or shrinking?

Market strategy: Is there a new initiative and is it successful?

New product: The puzzle and drama of a new product, how it's launched, and how it's received.

Now conjure the best way to word-paint your Most Important Point – your MIP. For instance, let's say that your MIP is that the specific demographic for Axe is young men ages 12-18, and this market is growing rapidly. You *could* take the usual staid approach as say something like:

"Our US target market is young men aged 12 to 18. It's growing rapidly, and we believe that this translates into continued growth for the foreseeable future."

There is nothing particularly wrong with this sentence, aside from its vagueness. It is not sharply drawn, and it does not showcase a key point of the presentation. It's forgettable.

---

9 David J. Hill, *The Elements of Rhetoric and Composition* (New York and Chicago: Sheldon & Company, 1886), 148.

Instead, you could do what a student of mine did in this very situation. Prior to the presentation, this student used birth-rate data to calculate the approximate growth rate of the target demographic in the United States of young males ages 12 to 18. Then, armed with this information, he pulled it out in the middle of his presentation segment this way:

He mentioned a rapidly growing target market segment, just as anyone would do in his position. The standard approach:

"Our target market segment of 12 to 18-year-olds is growing fast."

But then he transformed his presentation with a bit of concrete magic. He paused for effect. He then casually turned to a teammate and asked: "How long have we been talking here? Ten minutes?" His partner nodded. The speaker returned his look to the audience.

"Since we began this presentation 10 minutes ago, our target segment has grown by 27,000 potential customers." He paused again. "Now that's *growth!*"

The reaction in the audience was palpable. A murmur of approval rippled through the room. Students looked at each other, raised eyebrows, nodded. The audience exhibited all the visual cues that the speaker had actually connected with his listeners.

This was so much more powerful than a simple statement of market growth. You see how it works? This wasn't brilliant, and it wasn't rocket science. It wasn't a gimmick. It was simply appropriate use of the technique of *concreteness*. It resulted from imagination and creativity. The student chose his MIP, and answered the simple question: "How can I make this concrete for my audience?" His answer was to create an effective vehicle that enabled his audience to actually visualize – actually *experience*, in a way – the growth of the Axe target market.

Another way of projecting this fact visually is the use of PowerPoint's animation feature to portray the steady increase in the number of young men in the US – having cartoon figures of people appearing every three seconds, each figure representing 100 people.

The possibilities are many, and once you train yourself to think this way, to concretize your MIP and search for creative ways to illustrate it, you should have little trouble finding the proper visual or appropriate concrete terms to word-paint your MIP.

At first, it may sound and feel strange to seize words and phrases that you rarely use in your own conversation. Words and phrases that would never occur to you to use in a "business presentation." It is this plumbing of our imaginations that can lead to the most powerful and effective presentations – the use of creative examples, words, and images to startle and delight our audience. We want to get our audience to make satisfying connections, to visualize our points in unique ways, and to understand our points such that agreement comes logically and easily.

Conclusion

Business cases have inherent interest. There is natural drama, natural excitement. Gold is hidden in the numbers. Treasure is buried in the narrative. There is a story. A *natural* story. There are many stories, in fact. There is excitement to be found. Energy to be released. Emotions to be tapped. Enthusiasms to be kindled.

Storytelling is the one skill you can wield to tap into all that potential and lift your presenting into the stratosphere. It is so little practiced that it stands out in the best way possible. It gives your presentation depth, power and nuance. It colors your presentation and makes it memorable. Teach yourself to recognize a powerful story, and then adapt it for your own.

Start today telling business stories using the themes and techniques in this section of the book. Don't stumble through your stories or second-guess yourself. Don't mumble and shift your feet. Furrow your brow and tell me a story as if *you* believe it and desperately want *me* to believe it. Tell me a sincere business story the same way you grub for points for your GPA, the way you offer an impassioned plea for a class absence, the way you apologize to the professor when you've been called out for bad decorum in the classroom. When this happens to you, you instinctively give the professor a chance to be the hero and show compassion for a distraught student – *you*.

See how you already tell stories all the time? And when you want something from the professor, you tell that story with as much passion, emphasis, and emotion as possible. Try investing that passion in your next presentation.

PART IV

GROUP PRESENTATIONS

Introduction

Four of the most dreaded words in business school are: "Break yourselves into groups."

The group presentation is one of those universal experiences you face in business school, and it's one of the most dreaded, if not outright hated.

Many business students despise "group work," particularly those who do not enjoy relying upon others and instead seek evaluation for what we achieve as individuals. This is quite natural for us in the United States, who have a cultural climate that identifies us as mavericks, individualists, hardy pioneers, and entrepreneurs.[1]

But group work in business school is so ubiquitous now that almost every upper level course has some form of "group work" requirement. In most US business schools, you can expect to participate in more than 20 group presentations in your academic career. In other countries of the world, where the collectivist ethos is prevalent, particularly schools in Asia, group work is elevated to almost cult status and collaboration is highly developed.

There's a reason for all of this business school group work. Today's modern corporations expect their new hires to have experience working in groups *and* they expect superb communication skills. So your professor doesn't force you into groups because he simply enjoys making you miserable.

The upshot is that you *must* give "group presentations." *Many* of them.

This section of *The Complete Guide* takes you through the process of the group presentation and make plain what is expected of you. Rather than an arduous

---

1 See Geert Hofstede's Dimensions of Culture project that identifies the strength of certain cultural traits in more than 100 countries: www.geert-hofstede.com.

task, the group presentation can serve as a source of career benefit to you for years to come. With the right attitude and the knowledge to go with it, you can elevate and accelerate your career by developing superb individual and group presentation acumen. Moreover, you can test your mettle against the best business teams in the country and in the world by participating in case competitions. The last chapter of this section provides the only published full-blown guide to case competitions.

THE CURSE AND BLESSING
OF GROUP PRESENTATIONS

Students abhor group presentations for several reasons.

First, it removes control of your classroom fate from you and puts your grade in the hands of others whom you don't know well. These classmates are people you may not even *like*. You don't even get to choose them. This also happens in the real work world.

Second, your professor probably did not tell you how to deliver the presentation, what he expects, or even how you'll be graded. It's all kind of vague. Much like the real working world.

Third, your professor seems impervious to any complaint you make regarding the first two points above. In fact, he's downright cold about it. Much like your boss in the real working world.

All of this perplexes you and frustrates you. You're accustomed to learning, reviewing, and then regurgitating material – pretty straightforward stuff. But this? This is ambiguous.

You find all sorts of difficulties in group work. Anyone who has participated in a group project in college knows this. Perhaps you believe these problems are external? *Others* cause them, right? Surely *you* must not be contributing to the challenges facing your group? Let's examine the sources of group work agitation so that we can understand and overcome these challenges before they get out-of-hand.

The Challenge of Group Presentations

The first major challenge of group work is the unpredictability of your situation. One key characteristic of group presentations is that there are many uncertainties over which you have no control. The project appears submerged in ambiguity that you seem powerless to affect. It is bad enough to face the unknown variables of case analysis in a business presentation, but in a group presentation, several *other* variables are added to the mix. The most unpredictable variables of all – other people.

We *all* prefer to control our own destiny. Most all of us want to be judged on our own work. We like to work *alone*. This is very much the craftsman's view. Our labors are important to us. We take pride in our work.

But with group work, the waters muddy. It becomes difficult to identify who is doing what, and consequently, we worry about who will get the credit. We worry if there will even *be* any credit to distribute if our presentation collapses under the burden of multiple minds, differing opinions and people who seem not to care. We worry that our contribution will be overlooked, that someone else will take credit for *our* work.

We see ourselves becoming submerged. As we sink into kind of group ethos, our individual identity is threatened. How will the boss, the professor, or anyone else, know what we do? How will they know *our* contribution? Worse, what if we get saddled with a reputation for poor work because someone *else* screwed up?

The second major challenge is the ordeal of time management and schedule coordination. Six different students, each with differing class schedules and who may work part-time, must somehow schedule time to work together. You may be involved in several classes that require group projects. And you invariably are faced with the pathology of one or two team members who "don't have time for this." So the difficulties mentioned here multiply.

Why the Group Presentation? It's a Complex World

The group presentation is not an easy task. It can be downright painful and infuriating. It can turn student–against–student faster than anything else in college outside of Greek rush. So why do your professors require them? Why do *all* of your business school professors seem determined to put you through this misery?

You've probably heard the spurious reasons. One student myth is that professors assign group work so they can cut their own grading work load. The reasoning goes something like this: it's easier for a professor to grade six presentations or papers than to grade 30 individual papers. This myth is so pervasive that it has become conventional wisdom among students. There are three big problems with this.

First, by definition, individual work is not group work. If group work is an essential part of the workplace experience, then individual papers or other assignments do not contribute at all to the learning experience that is specifically designed to prepare you for the workplace.

Second, professors often are *required* to assign some form of group work in their courses. The prevailing pedagogy in many business schools advocates the group work experience as essential to prepare students for the twenty-first century workplace. Frankly, this is the way it should be.

Third, this myth assumes that professors enjoy watching students stumble their way through awkward presentations that are poorly prepared and half-heartedly delivered. While you, as a student, prepare for only one or two presentations, the professor oftentimes must watch 15 to 20 presentations in course of a semester and then evaluate them. I assure you that this can be an unpleasant experience.

The proverbial bottom line that we all talk about in business school is that you do "group work" because it is essential to the twenty-first century business world.

The Second-Most-Desired Skill

Corporate recruiters have cited Dartmouth's Tuck School of Business as topping the national rankings precisely because of the school's emphasis on teamwork and collaboration.[1] So why not embrace the group presentation as a necessary component of your school experience and one essential to your transition into the corporate world?

---

1 "Of all the attributes, recruiters said interpersonal and communication skills, a teamwork orientation, personal ethics and integrity, analytical and problem-solving abilities, and a strong work ethic matter most to them."

"Dartmouth's Tuck School of Business in Hanover, N.H., resumed its winning streak as survey respondents repeatedly praised its students for being down-to-earth team players. Tuck received its highest ratings this year for its 'well-rounded' students, their personal integrity, interpersonal and communication skills, and teamwork abilities."

"Tuck students live and breathe teamwork," says Douglas Asano, a survey respondent and director, inside sales, for J.M. Huber Corp. in Charlotte, NC. "The admissions process requires applicants to have a demonstrated excellence in teamwork, and then the faculty, curriculum and culture inculcate a practical understanding of teamwork at every step of the Tuck experience." Many recruiters also cited Tuck for excellence in teaching strategy and general management. Ronald Alsop, "Recruiters' Top Schools," *Wall Street Journal,* September 17, 2007. http://online.wsj.com/article/SB118961224646225232.html (accessed July 26, 2012).

The days of the business generalist are all but dead in modern multi-national business. Specialization rules the business workplace, and the manipulation of knowledge is ascendant. This means, from a practical standpoint, that we cannot produce major products by ourselves. We must collaborate.

There is little doubt that you will become one of these knowledge-workers at some point after graduation. You also will begin to specialize in certain work, especially if you join a large firm. This is because business operations today are incredibly complex and fast-paced. These two factors make it almost impossible for any one person to isolate themselves from the combined operations of the firm. Major tasks are divided and divided again. Think of it as an extreme form of division of labor. So we *must* work with others. The globalized and complex business context demands it.

"Cross-functional teams" is business-speak for how we deal with operations complexity. With increasing specialization of the workforce comes the necessity of integrating these specialized niches into a smoothly functioning unit.

Is this process pleasant? Judging from the reactions I get in class-after-class, year-by-year – no it is not pleasant. In fact, students seem to think it is akin to pulling teeth, a slow torture that drags on for weeks. They'd rather be doing… what?

What would you rather be doing?

You see this is the great conundrum and truth. You'd rather be doing something else, but that unnamed and imaginary "something else" that you *think* you'd really enjoy *does not exist*.

Moreover, this imaginary something will not help you acquire the job of your dreams. It surely won't help you more than the group work you've been assigned in your classes – group work that is designed *explicitly* to prepare you for your chosen profession.

Surely there is the outside chance that you can land a post-graduation position bereft of group work. You may find some semblance of your ideal solitary work-position in a highly technical job that commits you to laboring in a fuzzy fabric-board cubicle for the rest of your four-decade career. If that appeals to you, I wish you well. *But…*

I wager that you want to succeed in the world of the corporation, where high finance meets strategy meets marketing. Or in the world of entrepreneurship, where close collaboration means you daily rub shoulders with small, tight groups. This requires you to develop skill in two areas outside of your narrow specialization:

1. Presenting

2. Group work

The sooner you embrace the presentation and group work as essential components of your school experience, the smoother and more successful your business school experience, and the more successful you are upon graduation.

In fact, you might actually start to enjoy group work. Here's how.

Uncertainty: The Source of Dysfunction, Dissatisfaction and Anger

Stripped of fancy jargon, here is *the problem*. The professor requires you to organize and deliver a group presentation, but you *don't know how to organize and deliver a group presentation*. The professor often won't tell you how or what or why, except in vague terms.

It's up to you to meet with five other people you may not like or even know and somehow *work things out*. This is the critical juncture where most of the friction in group work is generated – needless uncertainty.

Oftentimes, it's this uncertainty that challenges us the most. This is the case with presentations. But we can often improve our situation by subtraction; by simply removing what it is that nettles us. In this case, it's the uncertainty revolving around *how to organize and deliver a group presentation*. In learning how to organize and deliver a group presentation, many of the personality and work habit problems that plague us simply won't come up. If they do come up, you'll know how to deal with them.

Let's get started.

Some basics: What is a group presentation?

Unless you're a freshman, you have been forced into this mode of work so many times that you've grown familiar with it. I fervently hope that I've caught you at the beginning of your business school career so that you launch your "group work" ethos properly.

Group work can vary according to professor, class, and subject, but its elements are standard. We're concerned at this point with the group assignment that requires you to analyze a case as a team and then to present your findings in a public presentation to your class.

Your professor assigns you a project with a specific time frame that requires you to work with other students – usually three to five others – and to produce a final written group project that usually culminates in a *presentation*.

The group presentation can be delivered in any number of forums, but in the business school you will deliver most all of your presentations in front of your classmates and your professor. The venue is usually your classroom.

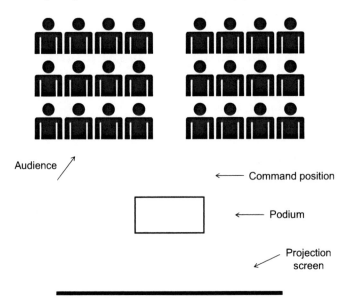

Your classroom could feature several seating arrangements, but you will face only one or two variations – perhaps a tiered semicircular amphitheater arrangement or a traditional classroom style.

The illustration depicts a typical classroom arrangement that we will use throughout these chapters to demonstrate various facets of the group presentation. Familiarize yourself with the components, which are simple and straightforward.

Audience

Your audience is almost always your fellow undergraduates, although you may have the chance to present before groups of professors, graduate students, administrators, or outside business people.

For some reason, I observe that it appears more difficult for students to present seriously and earnestly before their peers. Perhaps the air of familiarity leads to lackluster performances. Maybe it's peer pressure *not* to excel at this particular activity, a fear of appearing "uncool." Perhaps it's a tacit cooperative arrangement to depress performances so as not to make other groups look bad by comparison.

Regardless of the reasons why you may shy from performing at your best for the audience, *every* opportunity to present before a live group should be seized with relish – it's a rare chance to sharpen skills in a cost-free environment. Your audience is your main purpose for delivering your presentation. Don't lose sight of that fact. It does not matter how "good" your material is in the abstract if your audience cannot receive the message, digest it, and understand it during your presentation.

Podium / lectern

This monstrosity comes in a limited variety of shapes and sizes, none of which aid your presentation. No worse crutch could have been invented to prop up the ineffective speaker, both literally and figuratively. By turns it is a shield, a fence post, an isometric exerciser. The podium offers little in the way of added value.

This negative can be turned to your advantage; the more people who grip the podium with white knuckles, the more your 3D presentations shine. However, the podium sometimes provides you the electronic control panel from which you manipulate your presentation, so consider it a necessary evil.

Command position

Refer to the illustration and note the "command position" directly in front of the podium and facing your audience. I refer to this *command position* often. This is your new home, and I want you comfortable with it. It's an area ripe for exploitation in delivering a powerful message. You can double the impact of your presentation by stepping out from behind the podium and utilizing the magic of the command position.

This simple stepping away from the podium is such a powerful technique, because by doing so, you remove a significant physical barrier between you and your audience. You step closer to your audience physically and metaphorically, and you have gained immeasurable communicative power.

Projection screen

The screen that displays your PowerPoint slides is not a magical totem. You and the audience are not gathered to worship the PowerPoint. Do *not* turn to read your slides or stare at the screen when you lose your train of thought. Sure, glance at the screen to ensure that the proper image is displayed, but then immediately return your attention to your audience.

Interact with your slides as appropriate when they appear on the screen. I have emphasized this in earlier chapters, but it bears repeating. When you want audience attention directed to the screen for detailed viewing, walk to the screen and interact with it. *Touch* it to emphasize points if you must.

When you walk to the screen and stand beside it, it closes the distance between you and what your audience must look at – there is no divided attention.

Conclusion

This chapter has provided the basics of the group presentation – what it is, why it's important, and some of the rudimentary elements of presenting in a group. The following chapters continue to flesh out the concepts and principles of group presenting so to make them as painless as possible and as superb as they can be.

GROUP PRESENTATIONS I:
GETTING READY

Group Dynamics – "How come I never get a good group?"

You have been assigned to a group and a business case. Now, you must deliver a group presentation. Recognize that you have been thrown together with a purpose in mind and that you will disagree with one another, perhaps often. You *will* disagree with each other on aspects of the presentation. *How* you disagree and *how* you resolve those disagreements for the good of the team and your presentation is as important as the presentation itself.

It's essential that you maintain civil relations, if not cordial relations, with others in the group – *don't* burn bridges. You do not want to engender dislike for people, perhaps for the rest of your life. The people in the various group projects will form an important part of your network in years to come. Remember that the relationship is paramount, the presentation itself is secondary.

Your job is to craft a group experience, assign responsibilities and develop a reasonable schedule. Some members of your group will make time commitment choices that do not appear aligned with the objectives of the group. You hear phrases such as "I'm not able to be at the meeting." You may hear the outright arrogance of "I don't have time for this." *This*, of course, is simply a choice to be somewhere else to spend time in other pursuits, because everyone has the same amount of time, no more and no less. Different people make different choices about the use of their time. Recognize that this will happen and that it is neither good nor bad – it is simply the hand that you are dealt. How you react to it will in large part determine the success of your group.

I always communicate to my students what to expect in a six-person group. The 2-2-2 rule will usually hold. Two people work hard, two cooperate and are damned happy to be there, and two rarely show up, because they have "busy schedules." Another popular take on it is to apply the Pareto 80-20 rule: eighty percent of the work is done by twenty percent of the people.

Regardless of how you couch it, do not take your group woes to the professor for solution. Your professor doesn't appreciate it any more than your CEO or VP superior appreciates solving your personnel issues. It reflects badly on you and gives an impression of weakness.

How to Attack the Problem of the "Case"

Most business schools use the "case method." This is a superior teaching tool to learn how to solve contemporary business problems. You are required to read and analyze a "case." Then you present the "solutions" – the results of your analysis and your consequent strategic recommendations.

A case is a story, a little slice of business history. It is a story about a business situation that usually involves the challenges facing a particular company in a specific industry at a specific time in its history.

Cases don't just "happen." They are written with instruction in mind, to the end of solving certain clearly identifiable problems that face many businesses.

The European Case Clearing House (ECCH) is the world's largest repository of business cases from around the world. The ECCH describes its case studies this way: "Case studies recount real life business or management situations that present business executives with a dilemma or uncertain outcome. The case describes the scenario in the context of the events, people and factors that influence it and enables students to identify closely with those involved."[1]

A business case provides you with information about the business situation in narrative form. At the end of the case, you usually find data in the form of statements, photographs, annual reports, and such like. This information varies from case-to-case and depends on the purpose to which the case is directed.

What should you do with this "case?"

The first thing to recognize in the situation is that cases are not written about mundane or routine situations in the life of a company or industry. *Something has changed.* Something has changed either in the company, in the industry, or in the greater business environment. You would not be reading the case if

---

1   "ECCH: The Case for Learning," European Case Clearing House, http://www.ecch.com/educators/casemethod/introduction/whatis (accessed June 19, 2012).

something significant had not happened to the company in question, either positive or negative. Let's take an example to illustrate the point: the case of our imaginary firm ToughBolt Corporation.

ToughBolt Corporation has been a profitable firm for more than 30 years, manufacturing and selling widgets in several countries. The company has been profitable and successful by the usual business metrics – market share, company growth, return on capital. But *something has changed*, and now ToughBolt must respond to the change. This has prompted the writing of the "Toughbolt Case."

What's going on here?

What could have changed? This is the question you should ask yourself as you read any case.

Perhaps several new competitors have entered the market, changing the industry dynamics. Perhaps ToughBolt's margins and market share are shrinking. Perhaps new products and processes are making ToughBolt's products obsolete. Perhaps ToughBolt has not adapted to demographic changes in the workforce and is suffering labor discord. Perhaps customer tastes and preferences are changing.

Your team goes to work on the case, discussing possible answers to these questions. Your team brings to bear various tools of analysis to disassemble the case, discover what is really happening, what forces are at work, identify the problem(s), and recommend courses of action that can return the firm to solvency and success. You then aggregate all of this and prepare a presentation.

If you are presented with a case and guidance questions, everyone should, of course, read the case. At your meeting, rather than jumping in to divvy-up and assign research areas to your members, *first* discuss the case and decide on the situation statement. It helps if you understand how and why a case is written. Discuss and agree upon the elements of the case – identify the industry, identify the company, identify the product, identify the *problem*.

Ask what is happening in this slice of business life and why. What should be fixed, what should be changed, what should stay the same? I have found a superb overarching question is "What's going on here?" The answer to that question is your situation statement.

You are producing a play. It *is* a show, remember? It must be choreographed and rehearsed. Above all, approach your task seriously. Prepare well and then practice hard. Should you not, your audience will know in an instant. You will earn its animosity.

A serious study of this subject should so increase one's respect for the power of speech and give one such a realization of the difficulty and the responsibility of holding the attention for ten minutes or an hour of a hundred or a thousand people, that speaking will not be undertaken lightly, without something to say worth saying or without due preparation.[2]

Preparation

Let's say that you are assigned the ToughBolt, Inc. business case, and your group has produced a solid written analysis, a task that you are more than capable of doing. It's finished. Now, what do you do? How do you "prepare?"

Your task is clear. You must present your conclusions to an audience. And here is where I give you one of the most important pieces of information necessary to giving a first-rate show:

> *Your presentation is a completely different product than your written report.*

Completely different. Do you wonder how this is possible, since you create your presentation from your written report? Since you create an information product from your own case, how can the product be different, simply because one product is written and the other visual and vocal?

It is different in exactly the same way that a film is a completely different product than a novel, even if the story is supposedly the same. It is different in the way that a play read silently from the page differs from a play acted out on stage. Your presentation is present-oriented and can be a precarious affair. Consider:

- You operate in a different medium
- You have time constraints
- A group is receiving your message
- A group is delivering the message
- You have almost no opportunity for repeat
- You have multiple opportunities for miscommunication

In short, you are in a high-risk environment and you are vulnerable, far more vulnerable than you might be in a written report where the risk is much more controllable.

---

2 James A. Winans, *Public Speaking* (New York: The Century Co., 1926), 17.

Medium	Vocal and visual	Silent and visual
Time	Constraint	No constraint
Audience	Many	One
Delivery	Several people	One person / no person
Length	Tight limit	Loose limit
Variables	Many and uncontrolled	Few and controlled
Production	Complex	Simple

These many differences between written and oral reports are, to many people, unseen. Countless folks believe that there *is* no difference. This is why those same people believe that delivering a presentation is "easy."

For these folks, it consists of little more than cutting and pasting a written report's points onto a half-dozen cramped slides, and then reading them in public. As absurd as this perspective might appear in print, it actually has currency. People believe this, because they haven't been told otherwise.

"How come I never get assigned an interesting topic?"

Perhaps you've said that? I've certainly heard it. "How come I never get assigned an interesting topic?"

I believe that there is no such thing as an inherently uninteresting topic. Nor is there an inherently interesting topic. Interest is something that *you* generate when you combine your unique gifts and training to create something special. Creating interest is *your* job. In fact, that's what you're paid to do upon graduation.

Cases are not assigned so that they will interest you – no one cares if they interest you. That's not the point. Whether or not you find your topic interesting is irrelevant; it is your duty to craft a talk that interests the audience.

We all would love to be spoon-fed "interesting" topics. But what's an "interesting" topic? I have found the following to be true:

The students who complain about never getting an interesting topic actually do get assigned topics that are rich with potential and ripe for exploitation. Students don't recognize them as "interesting" because their store of internal information and context either is not there or is untapped. So they invariably neglect their research, butcher a potentially interesting topic, and miss every cue and opportunity to craft a great presentation. The upshot is that if you don't take presenting seriously, then you won't do anything different for an "interesting" topic than you would for a "boring" topic.

Now let's shuck that attitude if it's anywhere in the room. In fact, it might be a good idea to begin your group meetings by weaving into your discussions the best points of the case for potential exploitation in your presentation.

Good students recognize the drama, conflict and possibilities in every case. They invariably craft an interesting presentation regardless of the topic. How do you generate interest? Public speaking master James Winans provides several suggestions:

> [I]nterest is, generally speaking, strongest in old things in new settings, looked at from new angles, given new forms and developed with new facts and ideas, with new light on familiar characters, new explanations of familiar phenomena, or new applications of old truths.[3]

Let's have a look at how to assemble a winning presentation. The typical start to a presentation project is procrastination. You put it off as a daunting task. Or you put it off because you believe you can "wing it." Or you lament that you don't have an "interesting topic." Or a "good group." Or you "don't have time for this." These are just excuses for refusing to grapple with a task that seems amorphous. Instead, let's make it real and vow to tackle its initial stages *immediately*.

Start by selecting the best overall framework for your case, then decide on the major points to include.

Your presentation framework

There is no single prescribed method for organizing your presentation, but the guidelines in this section chart the way. Organizing frameworks help you make sense of a bewildering array of facts, data, and opinion.

Regardless of your station in school, your position in a company, or the industry in which you work, organizing a presentation is virtually the same process. Several frameworks can get you started quickly.

---

3 James A. Winans, *Public Speaking Principles and Practice* (Ithaca, NY: The Sewell Publishing Company, 1915), 72.

Think of these organizing frameworks as the skeleton around which you build your presentation. The framework you select is not your story. It's the structure – the *vessel* – for your story. David Nowell of Sheridan College suggests several ways to organize the presentation:

- Here is a problem, here is why it is serious, here's a solution

- Here's how it was then, how it is now and the implications of these changes

- Three reasons to…

- Past, present, future

- From the general to the particular (deductive approach), or from the particular to the general (inductive reasoning)

- Thesis, then list pros, cons and a conclusion

- The Good, the Bad and the Solution

- Problem / solution[4]

These are simple and powerful guides to presentation structure, and you are bound to find one that serves to showcase your assigned case in the best manner.

What to include

You have a welter of information and keen analysis that you would love to include in your case, but you can't present it all. How do you select what to include and what to omit?

Let's say that your task is to provide a SWOT within the body of a group presentation, and your time is four to five minutes. What is your actual task here? Think about it. How do you usually approach the task? How do you characterize it?

Here is my guess at how you approach it. You define your task as:

How can I fit X amount of information into this limited time?

In your own mind, the objective is not to communicate clearly to your audience. Your implicit objective is to "fit it all in." And if you "achieve" this dubious objective, then in your mind you will have succeeded.

---

4 David Nowell, "The Group Presentation," *Building Group Presentations* (2005), http://www-acad.sheridanc.on.ca/~nowell/presentations/grouppres.htm (accessed June 20, 2012).

Unfortunately, your professor might agree with you, since many business school professors look only for "content." They don't usually evaluate whether the content has been communicated clearly and effectively.[5]

So this is the missing component – you typically don't analyze how, why or in what way you can present the information in a public forum, shaping it to the visual/vocal medium. Instead, you attempt to twist the medium itself to match the written analysis – without success.

If a written paper has already been produced, this complicates your task, and the result is predictable. You end up trying to shovel 10 pounds of sand into a five-pound pail. The result is less than stellar. Your slides are crammed with unreadable information. You talk fast to force all the points in, so no one can possibly digest it. You run over-time.

This time Procrustes has it right

To fix this problem, I recommend a radical solution. I advise that you take the Procrustean approach. This approach is named after Procrustes, a figure from Greek mythology. The Columbia Encyclopedia describes the myth thus:

> He forced passersby to lie on a very long bed and then stretched them to fit it. Some said that he also had a very short bed; to make passersby fit this he sawed off their legs. Using Procrustes' own villainous methods, Theseus killed him.[6]

Surely Procrustes was a villain, what with sawing off people's legs or stretching them to fit an arbitrary standard. In modern-day parlance, it has retained its negative connotation with the term "Procrustean solution." The "Procrustean solution" is the undesirable practice of tailoring data to fit its container or some

---

5 Of course, there will be vociferous disagreement from my colleagues who *do* care much about style and communication and who *do* evaluate presentations apart from the criteria they use to grade written work. These hardy souls are in the minority, and of course I do not refer to them. But the unfortunate truth is that too many business school professors do not take seriously enough the presentation process with regard to presenting *as a skill*. Is there hard data to back up that claim? Of course not, and I welcome suggestions as to how one might go about collecting data on professors, data that might indicate that their skills are substandard in a particular area. That won't happen, of course. And so we must rely upon what is derided as "anecdotal evidence." And because we rely upon anecdotal evidence, you have my full cooperation in dismissing my comments here as unwarranted. Meanwhile, let's learn something new.

6 "Procrustes." *Columbia Encyclopedia*, 6th ed. (2011), at Encyclopedia.com, http://www.encyclopedia.com/doc/1E1-Procrust.html (accessed June 20, 2012).

other preconceived structure. A common example from the business world is embodied in the notion that no résumé should exceed one page in length.

But in this case, let's give Procrustes a break. Let's take a Procrustean approach and make a better presentation. Consider this: we have no choice in the length of our presentation. It's four or five minutes. That's our Procrustean Bed. So let's make the most of it and manipulate the situation to our benefit and to the benefit of our audience.

We're not stretching someone or something. And we're not hacking off legs. We are using our mind and judgment to select what should be in our show and what should not be in our show. If you find the decision of what to include too difficult, then let's do even more Procrustean manipulation. Pick only three major points that you want to make. Only three. Now, here is your modified task:

Pick three points to deliver in one segment of four to five minutes. If you must deliver an entire SWOT, then select one strength, one weakness, one opportunity, and one threat.

Here is why we do this: if you try to crowbar an entire SWOT analysis into a four-minute presentation, with multiple points for each category, you overwhelm your audience. They turn off and tune you out. You lose them, and you fail.

Presenting too many points is worse than presenting only one point. If you present, say, a total of five strengths, three weaknesses, four opportunities, and three threats, no one remembers any of it. Moreover, you irritate your audience mercilessly. Your presentation should offer the results of analysis, not a laundry list of facts on which you base your analysis. The SWOT is, in fact, almost raw data.

Your job is to sift through the mountains of information available, synthesize it, compress it, make it intelligible, then present it in a way that is understandable and, if possible, entertaining. You are taking information and transforming it into intelligence. You winnow out the chaff, and leave only the wheat. You reduce the static and white noise so that the communicative signal can be heard. You are panning for gold, washing away the detritus so the nuggets can be found. When you buy gold, you don't buy the waste product from which it was drawn. You don't want the audience to remember how you massaged the data, analyzed it, and arranged it. You want the audience to remember your *conclusions* and *recommendations*.

Practice

There is good practice and there is bad practice. But how can you say, Professor Ridgley, that there is such a thing as "bad practice?" Aren't you pleased that students who practice are at least practicing?

No, I am not pleased. Bad practice is pernicious. It can have an insidious effect. It can create the illusion of improvement and yet be a prelude to disaster. Let me explain. Practice is one of those words that we never bother to define, because each of us already "knows" what it means. Certainly your professor thinks you know what it means, since he urges you to "practice" your presentation prior to its delivery.

But what does it mean to "practice?" How do *you* practice?

Practice – the *right* practice, *good* practice, *proper* rehearsal – is the key to so much of your presentation's success and to your ultimate triumph. The Russians have a saying much akin to one of ours. We say "practice makes perfect." The Russians say *"Povtoreniya mat' ucheniya."* It means "Repetition is the mother of learning."

The key to confidence is knowledge and preparation. We lack confidence when we are unsure. With every practice, we gain confidence. The nerves that go with public speaking are like the nerves a soldier feels as he walks through a minefield – he fears a single misstep will trigger an explosion. But once the minefield is traversed a single time, the path is clear. With a clear and predictable path, the fear evaporates. The danger is avoided. The fear is gone, replaced with confidence and the soldier strides the open path with confidence.

Likewise, once you have practiced your talk, your fear dissipates. Once you have practiced it *exactly* like you will deliver it, straight to completion without pause, *then* you will have reduced the unknown to manageable proportions. The gigantic and fearsome phantasmagoria is shrunk. Your way through the minefield is clear, and the fear evaporates.

It really is that simple. "The best way for a young speaker to master his nervousness is to let the subject master him, to yield himself to his theme, to sink his own fears beneath his enthusiasm for truth."[7] This doesn't mean that you won't have butterflies before a talk or that you won't be nervous. We all suffer stage fright to some extent, and we never know when a fit of nerves might strike.

Before every game, professional football players are keyed up, emotional and nervous. But once the game begins and they feel the first "hit," they get in stride. Most high-performance athletes are like this. As are high-performance presenters, those who enjoy the challenge. Likewise, a bit of nervousness is good for you. It ensures your focus. But it's nervousness that is borne of anticipation. It is *good* nervousness, not the same as fear.

---

7 R. D. T. Hollister quoted in George Rowland Collins, *Platform Speaking* (New York and London: Harper & Brothers Publishers, 1923), 13–14.

This is as good a place as any to dispel an old chestnut, part of the conventional wisdom that passes as sage advice – practicing while looking at a mirror. Do you make the mistake of that old cliché and "practice in the mirror?" *Don't* practice in the mirror. That's dumb. You won't be looking at yourself as you give your talk, so don't practice that way. The only reason to look in a mirror is to ensure that your gestures and expressions display exactly as you think they do when you employ them. Other than that, stay away from the mirror.

Remember this dictum. Sear it into your mind.

Practice exactly the way you deliver your presentation.

I mean this literally. Stage your practices, both individually and as a group, as close to the real thing as you can. Make it as realistic as you can. If it's possible, practice in the room where you are to deliver your show. You want to remove as much uncertainty beforehand as possible.

One of the most prevalent and serious practice mistakes is to restart your presentation again and again when you make a mistake. Do *not* start over when you make a mistake…

When you stumble, practice recovering from your error.

This should be common sense. You *must* practice how you respond to making an error. You must understand how you to fight through and recover from an error. Then you have to practice doing it. So if you stumble in your presentation, you will have the confidence and prior experience to weather the minor glitch because you will have faced it before.

Think of it this way. Does a football team practice one way all week, and then employ a completely different game plan on game-day? Of course not, and neither should you.

Moving On…

Those are the preliminaries. Principles, preparation, practice. Those three Ps will serve you well as you craft your presentation. In the next chapter, we grapple with the interior elements of the group presentation.

16

GROUP PRESENTATIONS II: WHAT TO DO?

Let's say that your group is assigned a case presentation on the ToughBolt Corporation. Your group meets, and you decide to divide the work according to your own calculus. How might you divide up the work for your case report and, then, your presentation? It depends on the nature of the case, of course. And since this is a book on presentations not written analyses, you will not find information here on how to conduct your research. Here you learn how to present your research and your conclusions.

Tasks facing you likely include translating the following sections from an extensive written report into a form suitable for an oral and visual presentation.

- Strategy

- Environmental scan

- External analysis

- Value chain

- Internal analysis

- Industry analysis

- PEST or STEEP analysis

- SWOT

- Conclusion and recommendations

Your Section of the Presentation

First, here's what *not* to do.

The last chapter introduced us to the ideas of the Procrustean Solution and the Rule of Three. They come into play here. The typical wrong way to start is to eyeball the written paper, then eyeball your time available – usually between four and six minutes for each person. You end up stuffing ten pounds of sand into a five-pound bucket, which *never* works. You've seen the results of this approach; you have doubtless produced reports like this yourself.

You crowd your PowerPoint slides with data, numbers, information and sentences. You jam as much as you can from your paper onto the screen. You talk fast, and you don't even *attempt* to communicate anything. No one understands what you say, because that wasn't even your goal. Comprehensive but largely unreadable slides characterize your presentation. Let's fix this problem. Here is how to begin.

If your allotted time is four to six minutes, ask yourself this question:

"What *three* main points do I want to cover?"

In other words, observe the *Rule of Three*, as named by speech consultant Christopher Witt.[1] So instead of beginning by wading through your morass of information trying desperately to cram it all in, you begin with the restrictive framework of time and your three most important issues within your topic.

Observe the Rule of Three! Why three? Something magical resides in the number three, something that resonates with the human psyche, even as deep as the heart. Think of nursery rhymes and children's stories and songs: Three Blind Mice, The Three Little Pigs, Goldilocks and the Three Bears, The Three Wise Men.

Three points, no more. Then forget about the rest of the information for the presentation. *Know* the information, because you might be asked about it during the Q&A, but leave it out of your presentation. The heart of your presentation is comprised of your major points. Once you've identified them, you simply state them. This is an especially powerful technique that can result in memorable and effective business presentations.

The Rule of Three guarantees that you hammer home the major points of your topic so that your audience 1) remembers the main idea from your show and 2) actually is persuaded to your way of thinking.

---

1 Christopher Witt, *Real Leaders Don't Do PowerPoint* (New York: Crown Business, 2009), 78.

Beginnings, Middles, and Ends

Every presentation – every story – has this form and structure. You learned this in Part III: The Story. Beginning, middle, end. Each segment of the presentation has this structure as well. Your part has this structure; in fact, every member of the team has this same task – to deliver a portion of the presentation with a beginning, middle, and an end.

In other words, when you are the member of a five-person team and you are presenting for, say, four minutes, during that four-minute span, you tell a story that has a beginning, middle, and an end.

In the diagram below each of the boxes represents a speaker on a five-person team. The first speaker delivers the beginning. The second, third, and fourth speakers deliver the middle. The final speaker delivers the conclusion or the end. Note that each speaker uses the same beginning-middle-end format in delivering their portion of the show.

Your group presentation structure

Speaker 1	Speaker 2	Speaker 3	Speaker 4	Speaker 5
Beginning Middle End	Beginning Middle End	Beginning Middle End	Beginning Middle End	Beginning Middle End
Beginning		Middle		End

The above structure is not the only way you can build your presentation. It is, however, a reliable form. I suggest you use it to build your presentation in the initial stages. You may find that as you progress in your group discussions, you want to alter the structure. Please do so – but do so with careful thought and good reason.

One way to think of your part of the presentation is material sandwiched between two bookends. You should *bookend* your show. This means to make your major point at the beginning and then to repeat that major point at the end. Hence, the term "bookends." And in-between, you explain what your bookends are about.

Your beginning

I have found that quite often, students do not know how to begin a presentation. Do you tiptoe in like so many people in school and in the corporate world? Do you begin confidently and strongly? Or do you edge sideways into your show with lots of metaphorical throat clearing? Do you begin by thanking everyone in the room and other folks elsewhere for the "opportunity" and for the great refreshments? Do you deliver meaningless and forgettable introductions of your team members?

Here's an example of the pathologies of a typical presentation:

I viewed a practice presentation from one of my classes that purported to analyze a case involving the retailer Sears. The lead presenter was Janie. She began speaking, and related facts about the history of the company and its accomplishments over the past 40 years. She spoke in monotone. She flashed a timeline on the screen. Little pictures and graphics highlighted her points. As Janie continued, I wondered at what all of this might mean. I kept waiting for the linking thread. I waited for her point. As the four-minute mark approached, my brow furrowed. The linking thread had not come. The linking thread would *never* come, because *she had no point.*

At the end of her segment, I asked her, "Janie, forgive me, but I have no idea what any of that was about. How did your segment relate to Sears's strategic challenges in the case at hand?"

"Those were just random facts," she said brightly. She was quite ingenuous about it. She told me that she was "warming up" the audience.

Random facts

She was giving "random facts," and she thought that it was acceptable to begin a business case presentation this way. I do not say this to disparage her. In fact, she turned out to be one of my most coachable students, improving her presentation skills tremendously. But I must ask myself, what could possibly convince a student that an assembly of "random facts" is acceptable at the beginning of a presentation? Is it the notion that *anything* you say at the beginning is okay?

Let's go over the beginning, shall we? Together let's craft a template beginning that you can *always* use, no matter what your show is about. When you become comfortable with it, you can then modify it to suit the occasion.

We then move to the middle of the show, and finally to the conclusion. For this extended example, let's assume you have five people on your team.

Let's start – Put the "pow" in power

You begin with your introduction, and you lead off with your money line. Your money line is a grabber that hooks your audience. It isn't a gimmick.

It's not acting, nor is it "drama." Your money line is you applying your thought, energy and imagination to create a memorable line that sticks in your listener's mind. Start your section with a money line and end your section with a money line. Often, it can be the *same line*. Here is what you do:

Ensure that your audience is attentive. They should be watching you, expectantly. Never launch your presentation to an unsettled room, still bustling with small talk.

Ensure that you are ready, and ensure that your audience is ready. You don't want to waste a rousing beginning on a distracted audience. Here's an example of why this is important:

One of my students was presenting to an audience of corporate judges in a business competition. He was a tall, bald Nigerian student and dominated the command position. He paused, even before saying a word. He asserted control over the room and he waited interminably for the judges to settle themselves and to quit shuffling papers. He ensured that they were focused on him. He then spoke slowly and precisely in a deep and powerful voice. He said this:

"There's a deal on the table... *Don't* take it... Here's why."

With those three sledgehammer phrases, my student laid the groundwork for a powerful presentation.

He followed his grabber with a clear and direct situation statement that prepared his listeners for the subsequent 20 minutes of supporting analysis.

This is one of the most important lessons to learn in delivering your presentation. You must seize interest from the very first words. You must capture your listeners, grip them, and hold them. The great news is that it's not that difficult to do. You simply begin with your big idea or your tiniest detail. Deliver a money line to seize audience attention, then follow-up and deliver the goods.

Your money line

Think of your money line as the headline or as the lead of a newspaper story, the *first words* the presenter says. Here are examples of money lines leading into a presentation:

- *"Have you ever watched someone die? Actually die before your eyes?"*

- *"It's one of the most intimate things a woman can do to herself."*

- *"We have a rare and beautiful thing in common."*

- *"In the past ten minutes, our market grew by 27,000 customers."*

You find your money line in your story. It is buried somewhere in your case. Ask yourself "What is the most important thing happening in my story?" and then craft a money line that grabs and holds the listener.

Returning to our hypothetical example of the ToughBolt Corporation, here are examples of what's actually happening in the company and case. Ask yourself what money line emerges from the following?

- The need to slash our budget by 20 percent?

- Learning new skills?

- New competitor in the industry?

- Market downturn?

- Technology innovation threatens our market position?

- Change in strategic direction?

- A new company merger?

In all cases, you find what is dramatic and compelling in your topic and build your story around that point, leading off with the appropriate money line. This sets the stage for your **situation statement**.

The situation statement

The situation statement tells your audience what they will hear. It's the reason you are there, and the reason they have assembled to hear you. What will you tell them? Remember in any story, there must be change. The very reason we give a case presentation is because *something* has changed in the company's fortunes, for good or bad. So focus on that change. We must explain it and craft a response. This is why you have assembled your team: to explain the threat or the opportunity, to provide your analysis and to provide your recommendations.

The audience has gathered to hear about a problem and its proposed solution, to hear of success and how it will continue, or to hear of a proposed change in strategic direction.

Don't assume that everyone *knows* why you are here. Don't assume that they know the topic of your talk. *Ensure* that they know with a powerful situation statement.

A powerful situation statement centers the audience – *pow!* It focuses everyone on the topic. Don't meander into your talk. Don't tip-toe into it. Don't clear your throat with endless apologetics or thank you's. Don't "warm up" your audience. Direct and to the point is best. *Pow!*

Here's what I mean. Let's say your topic is the ToughBolt Corporation's new marketing campaign. Try starting this way:

"Today we present ToughBolt's new marketing campaign. We designed this campaign to regain the six percent market share lost in last year's downturn and to *increase* our market share by another ten percent. It's a campaign to lead us into the next four quarters and will result in a much stronger and more competitive market position 12 months from now."

You see? No "random facts." No wasted words. No metaphorical throat-clearing. No backing into the presentation, and no tiptoeing. *State the reason you are there simply and directly.*

Another more colorful introductory situation statement is this:

"We're all at risk right now. ToughBolt Corporation is under attack by forces that threaten our survival. Even as we sit here, drastic changes in our competitive environment attack our position in three ways. Our team presents the source of those changes, how these changes threaten us, and what our marketing team will do to secure our position in the industry and to continue robust growth in market share and profitability."

Do not be vague. Do *not* edge into your presentation with chummy talk. Do not begin like this:

"Good morning, how is everyone doing? Good, good. It's a pleasure to be here, and I'd like to thank our excellent board of directors for the opportunity to share with you the results of our work. I'm Dana Smith and this is my team, Bill, Joe, Mary, and Sophia. Today, we're planning on giving you a marketing presentation on ToughBolt Corporation's situation. We hope that by the end of our briefing you will—"

You've seen this kind of introduction, perhaps given one yourself. Make a commitment today that you'll never commit another abominable introduction like the one above.

Your middle

Your lead presenter – your opener – has just introduced the topic at hand. He has defined the problem. He has told of your efforts, and he has presaged your results. He has given the audience ample warning of what is to come. And finally, he begins the presentation by placing your firm into the context of its industry. Now it is time for your group to present, in sequence, exactly what was promised. The "middle" is simply the body of your analysis.

Your next three team members speak in succession, each to a different segment. Let's say: 1) your firm's place in the industry and the challenge facing it, 2) your firm's financial status and prospects, and 3) your analysis of the firm's prospects based on financial performance and competitive position.

Each presenter opens with a grabber, relates the facts of their section, and then closes the section with a *recapitulation of the grabber*. This, again, is called bookending, and each team member should bookend their segment.

Your conclusion

Your last team member – your closer – provides a quick overview of your results and offers a conclusion that reiterates your firm's recommended course of action and ends on a positive note.

The conclusion is at least as important as the introduction. It's the last thing your audience will hear that is crafted by you beforehand. It should reiterate your main points. It should repeat the major theme that you want your audience to remember. To transition into your conclusion, utter the magic words:

"In conclusion, we can see that…"

Then recapitulate in one or two sentences the situation statement and your recommendations. The final words should not be left to chance – memorize that last sentence, and it should be a blockbuster crafted by you to be memorable.

Pow!

What to Wear

Most presentations in business school require some sort of "business casual" attire. What does this mean?

For men, it means a jacket and tie. For ladies, it means a business suit. One exception to the "business casual" dictum is to dress with some sort of team uniform – with celebratory t-shirts or Izod shirts. If you choose to do this, do *not* call unnecessary attention to it as a gimmick. Let it be a natural part of your show. Aside from this exception, which should be cleared with your professor, business casual is the rule.

Business casual does *not* mean open collar shirts, chains, medallions, jeans, v-neck sweaters, "hoodies," and the like. It also means that there should be some coordination among team members with respect to dress. It doesn't mean color-coordinating, but it *does* mean that the general look of your team should be harmonious.

I have seen group presentations in which some students wore open collar shirts while others wore coats and ties. Some in jeans, others in suits. This is discordant and distracting. It also is a blatant disregard of instructions. Shouldn't you give yourself the best possible chance to succeed? If you think so, then why start your presentation by disregarding instructions?

What to Do

This section will show you exactly what to do and not to do while giving a group presentation.

First, remember that you are on-stage from the moment your presentation starts until the moment you walk off. Maybe you believe that you are only in the act of "presenting" when you are up-front in the command position, when you actually talk and gesture and relate to your PowerPoint slides. This isn't the case.

Regardless of who holds the command position, *you* are presenting 100 percent of the time. Every member of your group is "presenting" all the time. You present even when your teammates are talking. *Everything* you do during a presentation either enhances the show or detracts from it. If you've never thought about this point, then you are probably acting in ways that are detrimental to your group. Let's go through the entire process of delivering a group presentation *without sound*. In other words, let's look at what you should *do*. Let's look at what the audience should *see*.

First, here is the room in which you deliver your show:

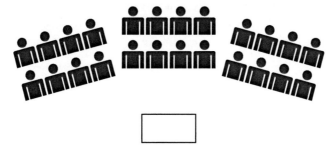

In the diagram above, the audience is seated in amphitheater arrangement. A podium is centered in front of the audience, and there is a screen behind the podium. The PowerPoint slides are projected on the screen behind you. This layout is fairly standard and may deviate only in terms of how the audience is seated and the location of the podium.

Your entry

Your group enters the room single file. The opener should walk to the command position in front of the podium and wait until the entire group is assembled to one side. Do *not* straggle in and assume random positions clustered around a podium. *Do not gather around the podium in a gaggle.* I have seen far too many bad shows to believe that it is an accident that students cluster around the podium. We must fight this herd instinct. The figure below shows the disorganized layout of a typical presentation. Group members stand willy-nilly, with no awareness of where to stand or why.

By contrast, the figure below shows a highly desirable configuration. The opener should stride immediately, alone, to the command position directly in front of the audience. Only one person presents at a time from the command position. The non-speaking members of the group enter and stand to one side.

This is a powerful configuration. The speaker owns the space before the podium and in front of his audience. The speaker holds the stage alone. He commands attention, with no distractions.

Professors disagree legitimately as to whether the speaker ought to stand in front of the podium or behind it. This is a matter of preference. It is acceptable for the speaker to position himself behind the podium, however this position is less desirable, because it puts a barrier between the speaker and audience. It also restrains the speaker, anchoring him to one spot and hindering communication. You cannot use all of your communication tools anchored behind a podium. I consider it less desirable, but it *is* acceptable. Some speakers may prefer the comfort of a podium anchor. But keep in mind that you give away a tremendous competitive advantage by hiding behind a podium.

Common Errors

I view dozens of student presentations each year, and I've noticed the same errors of commission and omission. They recur again and again. Take note of these and avoid them.

You don't practice as a team. It shouldn't be difficult to understand why we practice as a team prior to any presentation. How well would your favorite baseball, football or basketball team perform in a game with no team practice beforehand?

What if a football team prepared this way for the upcoming game: The team meets to "discuss" the upcoming game and "what we plan to do." Then team members go out individually to prepare "their part" of the game plan. Each person, on his own, rehearses his bit prior to the game. Perhaps the team comes together just prior to the game for a "quick run-through" to ensure that "everyone knows their parts." Does this appear to be a formula for success?

It's a recipe for disaster and embarrassment. It's not enough to prepare individually – your presentation must be a cohesive whole, with clear and smooth transitions.

You don't know how to start. How do *you* start your presentation? Doubtless you've begun at least one of your presentations with a foray into what I call "chumminess." Chumminess? You may have heard somewhere that it's important to "put the audience at ease." I've seen hearty fellows step right up with a boisterous "So how are you all doing today? Good, *good!*" This is called chumminess. You are not addressing your "chums," so stay away from chumminess.

You don't know how to stop. This may seem absurd to you, but ask yourself how often you actually prepare a strong conclusion? A conclusion that sums what you've said and leaves the powerful impression you worked so hard to evoke? A conclusion that tapers down to a razor-sharp point a final sentence with punch and pizzazz? With *pow!*

When you walk to the stage, do you already know precisely how you will begin and how you will end? I've seen many presentations and presenters who reach a natural stopping point – it feels like they should stop. It's logical that they should stop. But they *can't* stop. They don't know how. They drone on for lack of an ending.

I see students spiral down out of control until they crash and burn. I see students fade and physically wilt. I can catch the moment of realization on a presenter's face when he or she discovers that they don't know how to finish, and they don't know where to go or what to do. You can avoid this disastrous situation completely. Know your first words. Know your last words. It may be something as simple and direct as this:

"In conclusion, we can see that _____. This concludes my presentation."

Fill in the blank with your concluding statement, usually your one sentence recommendation. Excellent presentations have a handful of certitudes that characterize them all, and this is one of them. This concluding phrase is a workhorse, and you may always rely upon it. Try it now. Say it aloud:

> *"In conclusion, we can see that* _____. *This concludes my presentation."*

You don't know how to transition. How do you move smoothly from one speaker to the next during your presentation? This presents a problem in every presentation. It's the source of much handwringing yet is much easier than you imagine.

Think of the transition between your team members as links in the chain of your presentation. The links should be strong and decisive. Ask yourself: "Have I thought of how I will end my story and transition to the next team member? Has our team discussed it? Do I know exactly what I will say and why?" Don't leave your transition to chance. Craft your transitions and then practice them.

Your entire team mills around during the presentation. Your team appears disorganized, inattentive, and is scattered willy-nilly about the stage. What do your team members do when not in the command position? Don't scatter yourselves across the stage, and don't scratch at yourself, shuffle your feet, or have mumbled side conversations with your teammates. And certainly don't scowl or grimace during your team's presenting. Disorganized, shifting, chaotic, aimless wandering – this gives the impression that your message suffers from the same maladies. To correct this, here is what you do:

Your group takes position *away* from the center, at either side of the stage. Know where each person is to stand for the entire show. Then each student moves, in turn, to the command position to present his segment. This is so the audience can focus attention on the speaker alone.

When you are standing to the side, stand attentively and listen to the speaker. Don't move around or look down. Don't roam your eyes over the audience. Minimize your body movement, which is a distraction. Pay close attention to your teammate's message and fully support that message in your facial expression and body language. Your teammates will do the same for you.

The Question and Answer Session

This is the time where unpredictability can buffet your presentation. If you have prepared properly and have mined the material of the topic, aiming to become expert on this little slice of company life, questions should prove no problem.

The professor asking the question usually wants to understand one thing – how you came up with a particular statement, assertion or recommendation. Perhaps you weren't clear in your reasoning during your presentation. If not, this is a chance to shine. The professor also would like to see that knowledge about the case is spread reasonably across several members of the team, and that it is not simply a one-person show, so several students should be prepared to answer questions.

When the question is asked, determine who is to answer it. Step toward the questioner with an open posture, hands apart, eyebrows raised – repeat the question to be certain that you understand what is asked. This has the additional benefit of getting the questioner nodding in agreement with you.

Your answer should have a beginning, middle and end. Keep your answers short and clear. Don't talk yourself into a blind alley. Probably the most difficult part of a Q&A is getting into and out of the answer in a crisp way. Here are some phrases that can help you *begin* your answer:

- "Our team evaluated that option and decided to go with the scenario that you saw today. It has three advantages—"

- "That was a point of discussion on the team, and we came to a consensus that—"

- "Certainly that issue is important, and you'll find an extensive analysis of it in the appendix to our written report—"

- "Our recommendation is the result of careful consideration and balancing of competing points-of-view—"

The middle consists of your factual exposition of what you did, why you did it, and what it means. Don't get fancy and don't go into needless rambles. Think spare and to the point. To conclude your answer with power, say something like this:

- "I think you'll find that our analysis is robust and substantiates our original proposition."

- "Surely there is room for maneuver on the question, and our conclusion isn't the last word. But we believe that it is prudent and well-supported."

- "Reasonable people can disagree on what ought to be done, and we believe that our logic is sound and that our assumptions are conservative enough to support our conclusions."

Conclusion

In conclusion, we can see that the presentation has a simple structure and need not be a burdensome affair. If you divide the tasks properly, focus your presentation on the big idea, observe the Rule of Three, and utilize your principles, preparation, and practice, you can present a presentation flawless in its structure and orchestration. The question period can be handled with aplomb when the team has embraced its topic and has reviewed the simple steps of how to get into an answer and then out.

In the next chapter, we look at how to handle tasks specific to the business presentation, translating them from the written page to the big screen.

TOOLS OF ANALYSIS: ORIENT, ELIMINATE, EMPHASIZE, COMPARE

As a business student, you're probably familiar with the multimedia software package called PowerPoint. Microsoft's PowerPoint is a superb tool, and it's a wonder of modern communication technology. But it presents us with a paradox. The paradox is that many people using PowerPoint have no idea what they are doing. As a result, this powerful communication tool can do more damage to a presentation than good. The greatest damage is done when PowerPoint itself becomes the presentation while presenters move themselves offstage as a slide-reader.

The PowerPoint Challenge

PowerPoint has been criticized because it has become such a ubiquitous part of the business presentation landscape, and it is almost always used incorrectly. This is not the fault of the software package. It's the fault of the business presenters. At the heart of the problem is that *most business folks* don't know how to use PowerPoint properly. This is a generalization about the business community, and I stand by it. This has resulted in a misdirected anti-PowerPoint bashing campaign that has enriched quite a few folks.

The anti-PowerPoint caricature has become a bestselling theme and has spawned a subgenre of business books. When books begin making their way onto shelves that mock the technology itself, it means a trend has become ubiquitous and irresistible. Several books go by the title *Death by PowerPoint*. There is Seth Godin's classic eBook *Really Bad PowerPoint*. Christopher Witt's excellent book *Real Leaders Don't Do PowerPoint* skewers those who depend on technology to make their points for them, but who do not realize that their points aren't being made.[1] Mockery of PowerPoint even found its way onto the front page of America's premier newspaper on April 27, 2010, as the *New York Times* headline shouted: "We Have Met the Enemy and He Is PowerPoint."

Bad PowerPoint is widespread enough that these words likely bring to your mind any number of bad presenters. You may see yourself in here. And if you do, that's good news, because it indicates a measure of self-awareness that is necessary to presentation improvement. It's good news, because if you do nothing more than change your behavior to just eliminate the bad PowerPoint habits, you can transform yourself into a better-than-average presenter. That's a worthy goal. But let's do even better than that.

The first thing – There is certitude

"Business communication" is a gray area of business life, and one problem with the gray areas of life is that as long as there is wiggle room for disagreement, strong egos will argue a point. The area of concise, clear communication provides smart people with *lots* of wiggle room where settled issues can become "matters of opinion."

But it's not a matter of being smart. You know lots of smart people. Many of these smart people have no idea how to communicate in the medium of public speaking or of presentations. But because they are smart people, you *cannot tell them this*. Or, rather, you tell them this at your peril, because our speaking is bound up with our egos.

For the smart person who delivers a presentation, if the audience doesn't "get it," this means that something is wrong with the audience. *They* simply must try harder. This smart person never questions the message or the messenger. It's the audience who shoulders the blame. This lack of self-examination is a malady that afflicts smart and popular people more than it does the average Joe. If the person is in a leadership position and has a reputation of not listening to or not permitting criticism or even the occasional suggestion, then that person's presentation skills will never improve. Ever.

---

1   Michael Flocker, *Death by PowerPoint* (Cambridge: De Capo Press, 2005); Cherie Kerr, *Death by PowerPoint: How to Avoid Killing your Audience and Sucking the Life out of Your Presentation* (Santa Ana, CA: ExecuProv Press, 2001); Christopher Witt, *Real Leaders Don't Do PowerPoint* (New York: Crown Publishing Group, 2009); Seth Godin, *Really Bad PowerPoint*, eBook (2001), 5: http://www.sethgodin.com/freeprize/reallybad-1.pdf (accessed July 26, 2012).

So we enter that gray area here in just a few paragraphs, where egos jockey for position and every opinion counts as much as any other. But let's pretend shall we? Let's put our egos aside and pretend that we might learn something new and powerful about our tools of presentation. Let's feel the relief of certitude. Yes, there *are* principles to guide you. They are rock-solid. When the world's most famous orators – Demosthenes, Cicero and Quintilian – address the *very same challenges* that you face today, this should tell you that their enduring answers can serve you well.[2]

Our presentation principles are not matters of opinion to be endlessly debated over espresso in a smoky euro-cafe. If you follow these certitudes rather than follow the flawed alternatives available to you, your presentation will be the better for it. *Much* better for it.

In this chapter, I address the nettlesome issue of how to display your analytical results in a PowerPoint presentation. Let's start with the blessings – and curse – of our chief communicative tool PowerPoint.

Visual Aids

Visual aids can enhance a presentation or can destroy it. By visual aids, I mean PowerPoint or some other presentation package such as Keynote or Prezi. Other visual aids, such as whiteboard, butcher paper, props, short film clips, audio recordings, and overhead projectors, are still in use and can be valuable when employed properly. For business school students, however, PowerPoint is the standard.

PowerPoint and other presentation packages have been widely used for more than 20 years. These superb presentation packages have transformed the way we handle the public transmittal of business ideas. Coupled with other tools of the information age – cell phones, PCs, the Internet, satellite communications – they are powerful instruments in conducting business.

PowerPoint has changed the way we communicate, persuade, display, and entertain in the business world. By using the graphics, sound and animation that are bundled onto our powerful computers, we can present big and complex ideas to large and small groups. PowerPoint displays have, in fact, become the default method in the American corporate world when "presentations" are required.

---

2 No, the ancient Greeks and Romans did not work with PowerPoint; their principles of speaker-centered presentation and persuasion, however, constitute a timeless wellspring of wisdom that touch the core of our objectives in presenting.

But there is a dark side to all of this. Like any tool, PowerPoint can be misused and abused. PowerPoint has been around long enough for bad usage to become widespread. Bad PowerPoint technique usually falls within a narrow spectrum of behaviors – from this moment forward, I simply call them *Bad PowerPoint*. You want to avoid *Bad PowerPoint*.

Why is so much Bad PowerPoint out there in the corporate world? It's not a technical problem, as most folks know how to manipulate the software. The problem comes with the artistic license that executives sometimes take with the full range of pyrotechnic options, such as multiple fonts, dramatic animation, sound effects, and head-turning slide transitions.

The problem is compounded with lack of training in the visual elements needed for a satisfying show. The people using PowerPoint are mainly smart, savvy, computer-literate business folks, and so the problem is in simply not knowing what constitutes *good* and what constitutes *bad*.

I suspect that the reason for this is mimicry and corporate incest. In the absence of good habits within an organization, bad habits perpetuate themselves, especially if senior leadership is the culprit. If the model within a firm is average or below par, then this becomes the norm. In this way, bad presenting breeds more bad presenting.

We unfortunately do not license users for competence or require that candidates complete a PowerPoint safety course to ensure that they commit minimal damage. As a result, bad PowerPoint technique thrives.

The natural tendency of people is to mimic the boss, to accept his style as proper. Moreover, we are taught by various books on power never to "outshine the master."[3] If that boss happens to be an excellent presenter, mores the better. But experience teaches us that this is rarely the case.

While mimicry may serve you well as a corporate survival tool, it stunts your personal growth. Like any principle, it can be followed mindlessly, or it can serve you well if you are judicious. Such is the case with PowerPoint. People see "professionals" use this tool in gross fashion, and they copy the bad technique. They think it's "the way to do it."

I'm certain that this is how students develop such bad habits. Some corporate vice president or successful entrepreneur shows up at your school unprepared to deliver a talk, believing that his professional achievements are enough to impress you. He or she believes that preparation is unnecessary, that *faux* spontaneity can carry the day. They feel no drive to deliver a satisfying talk.

---

3 Robert Greene and Joost Elffers, *Power* (New York: Viking, 1998), 1.

This worthy believes that *anything* he says will be treated as business gospel. Who can blame you for copying him and his bad habits?

But bad habits they are – they span the disciplines, and they run rampant the length of the corporate ladder. I separate these bad habits and actions into two broad categories: 1) the PowerPoint material itself, and 2) your interaction with that material during your presentation. The next two sections speak to each of these – your slides and your interaction with them.

Your slides

Oftentimes, students throw together half-a-dozen makeshift slides. They cut and paste them from a written report with dozens of bullet points peppered throughout. The results are slides that confuse the audience rather than reinforce your major points, delivered in awful, mind-numbing presentations. There is a cost for serving up what designer Nancy Duarte calls "bad slides."

> Making bad slides is easy, and it will negatively impact your career. Invest in your slides, but invest in your own visual skills as well. The alternative is to inadvertently commit career suicide.[4]

Absent specific instruction, you might believe that it's acceptable to simply cut and paste graphics from a written report onto a slide. You then project that slide onto the screen while you talk about it. Usually prefacing what you say with the words "As you can see…" The results are usually poor, if not disastrous. This is what I call the "As you can see" syndrome and more on that later. It is a roadmap to disaster.

But the insidious part is that *no one tells you* the results are disastrous. And they do not tell you *what* makes your presenting an abomination. So let's discuss the types of issues you face in assembling your show.

Start by recognizing that no slide show can substitute for a lack of ideas, a lack of preparation, and a lack of a story to tell. PowerPoint cannot rescue you with its colors, sound, and animation. This is akin to Hollywood filmmakers who spend millions of dollars on dazzling computer-generated special effects and neglect the story. The films flop one after the other, and yet Hollywood does not get the message.

You can craft a winning film with a superb story and drama, but with minimal special effects – see *12 Angry Men*. But you *cannot* craft a winning film with no story or a bad story populated with people the audience doesn't care about and who are buffeted by dangers and threats contrived by Industrial Light and Magic.

---

4 Nancy Duarte, *Slide:ology: The Art and Science of Creating Great Presentations* (Sebastopol, CA: O'Reilly, 2008), 3.

Slides are not a magic pill; they won't organize a disorganized presentation; they won't give a point to a presentation that doesn't really have one; and they never make a convincing presentation on their own.[5]

Orient, eliminate, emphasize and compare

In working with your slides, follow the formula: orient, eliminate, emphasize and compare. This formula produces superb results every time, especially if you are working with difficult financial information. As preface to this, on *all* of your slides ensure that your font is at least 30 point. Your numbers should be at least 26 point.

Here is how you proceed:

First, *orient* your audience to the overall financial context. If you take information from a balance sheet or want to display company profit growth for a period of years, then briefly display the balance sheet in its entirety to *orient* the audience. *Tell* the audience they are viewing a balance sheet: "This is a balance sheet for the year 2012." Walk to the screen and point to the information categories. Touch the screen. Say *"Here* we have this number," *"Here* we have this category."

Second, *eliminate* everything on the screen that you do not talk about. This means clicking to the next slide, which has been stripped of irrelevant data. If you do not refer to it, it should not appear on your slide. *Strip* the visual down to the basic numbers and categories you use to make your point. Sure, put the entire balance sheet or spreadsheet on your first slide, orient your audience as to what it is to provide context, and then click to the next slide. This next slide should contain only the figures you refer to.

Third, *emphasize* the important points by increasing their size, coloring them, or bolding the numbers. Illustrate what the numbers *mean* by utilizing a chart or graph.

Fourth, *compare* your results to something else. Remember that numbers mean nothing by themselves. Comparison yields meaning and understanding. For example, think of a children's dinosaur book. You've seen the silhouette of a man beside a Triceratops or a Stegosaurus, or a Brontosaurus. The silhouette is there to provide you a frame of reference that enables you to understand the physical dimensions of something new and strange. You can compare the size of a man with the new information on dinosaurs.

---

5 Aileen Pincus, *Presenting* (London: Dorling Kindersley, 2008), 24.

Likewise, we want to provide a frame of reference to enable our audience to understand the results of our analysis. We provide a comparison of sorts as a baseline.

For instance, if you are talking about financial performance, and you have selected an indicator (such as ROI, yearly sales revenue growth or something similar), don't simply present the information as standalone. *Compare* your company's financial performance against something else. Do this to make your point and to tell your story.

Compare your firm's financial performance against its performance in prior years or quarters.

Compare your firm's financial performance against a major competitor or several competitors.

Compare your firm's financial performance against the industry as a whole.

Compare your firm's financial performance against similar sized firms in select *other* industries.

Your tools of analysis

In developing your analysis and recommendation, you will have used various tools of assessment that you acquired in your classes. These analytical tools yield results that you then must incorporate into your presentation. The rest of this chapter suggests how these outputs may best be incorporated into your presentation for clarity and concision.

First, we review several of the tools of analysis that you are expected to use in analyzing business cases. Second, we evaluate the "output" of these tools, the end product of your analysis – your results. Third, we see how *not* to present these results in a business presentation and what *is* the best way to present them.

Words like "analysis" cause some students to freeze-up. It has a strange cast to it, as if it's an alien process that they don't have access to. It causes brain-lock. This is because analysis is an inexact process. There are no fixed and accepted answers derived from iron logic, as in mathematics and hard sciences. Instead, analysis actually relies upon you to produce an answer that is uniquely yours.

Analysis is little more than systematically applied logic, experience, and common sense. It's a line of inquiry designed to obtain a specific result, but the result itself is oftentimes a matter of judgment. No two analyses will be the same, so let's dispense with the notion that there is a "right" answer and a "wrong" answer. Good analysis rests in the domain of ambiguity. There is only *your* answer and how well you support it. You will find that your analytical skill will improve over time with practice.

You may obtain great results from your analysis. In fact, you may have teased out the most nuanced analysis the world has ever seen. But if your presentation suffers in form and content, you lose. If no one understands you, you lose. What's more, you lose because it's *your fault*. Now, let's *correct* it.

For purposes of your presentation, this answer – whatever it is – must first be supported and it must then be communicated. Communicate your results logically. Clearly. Concisely. Understandably. It's your responsibility to present an interesting, logical, clear, concise, and memorable message. Even if the only reaction you hear is: "What a great presentation!" you will have won a major battle.

But, you ask, "What can I do about dull material?"

This is the *best* kind of material to arrange for a presentation. The contrast between your imaginative and deft handling of "dull" material and the presentations that have gone before is stark, and this redounds to your advantage. You can transform even the most inherently dull material into an interesting message. You can distill facts and figures into a compelling story. Even if it's *not* compelling, then it will be at least a story far more interesting than a straight exposition of the "facts."

Your interaction with your slides

Your "output" is never the analytical *process*. It's tempting to show the audience "how I developed the project." Do not entertain the audience with your tools. They won't like it, and it wastes their time. Do not display the analytical model – instead, display the results.

Display the results

Your output is your conclusion, arrived at through the application of one or more of the tools we use – SWOT, PEST, or what have you. Your results give rise to options or alternatives. Among these alternatives you find your ultimate recommendation. To display your results think simple, clear and direct.

Simple. Clear. Direct

Two main mistakes plague business school presentations with regard to presenting analytical results.

• **Too much complex information:** You cram too much information onto a single slide, you bury your conclusion as you talk, and then you talk about it interminably.

• **Not enough context:** Your conclusions or numbers appear as if drawn from a hat, and you don't provide enough context to yield understanding of the numbers.

Now, let's see how this general guidance plays out in action. Here are some of the tools of analysis that provide you with gist and framework of your presentation. Here is how to utilize the tools in your presentation. I assume that you are already familiar with the tools and know how to wield them with aplomb. If you are not, then I recommend a book to refresh your memory – *Analysis Without Paralysis* by Babette E. Bensoussan and Craig S. Fleisher. The five tools of analysis I review here are:

• SWOT

• Five Forces

• PEST

• Value chain analysis

• Financial analysis

Each of these analytical tools has strengths and weaknesses according to its purpose. When used properly toward the appropriate end, the instruments can be powerful illuminators of your business case. But if you use a single tool reflexively every time you analyze a case, then weaknesses emerge.

Avoid tool rut

The overused tool is a common malady in the business school classroom. Again, evidence here is only anecdotal, but it is natural for each of us to be drawn to a particular tool we favor. We may favor it for any number of reasons: elegance, ease of use, unambiguous results, or an aura of precision.

Many professors emphasize financial ratio analysis above all other tools, and this actually seems to make sense when we consider how the performance of modern business is numbers driven and numbers measured. They may tip the hat to SWOT analysis and a bit of Porter's Five Forces, but financial ratio analysis is the *sine qua non* of the business case method.

Ratio analysis does reveal incredibly useful intelligence about the firm's present condition and past performance. It is surely the processed information we need, but financial analysis alone is not nearly enough. We need much more. Ratio analysis alone cannot tell us causes, conditions and context. In fact by itself it may give a distorted view of the firm and its actual strategic fortunes.

We need *more* refined intelligence and in greater quantity. This is where we look to other analytical tools. We need these other tools used in combination to understand the multi-variable dynamics that got the firm where it is today.

At the end of this chapter, I recommend some of my favorite books that address a broad range of tools, their applicability, their strengths and weaknesses, and how to apply them. For now, understand that each tool has a purpose and is not the sole answer to every strategic question. It is in their *combined* use that their real value is revealed. But we're not concerned here with tool efficacy – only how to present its results in the most powerful way.

When using each of our analytical tools, we should ask the question "Which of the PowerPoint options provide the best mode to communicate the results of my analysis. Shapes? Text boxes? Graphics? Charts? X and Y graphs? Let's see how to present visuals from the results of some of our most familiar analytical tools.

SWOT

SWOT is shorthand for Strengths, Weaknesses, Opportunities, and Threats. It's a business analysis tool that links the internal capabilities of the firm with the external competitive environment. The SWOT is an elegant conceptual tool that guides us in visualizing our strategic direction. It's a blunt instrument, yes, and subject to manipulation and matters of opinion. But as a method of consolidating the results of the environmental scan, it has earned its pride of place. Don't waste an excellent SWOT analysis with a substandard presentation.

Often the SWOT is *not* placed within the context of the business environment. Many students have no inkling of how the SWOT fits into the bigger picture and how it can provide a link to many of the other tools you use. SWOT links the firm to the outside environment, which consists of the industry environment and the larger global market environment. The firm has strengths and weaknesses – the environment provides the opportunities and generates threats. Make this link clear in your presentation. When you do this, you make it easy for both you *and* your audience.

Next begin a recitation of the actual content of the analysis. Here is where most SWOT analyses go awry. Begin with strengths. The natural tendency is to list the strengths of the firm in rote fashion, lifted directly from your written report. But do we really want to list *all* of a firm's strengths in our presentation? *No, we do not.*

This is a symptom of the biggest failings of business presentations: You display too much information. Oftentimes, you feel compelled to display on the screen *everything* you have learned. This can be as bad as not listing enough (which rarely happens). Here is how the mistake occurs: You discover the firm has eight strengths. Therefore, you think, I must list all eight. Too often, that is *all* you do – you display a laundry list of "strengths" with no link to what it actually means in terms of what the firm ought to do, given outside conditions.

Do not list all eight strengths! Display in your results *only* the strengths most relevant to the point or conclusion you want to make. In fact, as an exercise in discipline, restrict yourself to displaying just two main strengths or even *one* key strength. Then, explain how that strength relates to the overall strategy of the firm, perhaps even *drives* the strategy of the firm. You should ask and answer the question *"Why is this important?"*

Say something like this: "We focus on this strength, because it is at the heart of our competitive advantage and is key to the implementation of our expansion strategy in the coming three years. Here's how…"

Displaying your SWOT

The typical display of a SWOT features a familiar two by two matrix (see figure). It's natural that you would use this format to display your findings, particularly if you have just learned about the SWOT. Note that the Strengths box is filled with dubious material. Resist the impulse to display a matrix crammed with every strength, weakness, opportunity, and threat you identified in your research. Instead be selective, and by pruning the least important elements, you imbue your talk with power.

Strengths	Weaknesses
Supplier reliability Time to market Customer relations Training of employees	------------- ------------- -------------

Opportunities	Threats
------------- ------------- -------------	------------- ------------- -------------

It's acceptable to flash the matrix on the screen to *orient* your audience to the topic. Then move away from the matrix and instead focus on the strength you have identified as key, coupled with a visual.

Use *this* slide as backdrop for your discussion of the source of this strength, and why it is important to the firm in developing a strategy that meshes with the external environment to create competitive advantage. Here's an example:

Move from the matrix to a graphic illustrating the key strength and demonstrating its power. In this case, this key strength is the firm's short time to market, and the graphic shown illustrates this. In this way, the primary strength of the company, the firm's competitive advantage, is not buried in the midst of a half-dozen other peripherally significant strengths.

Don't even mention the other "strengths," because this dilutes audience attention and distracts from your major point – and that point is that *our product's superior time to market is key to our success."*

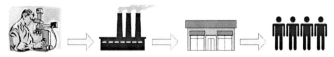
Average time: 38 days

The time to market slide should be animated from left-to-right to breathe life into the process. It then provides the backdrop for your brief discussion of how time to market superiority has led to robust growth and a large share of market. It forms the cornerstone of your business strategy in the near future, based on opportunities that you have identified.

"The environmental scan"

When you are told to do an "environmental scan," this means that you utilize analytical tools to assess the external environment your firm faces. We divide this external scan into micro and macro factors. The micro scan looks at the relevant industry and is called Porter's Five Forces Analysis. The macro scan looks at the macro forces that impact the firm, such as the relevant political, economic, socio/cultural, and technological factors and is called the PEST Analysis.

Industry analysis (Porter's Five Forces)

Harvard University's Michael Porter has contributed tremendously to our understanding of business strategy. This tool of analysis reveals much about an industry. How do we graphically illustrate the results of a "Porter's Five Forces" analysis? We must remember what we are trying to convey. Ask yourself, what is the best way to convey the *results* of my industry evaluation? Remember that your task here is *not* to illustrate the *method* you used to produce your conclusions, but rather to illustrate the *conclusions*.

No one cares if I know how to do a "Porter's Five Forces" and they won't care if you do either. It's likely that many people will never have heard of the technique or even of Michael Porter himself. The audience *does* care about the results of an industry analysis that informs them of crucial information that affects operations, for better or worse. These results are what you display.

Since Porter's model suggests that a "force" has a high, moderate, or low influence, you should choose your graphic display accordingly. Instead of simply printing words on the screen, use graphics that suggest the result in a powerful and clear way.

PEST

The PEST analysis is part of the "environmental scan" that every business student must perform at some point in his or her career, probably many times. The acronym stands for an analysis of the political, environmental, social, and technological environment. This tool is utilized effectively in cases involving international business, where differences across these dimensions between the home country and a target country can be great. It is also used, however, for domestic business analysis to provide a reassuring contextual framework within which all relevant factors have been considered.

The broadly sweeping character of the PEST analysis is daunting for many students. Maybe you feel overwhelmed at how to select relevant information to include. One result is that many presentations often include general information one can find in any Wikipedia article, such as annual rainfall, type of government, population size and the area of the country in square kilometers.

Obviously you should not provide irrelevant information. But oftentimes students begin this way in a kind of throat clearing exercise. You need no "warm-up," and this type of gobbledygook can actually harm your presentation, causing it to lose focus, momentum, and purpose. Moreover, deciding what to include in your PEST is relatively easy if you follow the following rule of thumb.

For your presentation, here is your basic rule: No information should be included in the PEST that does not directly relate to or impact the industry or product/service under consideration. Do not begin a PEST analysis without a specific product or service as your *unit of analysis*.

One you have determined your unit of analysis (whether fruit juice or cement manufacture), your PEST task becomes clear. The mass of information becomes manageable as you realize that you only include information relevant to your product or service, information and forces that may impact your market entry or choice of entry mode.

Value chain analysis

One of the most useful analytical tools available to you is value chain analysis. Even if you do not delve too deeply into any of the functional areas of the value chain, this tool provides you with a tidy framework to organize and display your information.

I recommend coupling value chain analysis with the SWOT. In fact, I *insist* on it. Breaking the firm into its functional parts makes it much easier to identify the areas of strength and weakness that are significant to the firm *in this instance*.

The value chain is the series of functions a firm performs that creates and adds value to a product from its conception through to its after-sale service. They form links in a chain. Most of our business labels are commonsense, and so if we think of these value-producing functions as links in a chain, we get "value chain."

To evaluate a firm's strengths and weaknesses, we break it into its five generic constituent parts – inbound logistics, operations, outbound logistics, sales and marketing, and after-sale service. Other functions, called secondary activities, add value all along the value chain – human resources, IT, finance. Once you have disassembled your firm into its functional parts, it's much easier to determine your strengths and weaknesses. This allows us to perform cost analysis at a fine-grained level in a step-by-step process:

1. Disaggregate the firm into separate activities

2. Establish the relative importance of activities in the total cost of our product

3. Identify the cost drivers

4. Identify linkages between interdependent activities that affect cost

5. Identify opportunities to reduce costs[6]

This process does not appear in your presentation, of course. Rather, its key points can appear in your written report proper, with more elaborate display in an appendix to your written report.

For purposes of your presentation, think *powerful graphic display* of your MIP – your most important point. Instead of reflexively cutting and pasting your written work onto a slide, ask yourself this question and work hard to provide an answer:

How can I most effectively display my results graphically so it drills my most important point into the audience consciousness so powerfully that they cannot possibly forget it?

Take the following simple diagram of the value chain. How can we enhance the illustration to display the results of our analysis?

Value chain

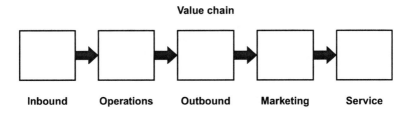

| Inbound | Operations | Outbound | Marketing | Service |

6 Robert M. Grant, *Contemporary Strategy Analysis* (West Sussex, UK: John Wiley and Sons, 2010), 240.

Simple color coding can illustrate the relative revenue state of the functional areas, with white indicating financial health, light grey areas for concern, and dark grey indicating unacceptable cost centers – our targets for reform measures.

Value chain

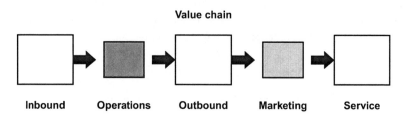

Inbound   Operations   Outbound   Marketing   Service

We can enhance our diagram with visuals that drive home the point, as seen below:

Value chain

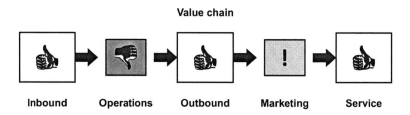

Inbound   Operations   Outbound   Marketing   Service

The foregoing diagrams are simple and direct. They indicate at a glance the general state of what we are trying to communicate. Your oral explication of the visual data brings a precision to the blunt impression that is given.

In the above visuals, it is apparent and memorable that our operations function needs our attention, and that our marketing function is heading south and should be monitored or tweaked. The audience remembers these salient points because of their visual depiction. Details of this conclusion and focus of our attention appear in the written report and, if it must be addressed in the oral presentation, you can provide details verbally during your Q&A. The above diagram should be animated to reveal each point *as it is made.*

The offered diagrams are simple, but not simplistic. They are elegant, parsimonious and transmit a great deal of information with minimal consideration by the audience. *You* shoulder the major burden as presenter to explain the results, putting the attention on you – where it should be.

By no means is this the only way to visualize industry analysis; many other visuals can be crafted, more appealing and pleasing to the eye perhaps. The key to remember, however, is the *transmission of results.* Your reasoning, your calculations, your substantiation should appear in an appendix at the end of your written report. For support, you can also prepare and *hide* a slide with specific points of support for your analysis. If questioned, you can reveal your supporting slide at the end of your presentation during Q&A.

Financial analysis

There are only a few occasions when financial data does not make its way into a business presentation. Financial analysis is where you discover and present the firm's profitability, stability, health, and potential. Financial data carry great import, but they also carry great deception. Because of the *appearance* of rigor or "hardness," numbers tend to carry much more weight in presentations than they really ought to.

The results of your financial analysis invariably constitute the ugliest section of a presentation. Something about a spreadsheet mesmerizes students and faculty alike in a way that is ultimately destructive. A spreadsheet splayed across the screen gives the impression of heft and *gravitas*. It seems important, substantial. Everyone nods.

Too often, you display an Excel spreadsheet on the screen that is unedited from your written report. You cut-and-paste it into your presentation. You splash the spreadsheet onto the screen, then talk from that spreadsheet without orienting your audience to the slide. This is the terrible technique displayed by my finance students, in particular, that is accompanied by the dreaded words: "As you can see …"

I call this AYCSS, or *As you can see syndrome.*

It looks like this: As the presenter, you look back at the screen and stare at the phalanx of tiny and unreadable numbers. Perhaps you grip the podium with one hand and you wave your other hand at the screen with the words "As you can see—"

Then you call out seemingly random numbers. To your audience, the numbers seem random because you have not oriented the audience to your material; you haven't provided the context needed for understanding. Your classmates in the audience watch with glazed eyes. Perhaps one or two people nod. Worse, there is a loud rustling of papers as your audience tries to find the referenced page somewhere in the hardcopy you mistakenly handed out at the beginning. It was a mistake, because you don't want your audience to "follow along" with you – you want your audience to pay attention.

Meanwhile, your professor sits sphinx-like. And *no one* has a clue as to what you're talking about or how it actually relates to the real world. You get through it, finally, and you're relieved. You hope that you were vague enough that no one can even *think* about asking a question. This is a common and quite ugly scenario.

But there *is* a best way that makes things easier for everyone. Use the formula presented earlier in the chapter – orient, eliminate, emphasize and compare.

Apply the Formula

One of the most prevalent mistakes in business school presentations is the inclusion of irrelevant information on slide after slide. This problem is at its worst when it involves financial data. Think primarily of the *unreadable spreadsheet*. It's acceptable to display a spreadsheet on the screen *initially* for contextual purposes. But you should never use it to highlight *results* of your analysis. To illustrate this point, let's try an exercise of how to assemble your slides and then display them in a step-by-step process.

Say that you want to report financials from ToughBolt Corporation. Your spreadsheet displays several categories of ToughBolt financial data from multiple years, 2000–2010. Yes, you *can* display that spreadsheet on a slide, but *only* to orient your audience. In this way, you let them know the context of your data; you let them know that you draw your information from this context. Here is what you do and say…

CHANGE SLIDE. <Your spreadsheet appears>

Walk to the screen and gesture to it with one arm as you speak. You stand beside the screen and indicate the spreadsheet so your audience does not divide its attention between you and the slide material. Do *not* remain at the lectern off to one side while the audience divides its attention between you, your words, and the image on the screen. You want to be *part* of the presentation of the data. That is why you *join* the screen. In this sense, *you* are the animation for the PowerPoint display. *Always* orient your audience to a complex slide or slide with numbers. Say this:

"Here is a spreadsheet that displays ToughBolt financial data. It is a standard financial report, and you are familiar with its format. It covers the ten-year period from 2000 to 2010. [GESTURE] It incorporates several categories of data, including _____, _____, _____, and _____. [GESTURE AT EACH] We are concerned with only *these* numbers – the trend of _____ over the ten-year period."

At this point you gesture directly at the figures to which you refer, palm facing the screen, lying flat and almost touching the numbers.

"We apply ratio analysis to the categories. Here are the results."

CHANGE SLIDE. The next slide eliminates the spreadsheet and displays *only* the raw data – the specific numbers with which you are concerned. Point to the information you want to emphasize and explain briefly what it is.

CHANGE SLIDE. Here your slide displays the final results in graphic form. In this case, a graph or chart that synthesizes your conclusion. It simplifies your point into a clear visual. Here is what you have done...

You have taken the audience on a journey of understanding. The journey has led from the context of the initial spreadsheet all the way to your final conclusion. You have avoided the two critical mistakes I mentioned: too much complex information (with your conclusion buried on the screen) or too little context (as if you have drawn your numbers from a hat). Generally speaking, this method of handling numbers of any kind will serve you well.

Conclusion

Displaying your results with PowerPoint can add power and clarity to your presentation when done properly. Visuals should be spare and elegant. They should present the results of your analysis in a clear and direct manner. In orchestrating your interaction with your slides, you should orient, eliminate, emphasize, and compare.

First, orient your audience to the context of the data, then eliminate the extraneous material, then emphasize your key points in some fashion using size or color, and finally you compare your results with some benchmark so that your audience can understand the meaning of the numbers.

Further reading on PowerPoint and analytical tools

- Cliff Atkinson, *Beyond Bullet Points* (2008)
- Nancy Duarte, *Slide:ology* (2008)
- Nancy Duarte, *Resonate* (2010)

- Craig S. Fleisher and Babette E. Bensoussan, *Analysis Without Paralysis* (2009)

THE CASE COMPETITION

A rite of passage for the business school student is the "case competition." Many students shun these competitions precisely because they involve group work. But if you have not yet received the message, let's repeat it here – collaboration to analyze complex problems and deliver the results in public presentations is how the real world of business works. This means lots of "group work."

The case competition is your chance to demonstrate a wide range of corporate business skills in a collaborative effort. You receive recognition, valuable experience, sometimes monetary rewards, and perhaps an open door to corporate employment. You can win anywhere from $1,000 to $75,000 in a single competition.

How It Works

The case competition is an event in which business teams deliver business presentations, competing against other teams in front of a team of judges. Teams display how quickly, thoroughly, and skillfully they can ingest a case, analyze it, and then present their conclusions and recommendations to a panel of judges.

Case competitions vary greatly in the details, but they do have a typical format and purpose. The operative idea behind such types of competitions is to provide a standard case to competing teams with a given time limit and then to rate how well the teams respond. There is, of course, no direct competition between teams; rather each team is judged independently how well it handles the assigned case and how well it presents its analysis and recommendations. There is usually a time limit and specific rules, with all teams operating under the same conditions. Competitions can be internal to the business school, or they can involve teams from several different schools. Sometimes there are several rounds of competition, with the final round typically judged by outside company executives.

The teams prepare a solution to the case, deliver a written report, assemble a presentation of their analysis and recommendations, and then deliver the timed presentation before a panel of judges, sometimes consisting of executives from the actual company in the case. The University of Washington's Foster School of Business is particularly good about this in its renowned Global Business Case Competition. Twelve to fourteen schools from around the world compete in this weeklong event. Its 2010 competition featured a case written especially for the competition on the Boeing Corporation, with executives from Boeing acting as judges.

One excellent aspect of case competitions that are judged by outsiders is that they provide a true indication of the competitors' mettle. They are removed from the internal politics of particular institutions, where favored students may receive benefits or rewards related more to their currying favor than to the quality of their work.

Some competitions introduce their own twists, which can make the competition more interesting and more complicated. For instance, Ohio State University's Center for International Business Education and Research (CIBER) in its annual case challenge creates teams from the pool of participants (i.e., members will be from different schools) instead of allowing the group of students from each school to compete as a team. Once students are assigned to teams, there is a day of team-building exercises.

The key to doing well in case competitions is to differentiate yourselves beforehand. This is much easier than you might imagine. Start with the three Ps of Business Presentations; they provide a steady guide to ready you for your competition. Principles, preparation, practice.

Principles

You don't start tuning your instrument for the first time when it's time to perform a concert, and likewise, you don't begin honing your presentation skills when it's time to present. By the time of your competition, all of your team members ought to be thoroughly grounded in the principles of powerful presentations offered in this volume.

This part of your competition prep should already be accomplished, with only a few review sessions to ensure everyone is sharp on the Seven Secrets: stance, voice, gesture, expression, movement, appearance and passion. Each member of your team should be a capable, polished presenter.

Preparation

We can divide the competition into several phases:

Phase 1: Lead-in to the competition

You are made aware of the competition's rules. You acknowledge and embrace the rules and what they imply. Your entire team should become intimately familiar with the parameters of the competition – think metaphorically and spatially. Recognize that the problem has length, breadth and depth. Understand the finite limits of the context presented to you, what you can and cannot do.

Think of the competition as an empty decanter that you fill with your analysis and conclusions on the day of the competition. Later, upon receiving the actual case, you will conduct the same process – recognize that the case problem has length and breadth and depth.

But now, prior to the competition, take stock of what you already know you must do, and then do as much as the rules permit beforehand.

This includes embracing the problem situation long before you arrive on-site for a competition and before you receive the case in question. Learn the parameters of the context in which you will operate.

- Competition rules

- Length of presentation

- Total time available (set-up, presenting, Q&A, close-out)

- Number of presenters allowed or required

- Visuals permitted or required

- Sources you may use, both beforehand and during the problem-solving phase

- Prohibitions

You know that you are required to provide analysis of a case, your results and recommendations. Why not prepare all that you can before you arrive at the competition? Some competitions may frown on this or forbid it – fine, then do it when you can, at the first point that it is permissible. This way, you can spend the majority of your case analysis time filling in the content. Prepare your slide template beforehand according to the principles expounded here.

Business presentations have a small universe of scenarios and a limited number of elements that comprise those scenarios. A well-prepared team that is composed of team members from different functional areas will have generic familiarity with virtually any case assigned in a competition and have no problems dealing with it.

Determine beforehand generally who will handle the presentation tasks on your team as well as the analytical portions of your case. The following example is offered to show how the task might be approached.

Presenting Roles	Analytical Tasks
Opener	Financial analysis SWOT
Presenter 1	Value chain
Presenter 2	Competitor analysis
Presenter 3	Recommendations
Closer	Conclusion

As part of this preparatory process, prepare your slide template with suitable logos, background, dynamic graphics, charts and graphs requiring only that the numbers be filled in.

Leading into the competition, your team must become familiar with sources of data that you may be permitted to utilize in conducting your case analysis – market research, industry surveys, and such like. Familiarity with several online databases like Business Source Premier, Mergent Online, and S&P NetAdvantage is necessary since not all schools may have access to the data sources you use most often.

With respect to the delivery of your presentation itself, a case competition is neither the time nor place for you to polish your delivery skills. You should have honed them to razor's edge by now. As well, your orchestration as a team should be perfected before arriving at the site of the competition.

At the competition, you lift your performance to the next level by applying all the principles, precepts, and hard skills you have applied in business school – finance, accounting, marketing, operations, strategy, analysis – and using them in a tightly orchestrated and professional presentation that pops.

If you have engaged the competition context successfully during the lead-up to the actual events, then you will have a taut case-cracking team in place when you are finally issued the case – a team ready to methodically address the issues involved in the case problem.

Phase 2: The case

Phase 2 begins when you're issued the case. Recognize the nature of this case may differ from what you are accustomed to – it could very well be more incomplete and open-ended than the structured cases you have dealt with in class. In fact, it could be a contemporary real-world case with no "solution." It could be a case crafted especially for the competition by the company sponsoring the competition.

Your first step is to read the case once through for general information and understanding, to inventory issues, and to define the magnitude of the task at hand. In effect, you are drawing a philosophical and psychological box around the case to encompass its main elements, to make it manageable, and to prevent wasting time in discussions of unnecessarily open-ended questions. Discussion proceeds on defining the problem statement. Remember to let this question guide your discussion so that you can quickly generate your situation statement:

What's going on here?

At this point, your expertise and skill gained in years of business schooling should guide you in developing your analysis and recommendations. The difference in acumen and skill-sets among teams in a competition is usually small, and I assume that every business team will produce analytical results and recommendations that are capable of winning the competition. This includes your team, of course.

Because the quality of teams is high, and the output of analysis similar, victory is rarely determined by the quality of the material itself. Instead, victory and defeat ride on the clarity, logic, power, and persuasiveness of the public presentation of that material. I have seen great analyses destroyed or masked by bad presentations.

The presentation is the final battlefield where the competition is won or lost. So we devote minimum time here on the preparation of your arguments. Many fine books can help you sharpen analysis, and a list of my recommended favorites appears at the end of the chapter. *This* volume concerns how you translate your written results into a powerful presentation that is verbally and visually compelling. We are concerned here with the key to your competition victory.

Here is your competitive edge: While 95 percent of teams view their presentations as a simple modified version of the written paper that they submit, your team attacks the competition armed with the tools and techniques of power presenting. You understand that the presentation is a distinct and significantly different communication tool than the written analysis.

Many teams cut-and-paste their written paper/summary into the presentation, unchanged. This usually makes for a heinous presentation that projects spreadsheets and bullet points and blocks of text on a screen. Such monstrosities obscure more than they communicate. It's a self-handicap and a horrendous mistake. Sure, at times you will see winning presentations that do this – I see them myself on occasion. This usually happens for one of several reasons, none of them having to do with the quality of the visual presentation.

1. Substance trumps: The business analysis and recommendation is substantially better than all other entries and overcomes deficiencies in presentation.

2. Mimicry: All entries utilize the same defective method of cutting-and-pasting the final report onto PowerPoint slides, thus leveling the playing field to a lowest common denominator of visual and verbal mediocrity.

Don't present all the fruits of your analysis in your presentation. Too much information and too many details can cripple your initial presentation with crowding and confusion. Remember that you should hold back details for use and explication during the Q&A period. A parsimonious presentation delivers your main points. Deciding *what to leave out* of your initial presentation can be as important as deciding what to include and emphasize.

Phase 3: The presentation

Recognize that your presentation is a wholly different communication mode than your final memorandum or report. Treat it as such, and your chances of winning your competition increase dramatically.

If your analysis is robust and your conclusions are sound, as should be the case with *all* the entries, then a powerful and stunning presentation delivered by a team of confident and skilled presenters wins the day most every time. With the competency of most competition teams relatively similar, if a team lifts itself above the competition with a stunning presentation, it wins.

If you have read this book to this point and internalized its message, you understand that you and your teammates are not something *exclusive* of the presentation. You *are* the presentation. By now, you should be well on the way to transforming yourself from an average presenter, ignorant of the techniques and skills of the masters, into a steadily improving speaker who constantly refines himself or herself along the seven dimensions we have discussed: stance, voice, gesture, expression, movement, appearance, and passion.

When I coach a team in a case competition, the team members prepare all of their analysis, conclusions, and recommendations on their own for their written report, which should be a final product worthy of victory. Then, the team produces a first draft presentation. It is at *this* point that the competition is most often won or lost, when a team translates the written report to a presentation format. I enter the process at this point as a coach to provide insight and feedback, but *not* on the material conclusions, recommendations or analysis. I provide feedback on the way that material is offered to an audience and how the team members each make their case in their show.

Powerful winning presentations do not spring forth unbidden or from the written material you prepare. The numbers "do not speak for themselves." The "power of your analysis" does not win the day. Your case solution is not judged on its merit alone, as if the brilliance of your solution is manifest to everyone who reads it. It is judged on how well you communicate the idea, powerfully and persuasively.

Each member of your team must be a tangible, active and compelling part of the presentation. You must orchestrate your presentation so that you work seamlessly with each other, with the visuals you show, and with the new knowledge you create.

As you prepare the substance of your presentation, and as you prepare your own parts according to your own temperament and skills, remember that one of the most important injunctions of any public performance is a positive attitude.

Positive attitude

Maintain a positive attitude throughout, especially where criticism of current company policy is concerned, or when your team must convey bad news. Examples include suggesting that the current strategy is "bad" or that the current executive team is not strong enough.

Sometimes in class presentations I see that students take a sharp adversarial attitude. Being honest is important, but you should be cognizant that you also need to use the "right" words to convey the bad news to the people who are paying you and are responsible for the bad situation in the first place, or who are emotionally invested in a specific strategy.

As much as we would like to believe that our superiors and our clients are mature and want to hear the "truth" – warts and all – human nature is such that we are easily hurt where our own projects and creations are concerned. If you wound someone's ego, you will pay a price. So if you attack the current strategy as unsound, and the person or persons who crafted that strategy sit in the audience, you have most likely needlessly doomed yourself to an also-ran finish in the competition.

Musical chairs

Do not yield to the tendency on the part of a team of three or four people to treat the presentation as a game of musical chairs. This occurs when each member presents a small chunk of material, and the presenters take a number of turns at presenting. The passing of the baton can be disconcerting and can disjoint your show. Minimize the passing of the baton and transitions, particularly when each person has only three or four minutes to present.

In most competitions, you are not permitted to have a faculty coach. At this point in the competition – when you have only a 24-hour period to prepare your case – you must *self-coach* yourself in the principles of superior presentations, applying the Seven Secrets you developed in the run-up to the competition. You must also coach each other in the delivery of each part of the presentation and assemble a seamless group-rendering of your material.

In your delivery, you must *harmonize* your messages. Everyone should be prepared to deliver a serviceable version of the entire presentation, not just their own part. This is to prepare for the chance that one or more of the team is unable to present at the appointed time for some unforeseeable reason. Ensure that all team members are on the same page, speaking with one voice; this means that one member does not contradict the other when answering questions. This is *not* the forum to demonstrate that team members are independent thinkers or that diversity of opinion is good. This brings us to the third "P" of practice.

Practice

You know that the key to a successful and confident performance is successful and confident practice. The effect of the right kind of diligent rehearsal is twofold: 1) your material is delivered in a logical, cogent fashion without stumble, and 2) the practice imbues your team with confidence so that stage fright is reduced to a minimum and your team's credibility is enhanced. Practice strips away the symptoms of stage fright as you concentrate on your message and its delivery.

To recap several points mentioned in earlier chapters, it is absolutely essential that you practice the correct way.

This means that you *practice the way you perform*. You do not start and restart your presentation repeatedly, as almost all of us have done at points in our presentation careers. There is something in our psyche that seems to urge us to "start over" when we make a mistake. When we stumble, we want a "do-over" so that we can put together a perfect rehearsal from start to finish. But when we do this, what we are actually practicing is the "starting over." We become very good at "starting over" when we make a mistake. But is that what we plan to do when we err in our actual presentation? Start over? No, of course not. But if we have practiced that way, what will we do when we stumble? We won't know what to do or how to handle the situation since we have *never practiced fighting through an error and continuing on*. We have practiced only one thing – starting over.

Instead of starting over when you err, practice the gliding over of "errors," never calling attention to them. Practice recovering from your mistake and minimizing it. Perform according to the principle that regardless of what happens, you planned it. Practice according to the principles enunciated in this volume and according to the hard preparation you have conducted leading up to the competition.

Q&A

Recognize the purpose of the question period, which is to probe your reasoning, your logic, and to identify the soundness of your assumptions. You must offer cogent and at least rudimentary answers to the Journalism 101 questions of who, what, when, where, why, and how (much). It behooves you to ask and answer these questions beforehand so that you are not blindsided in Q&A and struck dumb.

How you answer the questions is as important as the answers themselves; moreover, your team *must* demonstrate that you considered and discussed the issue deeply. Nothing undercuts a team's credibility as much as revealing that it "hadn't thought of that."

Practice your Q&A segment by determining where the most obvious questions will center – on the logic and soundness of your analysis, on the assumptions that undergird your recommendations and calculations, and on implementation of your recommendations. In particular, judges like to unpack and scrutinize your analysis; particularly focusing on the assumptions you used to derive your projection of reality. Be ready to explain those assumptions, and *never in a defensive manner.* Strike a positive posture and attitude that is midway between obsequious and belligerent – exhibit serene confidence in your answers. And utilize the Q&A structure provided to you in Chapter 16.

Delivery

At this point it is a matter of putting everything together exactly as you've prepared it, according to the principles in this book and harnessing them to the analytical tools and substantive education you have received in the various subdisciplines of business. You have reduced uncertainty to a manageable level, your team is confident, and you've prepared a presentation that you know will wow the judges. Delivering your actual presentation can actually be anti-climactic. It is the culmination of your logical preparation and is a matter of confidence and control.

Further reading on case competitions

- David A. Frank, *Creative Speaking* (1995)

- Brent C. Oberg, *Forensics: The Winner's Guide to Speech Contests* (1995)

- Richard Earl Edwards Page, *Competitive Debate: The Official Guide* (2008)

- William Schrier, *Contest Oratory: A Handbook* (1971)

- Jerry Weissman, *In the Line of Fire: How to Handle Tough Questions* (2005)

CONCLUSION

In the end, the test of any book like this is how much it helps you achieve your goals. Does it contribute to your development as a presenter, as a competent analyst who can present his or her ideas with confidence and poise? Does it contribute to your growth as a professional?

I hope that you have found *The Complete Guide* useful, and I look forward to hearing from you. Because my desire is that *The Complete Guide* becomes, in a sense, a living document – that it should in the future incorporate anecdotes and suggested techniques from readers in business education who apprise me of the latest requirements across the spectrum of our fine business schools.

You know that I've said in the past that we are all blessed and cursed in the realm of business presenting – the blessing is that all of us possess the native abilities to become competent, capable business presenters, comfortable before any audience. The curse, of course, is that it's doggedly hard work. It takes practice, and – for some of us – courage and persistence. But if you embrace the powerful techniques offered in *The Complete Guide*, you develop more much more quickly than you thought possible – you see yourself improve dramatically.

The path is clear. When you embrace the techniques offered here and apply yourself to the task, you gain immense personal competitive advantage *vis-à-vis* your peers in today's corporate world. In fact, no other single business skill today can offer you so much value in so short a time.

Why, then, if the path is so clear do so many refuse to take it? The reason for this is a paradox. It's a mystery that remains closed to me. For some reason that remains shrouded, the vast majority of students do not embrace superb business presenting as the panacea that it truly is. To offer a sports metaphor, it's like a football laying on the field and all the players are indecisive, confused, ignorant of what to do. The coach yells to pick up the ball and *run*, but no one does. Because of this reluctance, the field remains open to anyone who wishes to race for the end zone to score a touchdown.

That someone can be you. Will you heed the call? I hope that you do, because you have so much potential. And I believe that you *will* heed the call. We've never truly met, but I believe I know you, because inside every business school student is a desire to excel. You need only a bit of direction and the willingness to tease out that desire and let it drive you to success.

When I see untapped potential, I try never to let it pass without guidance, without a nudge in the right direction. Untapped potential is a tragedy, especially in the young. This, as I see it, is the task of the professor. I see such potential every day – talent that goes undeveloped and energy that goes misdirected. Perhaps it shouldn't bother me so, but if it did not, then I would not be a professor worth the name, and I would not have written this book.

And so I penned this volume in hopes that the bright young people drawn to business might flourish and reach their fullest development in the realm of presentations. It's a guide through a dark forest, through uncharted territory of business school and on into the corporate world proper. It may not be the perfect book, but I think it worthy of your attention.

You have reached the end, but this point is not your final destination – it is but a way station on your presenting journey. To achieve personal competitive advantage in a chaotic and sometimes hostile world of work is a difficult task. I encourage you now to try new techniques, to embrace older techniques, and to attempt techniques that have been forgotten over the years but resurfaced in modern form.

Come back to this volume for refresher, for a reminder that you can, indeed, become a great presenter and achieve unbridled advantage in the competitive world of business.

We find ourselves now having come full circle. You have reached this brief stop along your presentation journey, and I congratulate you. Now it's time for you to continue on, and I wish you good luck, Godspeed, and may all of your presentations be *especially powerful!*

GLOSSARY

"What Does *That* Mean?": A Presentations Glossary of Who, What, Where and How

Glossaries and lists of terms usually don't get much play in a book, and my experience is that people rarely look at them closely. This probably is no exception. But if you're new to business school and to the world of presentations, this glossary can help you tremendously. Throughout the book, I use specific words to get my point across, words or concepts that may not be familiar to you. And so, for you, I list here a compendium of words and phrases that I believe are essential for you to understand the world of business presenting.

Anchor – This is my term for anything that provides you confidence and comfort on-stage as you give your show. It can be anything including a particular posture, pose or prop. Usually it's a lectern, sometimes called a podium.

Elsewhere I criticize lectern use as a crutch, but the lectern is not entirely a bad thing. It simply should not dominate your talk or serve as a physical and psychic shield to separate you from your audience. Use it as an anchor, occasionally touching it, but *never* leaning on it.

As You Can See Syndrome (AYCSS) – The phrase "As you can see" is so pervasive, so endemic to the modern business presentation that there must be a school somewhere that trains people to utter this reflexive word gesture. Is there an AYCSS Academy? It would seem so.

The paradox of AYCSS is that it is usually accompanied by a vague gesture at a screen upon which is displayed some of the most unreadable nonsense constructed for a slide – usually a financial spreadsheet of some sort. The audience most assuredly *cannot* see.

Finance students seem particularly enamored of AYCSS. In fact, rogue finance professors doubtless inculcate this in students.

To Bookend, Bookending – This term describes the technique of sandwiching your portion of a presentation between a common theme, slogan or expression. You begin with a "money line" and you finish with the same "money line." This bookending is satisfying to the audience for several reasons; not least of which is that it hammers home understanding of your main point. The entire presentation should be bookended as well, preferably with the same person beginning and concluding the presentation.

Business Case – A business case is really just a little slice of history. It's a short narrative of a real-life business situation that focuses on a particular dilemma. It usually concerns one firm and a major change that it undergoes. Topics can include profit decline, personnel issues, cultural conflicts, market share decline, organization change, strategic direction, competitive advantage, and such like. The case is told like a story.

One key to understanding a business case is to recognize that, for the firm, something has changed or *should* be changed, and this is the reason for telling the story/case in the first place. In some cases, you might find that nothing should be changed. "Change" is the operative word. The business case provides you with the basis for your presentation.

Cartoon Voice – This is a high-pitched, scratchy voice that many people have, especially college women. The voice sounds like a cartoon character. They don't mean to have it. Think of Kelly Ripa or Elizabeth Hasselbeck or Kim Kardashian, three forgettable television "celebrities."

It's fixable, but only if you *want* to fix it. Unfortunately, many folks believe that their current voice has been bequeathed to them by the gods and should not be tampered with, when actually their voices are likely the product of haphazard development and benign neglect.

Oddly, because this voice has slipped into vogue on what is known as "reality television," it has gained a kind of quasi-legitimacy. The lowest common denominator mimics this voice, and the scourge of cartoon-talkers now plagues us. Disney Channel converts new tweener recruits daily to this malady.

You *choose* how you sound. Recognize that if you have a cartoon voice – or any other substandard voice pathology – it is not "you." You are under no obligation to keep it. It's your choice to keep it, or to modify it.

Case Competition – This is an event in which business teams, usually of two to five students, compete against each other. Teams display how quickly, thoroughly, and skillfully they can ingest a case, analyze it, and then present their conclusions and recommendations to a panel of judges. There is, of course, no direct competition between teams. Rather, each team is judged independently how well it handles the assigned case and presents its analysis and recommendations. There is usually a time limit and specific rules, with all teams operating under the same conditions. Competitions can be internal to the business school or involve teams from several different schools.

Case Method – This is a business school teaching method in which you analyze a business case and then present the results of your analysis in written and/or presentation form. The method is most closely identified with Harvard Business School, which generates 80 percent of the cases used in business schools worldwide.

The business case provides the unit of analysis in the case method of study, and in these types of classes you read and evaluate cases, offering your analysis and recommendations. Harvard Business School describes the case method this way: "When students are presented with a case, they place themselves in the role of the decision maker as they read through the situation and identify the problem they are faced with. The next step is to perform the necessary analysis – examining the causes and considering alternative courses of actions to come to a set of recommendations."[1]

Command Position – The position directly in front of a lectern or to the side of the lectern and four to eight feet from your audience. It extends approximately four feet to either side of you. As a presenter or speaker, this is your home. You own this space, so make it yours. You must always perform as if you *belong* there, never there as a visitor.

Communication Tools – Everything you use to send your message to an audience. Your personal tools include voice, expression, gesture, movement, and pause. Supplemental tools include PowerPoint projection, whiteboard and markers, butcher paper, props, and handouts.

Drama – Drama is a type of enactment, usually associated with comedy or tragedy involving fiction. In its common usage, it can encompass other situations as well. It involves in-depth character development and conflict.

You should always strive for a bit of drama in your presentations. I do not mean high drama of the sort you find in a taut film or novel or Latin soap opera. Rather, I refer to the drama inherent in business. Business cases are filled with the elements of drama – conflict, turning points, powerful personalities, struggles against the odds, good versus evil, battles between great firms,

---

1 "Academics," Harvard Business School, http://www.hbs.edu/mba/academics/howthe casemethodworks.html (accessed June 20, 2012).

subterfuge, and intrigue. The business case is dead without this drama. Strive to find the drama and incorporate it into your story.

Differentiation – This is a business strategy with which you should be familiar. It consists of adding value to a product or service in such a way that people perceive additional value and are willing to pay more for that value. One obvious example is the appeal of a brand, such as Nike, which enables that sports apparel company to charge a premium for basketball shoes that differ in no substantial way from major competitor shoes priced much less.

Apply the differentiation concept to you and to your presentations. How can you differentiate yourself? Watch your competition – your peers – and ask yourself how you can improve your skills and your content relative to their performance.

Dum–Dum – Placeholder words habitually inserted into speech that achieve a moronic effect. This is a presentation pathology of the grossest sort. Favorite dum-dums of the young generation are "like" and "totally" and "whatever" and "you know" and "uhhhh" and "ummm." Don't use dum-dums. They make you sound like a reality TV show airhead who is unable to speak in complete sentences. Speak like an adult.

Embrace –This is not human-resource-speak. It is a subjective measure of how close you get to your material. How intimately you know your subject. Do you *embrace* the material, or do you keep your distance? Embracing the material is the difference between surfing the wave and deep-sea diving. How much do you immerse yourself in the material of your presentation? Do you ride the surface or do you dive for the treasure that you can provide your audience? The opposite of "winging it."

Finger Play – A common pathology and bad habit that affects many students. It consists of tugging and picking at one's fingers while speaking, and it's often unconscious. It's distracting and debilitating for a presentation, transmitting lack of confidence.

Font – This is the style of type you use on your visuals. Fonts come in many styles, but the main distinction you must bear in mind is that between *serif* and *sans-serif* fonts. For your presentations, always use *sans-serif* fonts such as Calibri, Trebuchet, and Arial. Do not use *serif* fonts, such as Times New Roman or Garamond. The reason for this is that studies have universally shown that sans-serif fonts are easier to read in presentation settings. Here is an example of the two styles of fonts:

This is a serif font.   **This is a sans-serif font.**

Foot Scoop – This is a stage maneuver that I rarely see, although I see it enough to warn against it. It involves putting weight onto your back foot, while simultaneously lifting the toe of your front foot while rocking back on the heel of your front foot. You show the sole of the front shoe to the audience. It's distracting and unsightly, especially when repeatedly done in a cycling routine. Unless there is a practical reason to do so – your presentation is about shoe soles – avoid this maneuver.

Gesture – You gesture with your hands, primarily, to lend emphasis to the ideas and arguments of your presentation, but gesture encompasses much more. You also gesture with everything from your posture to your shifting of weight from one foot to the other, every lift of the eyebrow to every smile. The nonverbal communicative power of gesture is phenomenal – harness it to your use!

Hip-Shot – A cock of one hip to the side while speaking. It is common, and it is unacceptable in delivering a show. It radiates nonchalance and weakness. Need I tell you *not* to do this?

John Kennedy Thumb Press – This is a gesture you can adopt to give emphasis to your remarks. It is easy to do, it's fun to do, and it gives you something to do with your right hand. If you have finger-play problems, this is a good remedy. See **Obama Lint-Pick**.

Kinesics – This is the study of body language and its effectiveness as a communication tool. Body language plays an indispensable role in delivering a clear and powerful presentation. By body language, we mean posture, gesture, expression, stance, and movement.

Lectern – For many students, this is a crutch. It's a place to hide from the audience. I recommend using the lectern only once – to walk from behind it to approach your audience at the very beginning of your talk. Do not lean upon the lectern in nonchalant fashion, particularly leaning upon your elbow and with one leg crossed over the other. See **Podium**.

Leg-Cross –This maneuver is what it purports to be. Do not ever cross your legs while standing in front of an audience. Many folks do this, the majority of them female. It telegraphs instability and lack of confidence. It's visually unappealing, and it leads the audience to wonder when you'll fall over. Moreover, it puts you into a precarious balancing act that erodes your confidence even as it leads to a feeling that you will, indeed, fall over.

The Masters – When I refer to the "masters," I show respect toward the public speaking experts who developed presenting to a superb craft. The source for almost all our presentation wisdom originates more than 2,000 years ago as practiced by the Greek and the Roman speech masters such as Aristotle, Demosthenes, Cicero, Quintilian.

More recently, nineteenth- and early twentieth-century presentation masters, knew how to move a crowd to action – men such as Nathan Shephard, William Enfield, Henry Ward Beecher, Edward Everett, Grenville Kleiser, Russell Conwell, and Dale Carnegie. Today, internationally known presenters such as Patricia Fripp are role models for emulation.

The techniques and power of the masters comprise a secret trove open to anyone who cares to look, learn, and act. I draw upon the masters often throughout the book – when I mention a master, you needn't genuflect, but do show respect and absorb the lesson.

Obama Lint-Pick – This is a gesture similar to the Kennedy Thumb Press. It consists of the thumb and index finger pressed together, with the remaining fingers curled under in a semi-fist. Use it to indicate precision.

Orientation; to Orient – This is one of the most important techniques for reaching and touching an audience with your message. I use this term when discussing your interactions with your visuals. You *must* orient your audience to your visuals. When you display numbers or a graph or chart, you must first tell them *explicitly* what they are viewing, what the chart or graph represents or measures.

You walk to the screen and touch it, directing your audience to the framework of your discussion. If it's a graph, you tell them *explicitly* what the X and Y axes represent and what the gradations along each axis mean. *Never* say "As you can see…"

Podium – The area, usually raised, where the speaker gives his or her talk. It's a platform and stage area that encompasses the lectern. In modern usage, podium is often used interchangeably with **lectern**.

Proxemics – Edward T. Hall, a cultural anthropologist, first created and developed the concept of proxemics in his 1966 book *The Hidden Dimension*. Proxemics has to do with the study of how our distance from other people can affect communication between us by either enhancing or decreasing relaxation or tension. Created in the context of intercultural communication, proxemics also has superb application in the conference room with regard to business presentations.

Rule of Three – Organize your presentation on the Rule of Three. Make three points and only three points in your talk. If you deliver only one part of a group presentation, such as a SWOT analysis, then cover only three main points.

The Rule of Three is universally acknowledged among speaking professionals as having almost magical qualities. We think in threes and accept information in threes. Consider examples from history and from fairy tales: Goldilocks and the Three Bears, The Three Little Pigs. "I came, I saw, I conquered." The genie from the lamp offers three wishes. The Three Wise Men. Select the three major points you wish to convey, and let those three points structure your show.

Show – This is my shortened term for "presentation." A presentation is a show. You perform, act, and deliver a message in the same medium that actors use. "Show" is also somehow less intimidating that the stodgy four-syllable term "presentation." It evokes what I expect from my students. I sometimes refer to my students as my "showpeople." As in, "Who are my showpeople today?" when I ask for group presenters to prepare for their shows.

Situation Statement – This is your introduction to your presentation. This is also known as the problem statement or thesis statement. I call it the situation statement, because you aren't necessarily bringing bad news, so there might not be a "problem" involved. Not all shows are the vehicle of bad news.

Moreover, using the term "problem" tends us toward negativity, oftentimes needlessly. And in reality, a "problem" always provides opportunity. It depends on your perspective. So instead of "problem statement," let us always refer to the situation statement.

Space – This is the distance between you and your audience. There are four kinds of space that vary according to the distance from your listeners – public, social, private, and intimate. Each distance carries its own effects. The farthest and most impersonal space is "public space." This is 12 feet and beyond. Then comes "social space," which is between 4 and 12 feet from your audience. Then comes private space, which is between 18 inches and 4 feet from your audience. Finally, is "intimate space," which is anything inside 18 inches. Don't ever violate "intimate space" unless you are given permission. See **Proxemics.**

Stick-Puppet Presenting – The technique of delivering a business presentation in minimalist fashion, standing hunched behind a lectern, head down reading notes and offering only a frontal view of the speaker. This stick-puppet posture is relieved only with the occasional hiccup of movement that results from either unconscious bad habit or from a misguided attempt to "move around" in an errant search for variety. I also refer to this as 2D presenting.

3D Presenting – This form of business presenting takes advantage of the many and varied tools available to the public speaker, including the multiplicity of techniques comprising the speaker himself. 3D presenting offers a rich and sensual multisensory experience to the audience, engaging emotions and tapping potential.

2D Presenting – This form of minimalist business presenting deemphasizes the speaker and focuses attention toward an ersatz altar, such as a PowerPoint screen. In 2-D presenting, it sometimes appears that we are all invited by the speaker to read his PowerPoint slides in unison. There is little depth, detail, or humanity in 2D presenting.

Verbal Grind – This unfortunate verbal pathology comes at the end of sentences and is caused by squeezing out insufficient air to inflate the final word of the sentence. The result is a grinding or grating sound on the last word. Primarily a phenomenon that affects females, its most famous male purveyor is President Bill Clinton, whose grating voice with its Arkansas accent became a trademark.

This tic is likely a manifestation of 1970s "valley girl" talk or "Valspeak." It is manifested by a crackle and grating on the last word or syllable, as if the air supply is being pinched off. It actually appears to be a fashionable way to speak, grinding out the last word of a sentence into a grating fade, as if a dog is growling in the throat. As if someone has thrown sand into the voice box. When combined with "cartoon voice," it can reach unbearable scale for an audience.

Verbal Down-Tic – This is also called the "falling line." This is an unfortunate speaking habit of inflecting the voice downward at the end of every sentence, letting the air rush from the lungs in a fading expulsion, as if each sentence is a labor. The last syllables of a word are lost in breath. The effect is of exhaustion, depression, resignation, even of impending doom. The Verbal Down-Tic leeches energy from the room. It deflates the audience. In your talk, you have too many things that must go right than to be needlessly spreading gloom in the room.

Verbal Sing-Song – The voice bobs and weaves artificially, as if the person is imitating what they think a speaker ought to sound like. Who knows what inspires people to talk this way, usually *only* in public speaking or presenting. It is an affectation. *People do not talk like this*, and if you find yourself affecting a style or odd mannerism because you think you ought to, it's probably wrong.

Verbal Up-Tic – This is also called the "rising line" or the "high rising terminal" or "uptalking." This is an unfortunate habit of inflecting the voice upward at the end of every sentence, as if a question is being asked. It radiates weakness and uncertainty and conveys the mood of unfinished business, as if something more is yet to come. Sentence after sentence in succession is spoken as if they are questions.

You create a tense atmosphere with the Verbal Up-Tic that is almost demonic in its effect. This tic infests your audience with an unidentifiable uneasiness. At its worst, your audience wants to cover ears and cry "make it stop!" but they aren't quite sure at what they should vent their fury.

In certain places abroad, this tic is known as the Australian Questioning Intonation, popular among young Australians. The Brits are less generous in their assessment of this barbarism, calling it the "moronic interrogative," a term coined by comedian Rory McGrath. In United States popular culture, Meghan McCain, the daughter of Senator John McCain, has made a brisk living off her incessant verbal up-ticking. Listen for it in any interview. Listen for it in the elevator between classes.

Winging It – This is a euphemism for an unprepared, off-the-cuff, contemptuous waste of everyone's time from a student who didn't bother with the assignment. Many students tend to approach presentations with either fear, *faux* nonchalance, or with *real* nonchalance. It's a form of defensiveness. This can result in the phenomenon of "winging it." No preparation, no practice, no self-respect, just a defiant contempt for the assignment and the audience. It leaves the easy out that the student "didn't really try." It is obvious to everyone watching that you are "winging it." Why would you waste our time this way? Don't "wing it."

INDEX

12 Angry Men (film) 217

A Time to Kill (film) 145, 166–7, 170–71
Act Natural (Howard) 106
acting skills 24
Aeschines 22
Aesop's *Fables* 150
Alamo 159
anchor 245
Analysis Without Paralysis (Bensoussan and Fleisher) 221
appearance
  dress 120–22, 206
  self-confidence 124–5
  "stage fright" 122–4
Apple 147
Armstrong, Neil 142
As You Can See Syndrome 217, 245
audience 32, 40, 145, 166–7, 185
Axe deodorant 173–4

Bacon, Albert M. 22n5
bad advice 41–3
Barzun, Jacques x
Battle of Gettysburg 164
Bell, Alexander Melville 18, 133
Bensoussan, Babette E. 221
Bible, the 37
body language 56–7
Boeing Corporation 234
bookend, bookending 246
Brees, Paul x, 128

Brooks, Edward 104
Buddha, storytelling 141

Caesar, Julius 36
Campbell, Joseph 141, 159
cartoon voice(s) 3, 246
Cather, Katherine 137, 142
case, business 246
case competition
  definition 233, 246–7
  and positive attitude 239
  practice 240–41
  and Q&A 241
  three Ps 234
case method 188, 247
Charlemagne 141
chess 141
Christ, storytelling 141
Churchill, Winston 36
Cicero 18, 22
CIBER 234
"clicker" 86
Clinton, Bill 22
Coca-Cola 28, 53, 54
Collins, Jim xiii
command position 5, 185, 247
communication theory xvii
communication tools 247
communications course xv
Confucius, storytelling 141
Crockett, Davy 159
Curry, S. S. 128

Death by PowerPoint 213
Demosthenes 18, 22
differentiation 248
drama 247
Duarte, Nancy 217
dum-dums 69, 248; *see also* voice

earnestness 100–101, 104, 134, 135
Easy Rider (film) 160
Eastwood, Clint 37, 159
elocution 19
embrace 248
Emerson, Ralph Waldo 169
emotion 130, 133; *see also* James–Lange
    Theory
environmental scan 225
Esenwein, J. Berg 125–6, 130
Eskew, Mike 155
esteem building 9
European Case Clearing House
    (ECCH) 188
expression; *see also* earnestness
    drama 105
    embrace 105

"finger play" 95, 248
financial analysis 222, 229–31
Fishburne, Lawrence 25
Five Forces: *see* Porter's Five Forces
Fleisher, Craig S. 221
font 248
foot scoop 249
Foster School of Business 234

Gap, the xiii, xiv
gesture
    definition of 249
    John Kennedy Thumb Press 93, 249
    Magic Dust 94
    Obama Lint-Pick 93, 250
    This Many 94
    Two-Fisted Passion 94
Godin, Seth 213
Goode, Kenneth 40–41
Goodman, Andy 12
Google 147
Gorman, James 78
grabber 34, 35, 202

Gracchus 22
grade point average (GPA) 7, 175
Graduate Management Admission
    Council 8n1
Greeks, ancient 18
Greenpeace 147
Grisham, John 145, 147, 166

Haven, Kendall 138–9
hero 20, 152
Hero's Journey 141
High-Demand Skill Zone xvii, 7, 13
"hip-shot" 62, 249
Holy Grail 159
Homer 141
Horner, Charles 72
Hortentius 22
Howard, Ken 106; *see also Act Natural*

Iliad (Homer) 141
inflection 77–8
Institutes of Oratory (Quintilian) 98; *see also*
    Quintilian
Isocrates 22

Jacobi, Jeffrey 65
James, William 58
James–Lange Theory 57–8
Jesse, Anita 24
Jones, Indiana 40
Jones, James Earl 75

Kaufman, Zenn 40–41
Kelley, G. Vernon x, 128
Kent, Muhtar 53–4, 54n3, 55
Kidd, Robert 82
kinesics 249
King Arthur 159
Kleiser, Grenville 147
Kline, John 41, 43
Knowles, Sheridan 130
Koontz, Dean 163–4

Lange, Carl G. 58
lectern 5, 185, 249; *see also* podium
leg-cross 249
Lippman, Doug 169
Logitech 86

MacArthur, Douglas 37
Mahabharata 141
Major, Clare Tree 72
Masters, the 249
Matrix, The (film) 25
McCain, Meghan 81, 253
McGrath, Rory 253
McTips! 23, 25
Microsoft 15
Mohammed, storytelling 141
money line 202–3
Morgan, J. P. 172
Mosher, Joseph 99
movement
and 3D presenting 111, 252
and space 111–14
and stick-puppet presenting 111, 251

National School for Elocution and
Oratory 7
"natural born" speaker 23
negative self-talk 6
nonverbal signaling 51
Nowell, David 193

Obama, Barack 22
Odyssey (Homer) 141
Ohio State University Center for
International Business Education
and Research (CIBER):
see CIBER
orient, orientation 250
Our Iceberg is Melting (Kotter and
Rathgeber) 149

passion 128–36
Paulson, Lynda 16–17, 90
pause 81
persona 19, 63
PEST analysis 225
PETA 147
Plato, storytelling 141
podium 250
Porter, Michael 225
Porter's Five Forces 221–2, 225
Powell, Colin 22
power posing 58
Power Zone x, 14, 25

PowerPoint 15, 19, 213–14
practice 195–6
preparation 190
presentation
definition of 183
framework 32
group 4
and uncertainty 183
Q&A 210–11
and uncertainty 183
presentation survey 12
presence
professional 5
personal 16–18, 24
presenters 18
McTips! 21, 23
"natural born" 6, 21
Prison of Freedom 66
Procrustes 194
Profitable Showmanship (Goode and
Kaufman) 40–41
projection screen 185–6
Prometheus 159
proxemics 250; *see also* space

Quintilian 39, 98–9

Reagan, Ronald 22
Real Leaders Don't Do PowerPoint
(Witt) 213
Really Bad PowerPoint (Godin) 213
Reeves, Keanu 25
Ripa, Kelly 67
Rodenburg, Patsy 78
Roosevelt, Teddy 159
Rule of Three 31, 36–7, 199, 250

Seaton, Matt 79
Seinfeld, Jerry 22
Shakespeare, William 36
show 251
situation statement 251
Sixth Sense, The (film) 163
Skywalker, Luke 160
Socrates 18
and storytelling 141
"soft skills" ix
space 251; *see also* proxemics

St John, Edward Porter 152
stance
    basic 60
    classic 61
Star Wars (film) 75
Starship Enterprise 160
starting, staging, stopping 33–9
story; see also Hero's Journey
    Big Idea 168–9
    concreteness 171–4
    Most Important Point 168–9, 173
    personal story 154
    sensory involvement 162–5
    story moments 154, 155–7
    theme story 154–60
    WIIFY 165–7
Story Proof: The Science Behind the Startling
    Power of Story (Haven) 138
style 45–9
SWOT analysis 5, 195, 222–4

Tarantino, Quentin 147
Targus 86
TOOTSIFELT 41
Target Corporation 35
three Ps 29, 234
Trojan War 141, 159
Tuck School of Business 181, 181n1

Ulysses 141
University of Paris 141
UPS 155
uptalk 78–9, 252

Vader, Darth 75, 76
value chain analysis 226–9
Verbal Grind 80–81, 252
Verbal Down-Tic 80, 252
Verbal Sing-Song 252
Verbal Up-Tic 78–80, 252–3
visualization 5
voice
    "bad voice" 65
    cartoon voice 67–8
    deep, deeper 74, 76

Watkins, Dwight E. 60
West, Robert 87
Who Moved My Cheese? (Johnson) 149
Willis, Bruce 163
Winans, James Albert 23–4, 192
Winfrey, Oprah 22
winging it 253
Witt, Christopher 168, 213; see also Real
    Leaders Don't Do PowerPoint

Zelazny, Gene 30

CPSIA information can be obtained at www.ICGtesting.com
Printed in the USA
LVOW131727150513

333964LV00007B/811/P